This meticulously researched book  fe-
changing testimonies. It will take yo   ver
been before. Your faith will be catapul   ns.

jui
Founder and Director, Faith Evangelistic Ministries Int'l

The lessons we glean from these forerunners of healing power are extraor-
dinarily important. It is critical that we learn from their mistakes as well as
their victories. I highly recommend *God's Generals: The Healing Evangelists*
to all who desire to receive the fullness of all that Jesus has for them.

—*Heidi Baker, Ph.D.*
Founding Director, Iris Ministries

Roberts Liardon is one of the great historians of those who have gone
before us in Christendom. His latest edition, *God's Generals: The Healing
Evangelists*, is especially touching. It is so important to study those who
have gone before us in order to learn from their amazing lives.

—*Joan Hunter*
Best-selling author

I am happy to recommend *God's Generals: The Healing Evangelists*.
Information relating to these men and women of the past is something
that can be inspirational, challenging, and informative to this generation.

—*John Partington*
National Leader, Assemblies of God, Great Britain

Other Titles by Roberts Liardon

Breaking Controlling Powers

God's Generals: The Revivalists

God's Generals: The Roaring Reformers

God's Generals: Why They Succeeded and Why Some Failed

John G. Lake: The Complete Collection of His Life Teachings

Kathryn Kuhlman: A Spiritual Biography

Sharpen Your Discernment

★★★★★
GOD'S

The Healing
Evangelists

GENERALS

Roberts LIARDON

WHITAKER
HOUSE

Editorial Note: Original spellings are maintained in all quoted material, and, because of the numerous differences between British and American English, as well as conventions of the time, these are not noted by a [sic]. Original capitalizations are also maintained, so that often "he" and "his," etc., are not capitalized when referring to God, Jesus, or the Holy Spirit.

GOD'S GENERALS: THE HEALING EVANGELISTS

trade paperback edition ISBN: 978-1-60374-269-6
Printed in the United States of America
© 2011 by Roberts Liardon

Roberts Liardon Ministries
P.O. Box 2989
Sarasota, FL 34230
E-mail: info1@robertsliardon.org
www.RobertsLiardon.com

Whitaker House
1030 Hunt Valley Circle
New Kensington, PA 15068
www.whitakerhouse.com

The Library of Congress has cataloged the hardcover edition as follows:

Liardon, Roberts.
  God's generals : the healing evangelists / Roberts Liardon.
    p. cm.
  Includes bibliographical references.
  Summary: "Roberts Liardon recounts the lives and ministries of the great healing evangelists of the twentieth century, including Oral Roberts, Lester Sumrall, Charles and Frances Hunter, F. F. Bosworth, and George Jeffreys"—Provided by publisher.
  ISBN 978-1-60374-268-9 (hard : alk. paper) 1. Evangelists—Biography. 2. Healers—Biography. 3. Pentecostals—Biography. I. Title.
  BV3780.L458 2011
  234'.1310922—dc22
  [B]
                          2011000699

2 3 4 5 6 7 8 9 10 11   ⊔⊔   18 17 16 15 14 13 12 11

DEDICATION

---⭐---

I dedicate this book to the passionate lives of Robert and Millicent Spilman, pioneering leaders of the charismatic movement in England. I liken their ministry to Priscilla and Aquila in the New Testament, who helped people find the more perfect way. (See Acts 18:26.)

Robert (Bob) was born in Watford, England, in 1924, and joined the Royal Navy due to the demands of the Second World War. After the war, Bob, a qualified mechanical and civil engineer, took a position with the Ministry of Works overseeing the building of new roads in Nigeria. It was there that he met Millicent.

As a teenager, Millicent had accepted Jesus as her Lord and Savior at her local church in Chadderton, England. In 1948, as a fully qualified nurse trained in tropical diseases and midwifery, Millicent desired to go to Africa as a missionary but was told that she would have to first attend a Bible college for four years. Impatient to get to work, she applied and was appointed to the position of Nursing Sister in a Leprosy Mission Settlement Hospital near Enugu, Nigeria, where she met Bob. The two were married in 1953 at the Ridge Church in Accra, Ghana.

It was through Millicent's steadfast witness to the love of God in her life that Bob came to know Jesus as his Lord and Savior. Returning to the United Kingdom, Bob and Millicent settled into family life with their three children as Bob's career soared. Soon thereafter, Bob and Millicent experienced the baptism of the Holy Spirit, which influenced Bob to leave his secure future in Industry and step out in faith by following the Lord's leading.

Bob became best known for his work with the Full Gospel Businessmen's Fellowship International. In 1975, the Cheshire Chapter of FGBMFI was formed in his living room. From there, the movement grew to some four hundred chapters through-out the UK and Ireland. Bob was appointed as the group's International Director but always insisted that he could not have done this work without Millicent's love and support.

Bob and Millicent frequently visited many countries with oppressive re-gimes, including trips behind the Iron Curtain, always taking the gospel in word and print, encouraging those who loved the Lord and introducing many more to Him. Together, they impacted thousands of lives without ever seeking to promote themselves.

A soft-spoken but well-read man, Bob saw the need for Spirit-filled books. He established a business, Faith Builders, and became the first to import these books into the UK and Europe. Today, there are thousands of believers living Spirit-filled lives due to their influence and his ministry.

Bob went on to heaven in January 1999. He was survived by his wife, Milli-cent, their three children, and their five grandchildren, all of whom are fully com-mitted to the Lord and following God's plan for their lives.

A true gentleman has gone ahead, one who is greatly missed.

Thank you for the example you both lived as a Christian couple. Thank you for walking through difficult times and not giving up. We are better because you were faithful to God's calling on your lives.

—*Roberts Liardon*
London, England

CONTENTS

FOREWORD

──✦──

I was not prepared for how much I would learn, be blessed, and receive encouragement from reading Roberts Liardon's *God's Generals: The Healing Evangelists*. I have no doubt that you will, too. The title of *God's Generals* is an apt one for the particular people Roberts has chosen to describe. Although these "generals" are largely from the Pentecostal and charismatic sector of the Christian church, they have impacted countless millions of people from every theological and ecclesiastical position. Although I myself was brought up in a different tradition, I have been blessed profoundly by men like those described in this volume. Oral Roberts actually wrote forewords for two of my own books, and he graciously entertained my wife, Louise, and me in his home a few years before he went to heaven.

Some readers may not know that Roberts Liardon was actually named after Oral Roberts, one of the generals of this book. Roberts Liardon's parents were charter members of Oral Roberts University. He was the first male child to come from that charter class! Oral himself wanted to help name the baby and they all came up with the name Kenneth Roberts Liardon.

Roberts is the principal of the International Bible Institute of London. This institute is part of the ministry of Kensington Temple, of which my close friend Colin Dye is the Senior Pastor.

Mr. Liardon has done a remarkable job in his research. He has uncovered details that have been remained hidden until now. What is more impressive is that he has not glossed over facts that don't always show his subjects in a good light. He gives praise when it is due but reminds all of us that even the best of men are men at best.

✫✫✫✫✫

What encouraged me most about reading this book is the undoubted presence of the miraculous that marked the lives of these unusual men. I have longed to see miracles in my own ministry. I have seen some, but not many. Indeed, some of these men knew the disappointment of not seeing everyone healed. In the end, God is sovereign. He said to Moses, *"I will be gracious to whom I will be gracious, and I will have compassion on whom I will have compassion"* (Exodus 33:19). This dimension of Christian theology is sometimes missing with some of these stalwarts and, just maybe, could have helped them to have a more balanced perspective in their ministries.

A healing presence is something none of us can "work up." When it is present, as in Luke 5:17, people are healed. When such an anointing lifts, there are those who carry on as if nothing happened. In any case, a genuine healing presence often accompanied the ministries of the generals portrayed in this book. It was thrilling for me to read of them – just to know what God is able and willing to do. I would hope that this book would drive us to our knees and lead us to plead with God to show mercy. When we ask for mercy as in Hebrews 4:16, we have nothing to give in exchange, so, when God grants it, He alone gets all the glory. Perhaps that is one of the reasons God sometimes withholds mercy; it keeps us from claiming too much credit for ourselves.

I highly recommend this book. It is a reminder that God has raised up men in previous times and we must ask him to do it again – not with a few but with many – in such a time as this.

—R. T. Kendall
Minister at Westminster Chapel (1977–2002), London, England

F. F. BOSWORTH

"Healing Pioneer"

"HEALING PIONEER"

On a cold winter morning in 1925 in a schoolyard in Scranton, Pennsylvania, a group of rosy-cheeked children laughed gleefully as they chased each other around the tall oak tree. Little girls giggled on the swing set as they swung higher and higher.

Suddenly, one little girl fell to the ground, crying as she clutched at her chest. Apparently, she had injured herself, but even as she wiped her tears, the adults who were supervising were not concerned. Nine-year-old Raffaela Serio continued to have pain near the "invisible" injury on her chest. Her parents were concerned, so they took her to see one doctor and then another. It appeared she had just bruised the area near her left breast, but as the pain increased, a small lump formed and then grew to the size of an orange.

Raffaela's parents called on a friend who was a pediatric specialist trained at Johns Hopkins University. After administering several difficult tests, the doctor gravely pronounced the diagnosis. Little Raffaela Serio had sarcoma cancer of the left breast.

The grieving parents watched as their precious daughter lost weight rapidly. The specialist determined that the cancer was rooted too deeply for surgery and said he could do little for the pain. There was also an open, seeping sore, but since not much was known about cancer at the time, the doctor prescribed a special brown salve to be applied on the affected area each day, which would then be wrapped with clean bandages. Although they tried to be hopeful, Raffaela's doctors saw slim chance for a recovery.

After months of ineffective treatment and worry, the Serios invited Raffaela's doctor to join them for dinner one Sunday afternoon. As they quietly conversed around the table, the doctor looked with mournful eyes at the sick little girl he had been unable to help. Turning to her mother, he made an unusual statement for a physician: "There is a man holding some kind of special meetings in a large tent in Scranton. He prays, and people get well."

"Doctor, really, you must be kidding!" the Serios responded.

"No, I'm not joking. I mean it. I had a patient with a very large goiter who has been healed. She said Evangelist F. F. Bosworth prayed for her, and she was instantly healed." Mrs. Serio looked at the doctor in amazement, and he continued, "Why don't you take dear little Raffaela down there? They may be able to help her also."[1]

The Serios drove to Scranton that very evening to hear F. F. Bosworth preach a sermon on Christ's salvation and divine healing. They purchased a copy of Bosworth's book *Christ the Healer*, which would become a Christian classic on the power of Christ to heal. For the next week, the Serios read large portions of the book aloud to Raffaela so that all three of them could understand the biblical promise of healing in Christ.

With their faith greatly increased, the family drove back to the crusade the following Sunday. During the time of prayer for healing, F. F. Bosworth stepped toward the little girl standing on the platform and prayed a beautiful prayer for God's healing power. He prayed that God would heal her and use her as a living monument for His praise and glory.[2]

When they returned home later that night, Mrs. Serio got the salve ready for Raffaela's daily treatment. Raffaela looked at her mother in astonishment. "Why, mother dear, where is your faith? Didn't you hear the man say that Jesus healed me? I don't need any more bandages. I am healed." Neither the large lump nor the swelling from beneath her arm to her collarbone had gone away, but the little girl had begun to see herself through the eyes of faith.

There was little sleep for Mrs. Serio that night as she tossed and turned, worrying about her sweet girl. But the next day, as she later recounted, "morning dawned and with it came a newness of life for our darling! She had stepped out into the faith life with Jesus and He had met her. Oh! the joy and glory of it!"[3] The morning sunlight revealed that all the swelling from the collarbone and under the arm was gone! Five days later, the lump was the size of a hickory nut; shortly after that, it disappeared completely!

"Praise our wonderful, precious Jesus" was the joyous mother's cry that summer of 1925 in the city of Scranton, Pennsylvania.[4] Her little girl had been miraculously healed because a man of God had been faithful to preach complete salvation in the atonement of Christ—salvation for the mind, body, and spirit. And God had been faithful to perform His Word.

An Early Pentecostal General

F. F. Bosworth was a frontier evangelist, a pioneer Christian radio broadcaster, one of the most successful healing evangelists of the 1920s, and a man who created a bridge to the healing revivalists of the 1940s and 1950s. From his visit to Azusa Street and on, Fred Bosworth was a cornerstone of the modern Pentecostal movement.

F. F. Bosworth

In his early revivals, Bosworth came in contact with other Pentecostal leaders, such as John Alexander Dowie, Maria Woodworth-Etter, Charles F. Parham, John G. Lake, Paul Rader, and E. W. Kenyon. Years later, in the 1950s, with his vast knowledge of the Scriptures and his broad experience as a healing evangelist, he became a mentor for men like Jack Coe, a young Oral Roberts, Ern Baxter, and many in James Gordon Lindsay's "Voice of Healing" group. He built an especially close mentoring relationship with William Branham and T. L.

Osborn. Baxter traveled with these men to South Africa and may have attended the Branham-Bosworth meetings in the States, as well.

F. F. Bosworth was a man of great integrity and honor. He was not overcome with emotionalism in the healing ministry but steadily looked to God to fulfill His Word. Because of this, he never wanted people to claim healings due to emotional responses. Bosworth faithfully recorded the names and addresses of those who were healed through his ministry. To him, they were the "witnesses," living proof that God's Spirit was at work among His people to heal. Bosworth welcomed doctors' confirmations of the healings, as well.

As a result, during his years in ministry, Bosworth accumulated over 250,000 letters and testimonies from people who had been touched by his messages. A number of those testimonies will be shared in these pages as we look at one of God's true generals, who led some astounding healing revivals in the early twentieth century. Yet Bosworth always stated that his primary focus was evangelism, then healing.

A Frontier Boy

When the Civil War finally ended after four long years, the United States was a wounded nation. The U.S. government decided to create a new national vision of change and expansion to encourage its citizens to look beyond the years of war to a future of hope and promise. People were enticed to move West and settle new territories. With the Homestead Act of 1862, which supplied homesteaders with affordable federal land, and with the expansion of the railroad, families were moving by the thousands to the Midwest.

Burton Bosworth had served in the war as a Union soldier, and he and his wife, Amelia, headed out to Nebraska, where they could buy land for a cheap rate. They bought a small farm in Utica, Nebraska, and began a family.

On a frigid winter day, January 17, 1877, Amelia Bosworth gave birth to her second son, Fred Francis. The Bosworths were grateful to have another son to help build their farm. It would have brought them greater joy if they had known that this son would also touch more than one million people with the love and power of Jesus Christ.

✶✶✶✶✶

F. F. Bosworth

Fred was a boy with steadfast determination. He was a hard worker who set some lofty goals, and he ultimately reached them. When he was only nine years old, Fred accompanied his father to a Civil War reunion at Fort Kearney, Nebraska, to enjoy the brass band and military ceremonies. A lover of music from his earliest days, Fred was mesmerized by the music flowing from the decorated stage. As the crowd cheered and sang patriotic songs, Fred inched forward to watch the cornet players. Fascinated by the instrument, Fred was determined to possess his own cornet and to learn how to play it. He had a yearning for music deep within his soul.

Being a farmer's son, Fred was adept at using the resources around him. For example, when his uncle gave him the runt of a pig litter to have as his own, he fattened up the pig and sold it at the local market. With that money, the industrious boy bought a cow, raised her, fattened her up, and traded her and her calf for a brand-new cornet. Now that he had his coveted instrument, he needed money for lessons. Undaunted, Fred pored over the old organ's elementary instruction book in their farmhouse parlor, and that is how he learned to read music and play notes.

Fred purchased the most advanced cornet music book he could find. While working in his father's feed store, he would practice for hours when business was slow. He studied the notes, learned the musical values, and practiced diligently. Early in his life, he showed the perseverance that would take him through difficult times and even persecution in years to come.

Soon, Fred was skilled enough as a musician to play in a community band. When his family moved to University Place, Nebraska, he auditioned and won a seat in the Nebraska State Band. One day, this young man's fine musical talent would even grace the stage in New York City.

By the age of sixteen, Fred Bosworth was itching to be out on his own. In addition to his natural aptitude for music, he was a natural salesman. He met a "general agent" who wanted him to sell a variety of products, including cement for building industries. Fred and his older brother "rode the rails" around the State of Nebraska, often jumping open train cars to ride for free, as they tried to make their fortune as traveling salesmen. On one of these adventures, Fred's life was changed forever.

★★★★★

Changed Forever!

Many of young Fred's sales trips took him to Omaha. On one trip, he stopped to visit Miss Maude Greene, who was several years older than he. She'd invited him to join her at an old-time revival at the First Methodist Church that week. The first two nights, he listened politely to the gospel singing and the preaching, then escorted Miss Maude home and returned to his hotel. On the third night, however, the Holy Spirit began to tug on his heart.

For the first time, Fred really *heard* the message of salvation and understood the sacrifice Jesus had made for him on the cross nineteen hundred years earlier. His heart was stirred within him. Sensing that something was happening, Maude encouraged Fred to take a trip down to the altar when the preacher called.

> **With the presence of God flowing through him, Fred decided to say yes to God.**

Reluctantly at first, but then with a firmer step, Fred Bosworth approached that little Methodist altar. While he knelt there, he knew that he must decide that very night if he was going to make a decision for Christ or walk away from Him.

With the presence of God flowing through him, Fred decided to say yes to God. Immediately, his heart was filled with joy to overflowing, and he erupted in holy laughter. "Such a happiness filled his heart he laughed for joy, till he actually felt embarrassed because he could scarcely stop."[5] Now, Fred had another decision to make. Much of his sales success had been based on dishonest methods and half-truths. He needed to quit his salesman's life and go home. But what would he do with his life in Christ now?

For the next two years, Bosworth held so many different jobs, it was hard to keep count. He worked in a windmill factory, then as a clerk in a grocery store. Following that, he was a department store clerk, a meat market butcher, a railroad maintenance worker, and a house painter. He learned more about his relationship with the Lord during this time, but he also struggled with an anxious soul.

✻✻✻✻✻

F. F. BOSWORTH
A Female Healing Evangelist

Fred's career was not his only struggle. His health was deteriorating rapidly. Eight years earlier, when the Bosworths lived in University Place, a young boy had been hurt, and the local doctor needed to perform surgery. There was not enough adult help available, so young Fred helped the doctor during the surgery. The operating room was kept very warm, and when Fred left, he walked out into an icy-cold Nebraska night. As a result, he developed a severe cough that weakened his lungs and resulted in a chronic lung condition that manifested as a dry, raspy cough.

Now, at the age of nineteen, his cough had worsened, and it had become painful to breathe. After spending several weeks in bed, Fred was finally diagnosed with tuberculosis—the "killer disease" of the late nineteenth and early twentieth centuries. And the doctor's verdict was hopeless. He predicted that Fred had little time left to live.[6]

What should he do now? His parents had moved to Fitzgerald, Georgia, for a fresh start one year earlier. Facing death at nineteen, Fred Bosworth decided to take a train trip to Georgia to see his parents one last time. He was seriously ill during the long, agonizing train ride and wondered if he would make it there alive. When he finally reached Fitzgerald, Fred stumbled off the train and into his mother's loving arms. She nursed him over the course of several weeks, until he was finally able to get out of the house for short periods of time.

On his first outing, Fred went to another Methodist revival so that he could be encouraged by the Word of God. Miss Mattie Perry, a healing evangelist, was teaching a series on developing a deeper walk with God. Fred coughed throughout the service, and she looked his way intently several times. At the end of the sermon, Fred went forward to pray for more of God in his life.

Miss Mattie walked directly over to Fred, looked him in the eyes, and told him that God still had work for him to do, and that he was too young to die. With that, Miss Mattie laid hands on Fred and prayed for him to be delivered completely from tuberculosis. From that very moment, Fred began to heal, and within days, his cough was gone completely. A doctor's visit confirmed that his lungs were totally restored. Fred Bosworth rejoiced in his healing, but he had little idea at the time that he had been healed to bring forth the truth of God's gospel message to thousands of people, believers and nonbelievers alike.

"God, I Still Need a Plan"

Fred's health returned quickly. He didn't know how he was to serve God, so he settled in Georgia with his family and found work, first as the assistant postmaster in Fitzgerald. Next, he was elected town clerk. After a time, he moved on to work as a banker. When Fred was twenty-three, he met and married a young lady named Estella Hayde. He had led her to the Lord shortly after they'd met, and she was also dedicated to finding a way to serve Jesus.

The Bosworth Musical Trio

Fred and his wife attended church faithfully, but a subtle anxiousness continued to plague his soul. To ease his unrest, Fred returned to music and played the cornet that he loved, which was possible because of the renewed strength in his lungs. Soon, he was playing and directing the Georgia Empire State Band, performing at weekend community events throughout the State of Georgia, and waiting for God to show him the next step.

God is faithful to His Word. He had a plan for F. F. Bosworth, whose life was about to make a sudden turn in God's direction. In God's providence, Fred and Estella had been given a copy of the magazine *Leaves of Healing*. Written by Scottish evangelist John Alexander Dowie, it proclaimed the healing power of Jesus Christ at work on the earth today. It also described a Christian community that Dowie had established in Zion City, Illinois.

Fred and Estella discussed the new city with great excitement. Fred already knew from personal experience that Jesus Christ still healed. Now, he was eager for the opportunity to learn from someone who believed the same thing and to serve the Lord in this new city. As soon as the young couple arrived in Zion City, Fred found a job as a bookkeeper in a local store. At each community church service, he played his cornet joyfully to the Lord.

✳✳✳✳✳

F. F. Bosworth

The Zion City Band was not very accomplished. John Alexander Dowie quickly recognized the scope of Fred Bosworth's musical talent, and when he asked Fred if he would take on the paid position of band director, Fred jumped at the chance. In the past, Fred had played with secular bands, and he thrilled at being able to play the music he dearly loved while lifting up the name of Jesus.

According to one of Bosworth's early biographers, "The Zion City Band rapidly changed from a discordant, amateur musical group to one of the largest and finest musical organizations in the entire United States."[7] Fred's reputation as a musician spread just as quickly. Within months, the forty-seven-member band received a great deal of recognition as a result of playing at Dowie's outreach services, even performing at Madison Square Garden in New York City!

Bosworth was to direct twenty consecutive concerts, two per day for ten days. In New York, critics initially viewed the Midwestern Christian band with cynicism and predicted cultural disaster, but they were unprepared for Bosworth's musical talent and his dedicated service to God. After the first performance, the press offered its praise, saying, "The Concert...was awaited with no little apprehension, but before the players on the stage had swept the first four bars of the first overture, all present knew they were listening to real music produced by masters of the art."[8] F. F. Bosworth was just twenty-six years old at the time of this musical victory.

The Sweeping Power of the Holy Spirit

Not everything in Zion City was going as well. Beginning in 1903, John Alexander Dowie became increasingly autocratic in his role as the city's leader. He proclaimed himself a prophet, "Elijah the Restorer," and donned the robes of an Old Testament priest. Financial and personal troubles surrounded him.

At the same time, a resident of Zion City named Mrs. Waldron attended a tent crusade under the ministry of Charles F. Parham and received the baptism in the Holy Spirit with the evidence of tongues. When she brought the exciting news to Zion City, John Alexander Dowie was determined to keep the "tongues movement" out of his community. However, Bosworth and evangelist John G. Lake, who also lived in Zion City at the time, were

F. F. and Estella Bosworth pose for a family portrait in Zion with Vivian and Vernon.

hungry for the presence of the Holy Spirit in their lives. When Parham came to Zion City to preach on the baptism in the Holy Spirit a few years later, the Bosworths welcomed him into their home to hold meetings. Shortly after this, Fred Bosworth and Lake received the baptism of the Holy Spirit. Together, they made a trip to Azusa Street in California to experience the Holy Spirit's revival there and to seek answers to their questions from the Reverend William J. Seymour concerning this "new" work of God.[9] After Bosworth received the baptism in the Holy Spirit, he looked back at his early days of nomadic movements from one job to the other and said, "I wish someone at that time had told me about being baptized in the Holy Spirit. I did a great deal of drifting not knowing what the right place was for me."[10]

The right place for Fred Bosworth became clear to him almost immediately. During the years that he lived in Zion City, he spoke of his fear that God would call him to preach the gospel. After receiving the baptism in the Holy Spirit, however, he became afraid that God would *not* call him to preach. At twenty-nine years of age, his life had been radically changed. He began to search the Scriptures on the Holy Spirit, such as Matthew 3:11, *"I indeed baptize you with water unto repentance: but he that cometh after me is mightier than I, whose shoes I am not worthy to bear: he shall baptize you with the Holy Ghost, and with fire,"* and Acts 19:2, *"Have ye received the Holy Ghost since ye believed? And they said unto him, We have not so much as heard whether there be any Holy Ghost."* Jesus had promised that the Holy Spirit would come, and that He would be the One to baptize the disciples in the Spirit.

Bosworth also read some of the writings of A. J. Gordon, who spoke out forcefully on the scriptural proof for the baptism of the Holy Spirit as a second and separate experience from salvation. "It is as sinners that we accept Christ; but it is as sons that we accept the Holy Spirit," Gordon wrote as he expounded on the baptism of the Holy Spirit. "We must withhold our consent from the inconsistent exegesis which would make the water baptism of the apostolic times rigidly binding but would relegate the Baptism in the Spirit to a bygone dispensation."[11]

✶✶✶✶✶

F. F. Bosworth

Bosworth admired the wisdom of using biblical logic and the Word to defend the good news of the full gospel. It would become a hallmark for him in future debates on the healing power of God on the earth in modern days.

At the Azusa Street Mission (clockwise from upper left):
Brother Allen, F. F. Bosworth, Tom Hezmalhalch, John G. Lake, and William Seymour

Committed in the Face of Death

Leaving Zion City, Fred and Estella Bosworth decided they would rely completely on the Lord for His provision. Fred abandoned his secular job and his music once again to preach the gospel wherever they were invited. In the beginning of this new life of faith, the Bosworths had to rely daily on the Lord for their provision. They now had a young daughter, Vivian, and they would pray for each meal to be provided, often up to the last minute. At one point in time, they ate boiled wheat for three meals a day. It sustained them for that period, but afterward, they never had boiled wheat on their table again.

When there was no food left, Fred Bosworth would stick his head into the empty bread box and shout, "Glory!" at the top of his lungs. Then, Estella and little Vivian would do the same. God always provided!

✯✯✯✯✯
23

The little Bosworth family traveled to South Bend, Indiana; Austin and Waco, Texas; Conway, South Carolina; and Fitzgerald, Georgia, before finally settling in Dallas, Texas. The year was 1909, and the Pentecostal movement was gathering momentum throughout the nation as the Holy Spirit moved. In Dallas, Fred began a church affiliated with the Christian and Missionary Alliance. They held tent meetings all over the area, sometimes four meetings in one day, introducing people to the power of God through His Holy Spirit.

> **Excited to see others come to know the Lord, Fred was always open to new opportunities to preach.**

Excited to see others come to know the Lord, Fred was always open to new opportunities to preach. One hot summer night in 1909, a friend told him of a camp meeting in Hearne, Texas, some miles outside of Dallas, where the Spirit of God was moving among a black congregation. Racial tensions were high in Texas at the time, so the tent meetings were segregated. The white folks didn't want to approach a "black altar." Thus, Fred was invited so that the white attendees might also receive the baptism of the Holy Spirit from a white preacher.

Bosworth took a train to Hearne and then followed the music to find the camp site. Excitement for Jesus filled the air, and the white people who were listening on the outskirts of the camp invited Bosworth to come and preach to them about the power of God. Standing on a platform between the two segregated groups, Fred gave a short message on the love of Christ and the power of His Spirit to change lives.

"Please stay at my house tonight," one of the other white ministers invited him, "so that you can continue your message tomorrow." Bosworth welcomed the opportunity, and they headed toward the man's home. Suddenly, a mob of angry white men carrying clubs and sticks rushed up behind them. They spit and yelled at Bosworth, accusing him of coming to preach to the black congregation. He explained that the white congregation had invited him, but the incensed men still threatened him and ordered him to leave town immediately.

✷✷✷✷✷

F. F. Bosworth

Filled with a hatred that comes only from Satan, these men meant business, and Bosworth knew it. He agreed to leave and walked rapidly to the train station to head back to Dallas. Standing in the dark station in the quiet of the Texas night, Bosworth was suddenly confronted with an even larger mob of drunken men, who cursed aloud as they stumbled toward the train station.

The mob fell upon Bosworth and knocked him to the ground. They threatened him, saying he would never leave there alive, and beat him with boat oars and sticks all along his back until the skin was torn and bleeding. Several cracks of a baseball bat on his left arm resulted in a broken wrist, leaving his hand to hang painfully at his side. Through it all, Fred Bosworth didn't put up a fight. He committed himself to the Lord's protection and did nothing to defend himself.

As suddenly as the beating had begun, it stopped. The mob, tired of its sport, picked up Bosworth and demanded that he leave town immediately rather than wait for the next train. Bleeding, and with his wrist pounding with pain, Bosworth picked up his suitcase with his other hand and began walking toward Dallas. An attempt to flag down a train on the way proved futile, so he continued on foot. Two days later, he reached home and collapsed in front of his frightened wife. It took a month of bed rest to recover, but Bosworth was thrilled that he had been able to walk all those miles in a glorious state of deep intercession. He was thankful to be alive and able to preach the Word of God. Not long after this, a report came to Fred and Estella that the two leaders of those mobs had met with separate and untimely deaths.

What follows is a letter that Bosworth wrote to his mother shortly after the beating:

We were so glad to get yours, Bert's and Bertha's letters this morning and will answer at once to save you the unnecessary worry about me. When I wrote you from Calvert on my way home from Hearne, Tex., I started a letter telling you all about the mobbing and then thinking how it, might worry you, I tore up the first, letter and wrote you the other one, not, mentioning the pounding I got.

I did this only to save you from worrying. I have never seen any paper with the account, of this mobbing so I don't know what the paper said, wish you would send me the paper. I heard day before yesterday. It was in one of the papers here and went and looked over the files but failed to find it.

At, the annual State Encampment (Pentecostal) of the Col. people at Hearne, the people built a brush arbor, (continuing from the end of their tent) to accommodate the white people of Hearne who wanted to attend the camp meeting. This full gospel had never been preached to the white people at Hearne and besides filling this brush arbor, automobiles and carriages and many white people standing surrounded the tent to listen to the preaching and testimonies of the Col. people. Many of the white citizens became deeply interested in the teaching and not wanting to seek the Baptism at a colored altar. The white people urged the Col. leaders to send for some white Pentecostal teacher to come and help them into the Baptism. And so to accommodate these white citizens, I was sent for and of course went, to the campground and on Saturday night preached to two large audiences, one white and one black. God gave me unusual liberty and blessing in teaching and explaining the truths for which this movement stands, both audiences receiving the truth with great enthusiasm.

I was tired and thought I wouldn't preach that night but the people wanted me to and then God anointed me for it. As I was on my way to spend the night with another white preacher who had also come that day we were attacked by several roughs, one of whom had a revolver with which (as he and the others cursed us for coming there as they said to put them on a level with the d.[irty] n—s) they seemed determined to shoot us both down at once.

God was wonderfully with me and with perfect coolness, I told them that, I was doing God's will the very best I knew how, was ready to die and would offer no resistance to anything God permitted them to do, (these are not, the exact, words), but if they had no objections I would like to speak a few words of explanation before they shot us. At first they refused me this privilege, but finally said I could say what I wanted to. I then told them that I came with no thought or desire of pushing them on a level with anyone but, that it, was the white people who wanted me to come to help them, that I had done the very best, I knew and was willing to take anything God permitted.

With this explanation, they decided not to kill, but insisted that we should take the next train, and so we went to the depot and I bought my ticket to Dallas and the other Bro. went to his room for his suitcase; and while he was gone and I was waiting for my train, a larger mob of about 25 took me horn the depot and knocked me down and pounded me with heavy hardwood clubs with all their power, cursing and declaring that I would never preach again when they were through with me. As they pounded me with these heavy clubs (made from the oar of a boat), I offered no resistance, but committed myself to God and asked him not to let the blows break my spine. God stood wonderfully by me and no bones were broken except a slight fracture in my left wrist. When they left off pounding me with the clubs as I got up others of the mob who had no clubs knocked me down hitting me in the head with their fists. I was knocked down several times but was not for a moment unconscious, which was a miracle of God's care.

I was then not allowed to take my train but had to walk 9 miles to Calvert where I got a train Sunday at 2 p.m. for home.

The suffering during this pounding was terrible but as soon as it was over I looked away from wounds and bruises to God and he took away all suffering and put his power and strength upon me so that I carried a heavy suitcase with my right arm over 9 miles. I never had the slightest anger or ill feeling towards those men who beat me so cruelly, and the walk to Calvert in the dark with moon-light was the most heavenly experience of my life and the Lord gave me wonderful intercession for those men that He should forgive them and prepare them for his coming.

My flesh was mashed to the bone on my back down nearly to my knees, but since the beating I have been free from all suffering.

Others been made nervous and have broken down and wept as they were shown the wounds on my bow, but I have been absolutely free from nervousness, no fear and not even tired.

He has been so precious to me since that I have thanked him many times for being privileged to know something of the "fellowship of his sufferings". If this moving was the result of some unwise thing I had done or for speaking anything but His own sweet message, I would be very sorry but since it came for plain obedience in preaching His gospel to every creature, it has given me great joy to experience this which was so common among the early Christians in the first centuries of the church.

I feel like I am several notches higher in the Christian life.

Already this experience God has used and made it a blessing to others and I have read some of the sweetest letters from God's people.

You need not worry one bit for we are not now preaching to Col. People and will not unless God clearly leads as he did when he led us to Queen City and other parts of Dallas. He put his seal upon this by saving many, healing many and baptizing over 225 with the Holy Ghost. The deepest and quickest work I have known of. We do not lay our own plans but wait for him.

We have just moved our tent from the corner of Weaskell and State Sts. To the corner of East Side and Washington Ave., and last night which was our first night in the new location, the tent was nearly full and the attention was fine. Pray that God will give us a great meeting there. We may move into some house near the tent in a few days.

Vivian is well and so sweet. God gives her at times the real burden for souls at which times the Spirit makes intercession through her in tongues. Bro. Graves (Fred A. Graves) is with us.

The paper just came from Z.C. (Zion City, Illinois) telling about my beating.

Not much like the facts. My face was not scratched but my head was bruised in several places, No marks left on my face.

Would love to see you all at home. We are all happy in the will of God.

I would much prefer to be faithful and have some little tribulation now than to fail to overcome and have to pass through the great

✶✶✶✶✶

tribulation soon to come. Praise God I am determined to have God's plan for my life carried out.

With much love to you all, I am Your Devoted Son.
Fred

Ten Years of Revival

As the Pentecostal wave moved through the country, Assemblies of God congregations began to spring up. In 1910, Bosworth established the First Assembly of God church in Dallas, and people flocked there from miles around to hear him preach. From the very beginning, seekers were saved and baptized in the Holy Spirit with the evidence of speaking in tongues. Bosworth didn't have any formal seminary training, but he was an intelligent man who studied the Bible with more diligence than he had displayed when teaching himself to play the cornet. God had placed him in the spiritual office of evangelist, as well as teacher, for building up the body of Christ. (See Ephesians 4:11–13.) This was evident to everyone who heard him.

In 1912, Bosworth invited Maria Woodworth-Etter, the famous Pentecostal evangelist, to lead a series of meetings at his church. During her six-month stay, revival rocked the city of Dallas. Scores of people were saved, filled with the Holy Spirit, and healed under her ministry. Bosworth became well-known among Pentecostals because of the success of Woodworth-Etter's meetings. Revival continued in his church for the next several years.

The number of Assemblies of God churches grew, and Bosworth was selected as a delegate to the General Council of the Assemblies of God denomination as it was being formed. In April of 1914, the first General Council met in Hot Springs, Arkansas, to discuss the new work. Bosworth was then invited to become one of the sixteen members of the executive presbyters. It was the role of the Council and the presbyters to set the tenets of faith for the new denomination.

Even while pastoring his church in Dallas and working as a delegate for the Assemblies of God, Fred Bosworth traveled over 75,000 miles throughout the Southwest and took every opportunity to preach. If there was even one ear open to the gospel of Jesus Christ, Fred was eager to bring the good news! He believed in an interceding church that also reached out to the lost, so he organized many tent meetings in different areas of Dallas that occurred simultaneously. The gospel was preached night after night, and more and more people turned to Christ for salvation.

From Pastor to Full-time Evangelist

As the revival began to slow down in Dallas, Fred and Estella's only son, four-year-old Vernon, became sick and suddenly died.

Within months of the loss, Fred resigned from the church he had pastored and loved. From years of studying the Word, Bosworth had come to the conclusion that speaking in tongues was not the only initial evidence of the baptism in the Holy Spirit. The other members of the Assemblies of God founding board disagreed with Bosworth; they believed unanimously that tongues as the initial evidence of the baptism should be one of the irrefutable tenets of the denomination. A fellow minister in the Dallas area began to spread rumors about Bosworth, accusing him of heresy among the Pentecostal churches.

Quietly and without protest, Bosworth turned in his Assemblies of God ordination papers in July 1918. He was invited to present his beliefs to the General Council one more time concerning why speaking in tongues need not be the initial evidence of the baptism of the Holy Spirit. Bosworth did so with a humble heart, presenting his beliefs passionately. The Council listened but still voted against his proposals, and they parted ways.

With little time to recover from these tremendous disappointments, Fred faced another, greater tragedy. Estella had been a hardworking helpmate for eighteen years, but in her exuberance for the ministry, she often overexerted herself. As her health slipped, she continued to ignore the bed rest that she needed. Early in 1919, she developed a cough, which quickly became pneumonia and then tuberculosis. Even though prayers for healing went up in earnest, Estella Bosworth died on November 16, 1919, leaving two daughters without a mother. Fred had seen countless healings as a result of answered prayer, which made his wife's death seem an even greater tragedy, but he never gave up his faith in a faithful, living God.

✭✭✭✭✭

Through these tragedies, Fred Bosworth became a more compassionate human being. He was seen as kind, self-effacing, and completely dependent on the Lord for everything. Through these trials, his faith was not moved, so God gave him a greater power in witnessing for Him.

After finding someone to take care of his daughters, Fred Bosworth turned his steps to national evangelism, answering the call to preach wherever he could. He had rejoined the Christian and Missionary Alliance Church and asked his younger brother, Burton, to join in his revival ministry as the worship leader. They began traveling wherever they were invited, carrying a burning passion to see the lost come to Christ. The decade of the 1920s would see F. F. Bosworth preaching the Word of God in power with signs and wonders following.

Healing Victories in Lima, Ohio

In the summer of 1920, Bosworth was invited to preach at a revival in Lima, Ohio. The pastor had one simple request—that he would bring a message on the healing power of Jesus Christ for today. Accepting the summons as God's will, Bosworth spent a great deal of time studying the Bible, both the Old and the New Testaments, to learn more about the healing presence of God.

God had brought Bosworth back from near death from tuberculosis through His healing power, so Fred knew that Jesus Christ healed today. Healing for the believer was a part of the salvation message; it was included in the price Christ had paid on the cross. Now, Fred studied the Word closely to find as much scriptural support as he could for his messages.

Fred still had one nagging fear. "I said to the Lord, 'But suppose I preach healing, and the people come, and they don't get healed?' And the Lord responded, 'If people didn't get saved, you wouldn't stop preaching the gospel.'"[12] With that, Fred went forth boldly to share the complete message of Jesus' atonement.

The Lima meetings were held in a large tent during the hot evenings of August 1920. On the first night, Fred Bosworth stood at the podium and announced to the expectant audience, "I am convinced that healing of the body is just as much a part of the gospel as salvation for the soul." He assured them that Christ longed to do for their "pain-wracked" bodies

Fred Bosworth stood at the podium and announced to the expectant audience, "I am convinced that healing of the body is just as much a part of the gospel as salvation for the soul."

what He also wanted to do for their lost souls. Then, he made a bold proclamation: bring your sick and infirm—whether they know Jesus or not, God wants to heal them.

The congregation was electrified by this announcement, and many planned to return with their sick and dying loved ones. Bosworth emphasized that the saved and unsaved alike should bring the sick to be healed by a compassionate Christ. He offered hope that they could be well again.

The next night, hundreds of people were present; the night after that, thousands made their way to the tent meeting. Soon, the meetings had to be moved into Memorial Hall. Some came expecting a miracle; others came ready to laugh at failure. But everyone present saw the same things: deaf ears could hear, blind eyes could see, the lame could walk. The Holy Spirit was moving among the people, and He was unstoppable. Doctors came and brought their most critical patients, and many of them were cured.

A woman without hope named Alice Baker attended one of the early Lima meetings. She suffered from cancer of the face, and her upper lip had been so eaten away that her teeth were visible. She kept her face covered with cloths so that no one would see the destroyed flesh. To ease her agonizing pain so she could sleep at night, the doctors had resorted to giving her small doses of ether. Alice had spent what little money she had on appointments with specialists in New York and New Jersey, but there was absolutely nothing they could do for her. Alice was filled with despair.

When she heard about the healing meetings taking place at Memorial Hall, she didn't understand what was happening there, but she decided to go and see if there was any hope left. The first thing she heard from the pulpit was the price Jesus Christ had paid on the cross for her sins. With a glad and grateful heart, she knelt and accepted Him as her Savior. Then, she went forward for a healing prayer.

She later recounted what happened when she met with the Bosworth team.

> After they prayed for me it seemed a rubber cap was drawn over my face, and it gradually slipped off, and I knew I was healed. I told a lady to remove the bandages and God blessed my soul, so I could not help shouting, and I shouted many times. It is so good to be without pain....Oh, I am so happy all the time. I went down the street shouting....The next morning after I was healed I went to the hotel where I worked and showed the lady that I was without the bandages and that the Lord had given me a new lip that night, and she was shocked....Many have come from other towns to see me...and hear about my healing. I am glad to tell them. My doctor came to see for himself, and all he said was it was wonderful.[13]

F. F. Bosworth was a simple man with a heart to bring the lost to Christ. He believed that physical healing was included in the atonement and that true healings would draw crowds to hear the message of Christ's salvation, the ultimate goal. He was also a very deliberate man, so he looked for confirmation of each healing that took place. Often, the local newspapers would record in detail the miracles that had occurred on those August nights in Lima.

In an article published in the *National Labor Tribune*, a newspaper in nearby Pittsburgh, Pennsylvania, Bertram Miller wrote of the miraculous Bosworth campaign, "There has been no criticism from the public press, no fanaticism or carnal emotionalism at any of the services.... Many denominations and nationalities were in attendance at the meetings, and many were saved and wonderfully healed, wondering why they had never heard the full gospel before...."[14]

Some were healed instantly, many at their homes in the following days. At one service alone, there were ten doctors present watching the proceedings with deep interest. Several of them had terminally ill patients of their own healed before their very eyes.[15]

✫✫✫✫✫

The Miracles Move to Pittsburgh

After several weeks of ministering in Lima, the Bosworth team moved on to Pittsburgh. Many of the newly healed went with them, eager to help in the work and pray for the sick themselves. Bosworth never believed that healing came through his hands alone but through faith in God's Word that built up in the hearts of those who needed healing.

The miracles in Pittsburgh surpassed those in Lima. No church was large enough to accommodate the crowds, so the meetings were held in Carnegie Hall in Oakland, a suburb near downtown Pittsburgh. The *National Labor Tribune* continued to report on the amazing meetings as they were occurring.

All denominations crowd the hall—Catholics, Episcopalians, Presbyterians, Methodists, Baptists, United Presbyterians, Primitive Methodists, Methodist Protestant, Pentecostal Nazarene, with many others, may be seen among those at the altar seeking Divine aid. Several hundred seekers after God crowd the platform daily....Doctors, lawyers, financiers, merchants, professional men of all types and caliber. Christian Scientists—including practitioners—nurses, and head nurses from the hospitals and sanitariums, all seeking soul salvation or bodily healing. It is a sight that astounds the onlookers to see those multitudes seeking their way to God....Beyond belief are the results.[16]

"John Sproul Can Talk!"

John Sproul had fought in WWI as a young soldier. While he was on a special assignment to secure supplies in France, he and a friend were hit with mustard gas. The friend died within a day or two, but John survived—just barely. He had to have fourteen operations in the French hospital where he was admitted. Six operations were performed on his throat and eight on his lungs. Following the operations, he completely lost the ability to speak, and so many of his neck muscles were cut away that he had a hard time holding his head up.[17]

Sproul returned to the States in constant pain, with hemorrhaging in his lungs and frequent bouts of stomach sickness or sudden

✷✷✷✷✷

unconsciousness. He traveled throughout the country trying to get medical help, but his case was declared hopeless. When he returned to his hometown of Pittsburgh, the mayor, Edward Babcock, took up his cause. The country was disturbed by the lack of medical aid for wounded veterans, so Mayor Babcock and the local congressmen sent Sproul to Washington, D.C., for special medical treatment.

When he returned from Washington, Sproul informed the mayor that he had been pronounced incurable by the physicians there and given a certificate of total disability for life. He was awarded a monthly disability payment, but he still faced a future filled with unrelenting pain.

By the providence of God, soon after Sproul's return from Washington, he saw an advertisement for Evangelist F. F. Bosworth's campaign in Pittsburgh. He went simply because he felt he had nothing to lose. As he sat and listened to the testimonies of those who had given their hearts to Christ, the Spirit moved in his soul. He later exclaimed, "Oh, the joy that filled my soul when I realized the Lord was ready to save me, right then, and I said, 'Yes' to God. How I longed to be able to speak, to tell people that I knew I was saved!"[18]

When Bosworth called for those who wished to be healed to come forward, John Sproul walked up to the platform with a heart full of faith. After prayer, a Christian brother exclaimed, "Praise the Lord," and Sproul thought the man meant that he should praise the Lord with his own voice. "Of all the foolish things," John reasoned, "to expect me to praise the Lord when I can't talk!" Then, he thought, *Well, that isn't faith. I'll try, even if nobody hears it.*[19]

The moment he made the effort to praise the Lord, a strange power seemed to fill his whole body. Pain coursed through him from his stomach through his throat and into his head. It was excruciating, but in an instant, it was gone. With it went all of the agonizing pain that John had experienced for four years. There was no more lung pain, no more throat pain, and no more wheezing! At the top of his voice, he yelled, "Praise the Lord! Praise the Lord!" Soon after the service, his family cautioned John to be careful with his newly recovered voice, but his response was, "I was shouting His praises, and I knew as long as I praised God, nothing would ever happen to my voice."[20]

★ ★ ★ ★ ★

John called his friends and his mother on the telephone to tell them the amazing news, but none could believe it was he. When the news reached the local newspaper reporters, they insisted on meeting with him, as did Mayor Babcock. Fred walked into the mayor's office with his head held high, and he smiled and spoke normally. The next day's newspaper hit the stands for the whole city to see the headline, "John Sproul Can Talk!"

The Sproul family rejoiced when John's three-year-old daughter, Mary Jane, who had never heard him speak, clapped her little hands and exclaimed, "Daddy can talk! Daddy can talk! Jesus made Daddy talk!"[21]

The Veterans Bureau ordered John to report for tests, after which they declared him well, indeed. He had to forsake his disability payments, but he had been healed by God and could work now. For years after his healing, he corresponded with F. F. Bosworth, letting him know how much he enjoyed perfect health in his body and his soul!

Christ the Healer

From his intimacy with Scriptures on divine healing, Fred wrote *Christ the Healer* in 1924. The book remains a classic work on Christ's healing power, and it is just as relevant to the body of Christ today as it was upon publication nearly one hundred years ago.

The primary question Bosworth wanted to answer in his book was, "Did Christ redeem us from our diseases when He atoned for our sins?"[22] To him, the Bible answered with a resounding "Yes!" He believed that the healing nature of God was revealed in both the Old Testament and the New Testament.

In the Old Testament, the book of Exodus recounts the Israelites' miraculous journey through the Red Sea, which God parted through Moses, as they fled captivity in Egypt. When they reached the other side of the sea, this same God of salvation introduced Himself as their healer for the first time, saying, *"I am the LORD that healeth you"* (Exodus 15:26). In Psalms, King David also recognized the healing nature of God's salvation: *"Bless the LORD, O my soul, and forget not all of his benefits: who forgiveth all thine iniquities; who healeth all thy diseases"* (Psalm 103:2–3). David realized that both the forgiveness of sins and the healing of the body were benefits that belonged to the people of God.

✷✷✷✷✷

Perhaps the most decisive Scripture of all for Bosworth was Isaiah 53:5: *"He was wounded for our transgressions, he was bruised for our iniquities: the chastisement of our peace was upon him; and with his stripes we are healed."*

In these Scriptures, the Lord is revealed as a complete Savior who forgives sins *and* heals diseases. Both benefits are offered equally for anyone who would receive them.

In *Christ the Healer*, Bosworth wrote that God's healing nature continued to be revealed in the earthly ministry of Christ, citing Matthew 4:23: *"And Jesus went about all Galilee, teaching in their synagogues, and preaching the gospel of the kingdom, and healing all manner of sickness and all manner of disease among the people,"* Matthew 12:15: *"Jesus...withdrew himself from thence: and great multitudes followed him, and he healed them all,"* and Luke 6:19: *"And the whole multitude sought to touch him: for there went virtue out of him, and healed them all."*

Bosworth was convinced that these Scriptures clearly revealed the will of God concerning healing. He declared, "Faith begins where the will of God is known."[23] The Word reveals that it is God's will to heal, and believers can accept His will by faith—faith that is produced by hearing the Word of God. (See Romans 10:17.)

Finally, Bosworth pointed out that the Greek word for salvation, *soteria*, implies all the deliverance, preservation, healing, and soundness that Christ promised with His death and resurrection. Full salvation was in the atonement of the blood of Christ.

Faith Cures a Young Girl

During the first half of the 1920s, Fred and his brother Burton traveled continuously throughout the nation. Their primary purpose at each meeting was to save souls.

During a seven-week campaign in Ottawa, Canada, the "conservative" Canadians showed a great enthusiasm for the Lord. Twelve thousand people surrendered their hearts to Christ, and ten thousand people attended the farewell meeting. The Canadians were so grateful for the powerful message that Christ heals soul and body that five thousand of them accompanied the Bosworth party to their train. They picked up the brothers and carried them on their shoulders all the way to the train station! Yet Fred Bosworth was always careful to give the glory to God and not to take it for himself.

It had been several years since Estella Bosworth had passed away, and Fred was perfectly content to remain unmarried while serving the Lord. But he also desired God's will for his life. When he was forty-five years old, he met a young lady named Florence Valentine, a post-graduate student at a New York campus of Nyack Bible School. When Bosworth met her, he realized that she shared his desire to serve God and preach the gospel. They both prayed that God's will would be done and were married quietly a short time later. Florence brought him great joy and was an excellent helpmate during their thirty-six years of marriage.

With Florence helping to spread the message of faith in God's healing power, the Bosworth brothers continued to hold healing meetings throughout the 1920s. After ministering together for five years, Burton moved on to minister on his own, while Fred and Florence conducted much of their ministry in the Chicago area. The revival meetings were often held in Chicago's Gospel Tabernacle, and people continued to be miraculously healed.

On Wednesday, March 28, 1928, the *Chicago Daily News* featured a front-page headline that read, "Deaf Six Years, Faith Cures Her." Beneath the headline was a large photo of Fred Bosworth teaching a smiling teenage girl how to use a telephone.

The girl was Ruth Peiper, age sixteen. Her mother had died when Ruth was only eight, and her father had refused to provide a home for her. So, Ruth had been sent to a home for dependent girls. When she was eleven years old, she contracted diphtheria and scarlet fever. Due to those illnesses, she lost hearing in both her ears. She also had to wear a body cast and walked with a noticeable limp due to a severe curvature of the spine. Her doctors had not been able to help her, and her stay in the home became far longer than that of most other girls her age.

Ruth had become a favorite at the home, and one of the volunteers had taken a special interest in her. This volunteer had urged Martha Dixon, the matron, to take Ruth to a Bosworth healing meeting at the

Chicago Gospel Tabernacle. Ready to do anything that might help Ruth, Mrs. Dixon took her to the meeting. That night, March 2, 1928, Ruth Peiper was completely healed!

Ruth came running into the front parlor of the home to tell the *Chicago Daily News* reporter more of her story. "'Yes, it's all true,' she said as she walked across the room without a limp. 'Something just suddenly happened to me as I stood on the platform being anointed by the Reverend Bosworth. It was like lightning and thunder in my head. Then there was a ringing in my ears.'"

Riding home on the bus that night with Mrs. Dixon, Ruth couldn't believe how loud everything was. Every time someone paid the bus fare and the bell rang, she jumped. The sounds were loud, but they were also wonderful! "'It's all in the Bible,' Ruth concluded to the reporter. 'It is just believing what is there that has made me well.'"[24]

The power of God to heal was still moving through the Bosworths' ministry at the end of the 1920s.

"What Manner of Man Is This?"

Without a doubt, F. F. Bosworth had become one of the most successful of the healing evangelists of the 1920s. But what sort of man was he? Many of his Pentecostal contemporaries were known for their loud meetings and emotional appeals. Bosworth was different. So, who *was* Fred Bosworth? With deep humility and compassion, Bosworth was confident in God, in His Word, and in the Lord's calling on his life. Because of these things, he never felt threatened by the successes of other ministries or felt that he was in competition with other preachers. He strived for purity in his actions and motives. The integrity of his life and ministry brought the respect of others, even those who disagreed with him. In temperament, he was a man of good humor who always tried to remain optimistic, no matter the circumstances.

One news reporter from Pittsburgh alluded to Luke 8:25 when he wrote, "The simplicity of the services and the wanton lack of any attempt to play upon the emotions of the great throngs who crowd themselves into the building naturally incites the onlooker to inquire, 'What manner of man is this?'"[25]

Eunice N. Perkins, Bosworth's early biographer, was a great admirer of his preaching style, which she described thusly: "No dramatics! A clear, convincing logic ofttimes, for altho uneducated in a worldly sense, he has an unusually bright mind, has studied the cream of Christian literature, and is continually being taught the Word of God, by the Spirit of God. Moreover, his simple naturalness, or natural simplicity, is delightfully refreshing to all who hear him, while it is, at the same time, more forceful than the most amazing pulpit oratory."[26]

> **Bosworth believed in the living power of the Bible to build faith in the hearts of those who read from its pages or heard it preached.**

Bosworth believed in the living power of the Bible to build faith in the hearts of those who read from its pages or heard it preached. Because he believed so steadfastly in the solid foundation of the Word, he preached with a quiet, firm authority that was uncommon at the time.

When the Bosworth party was conducting a crusade in St. Paul, Minnesota, the Reverend J. D. Williams reviewed F. F. Bosworth in the local newspaper. He admired "the wide scope of his message. The preaching was Scriptural and earnest and the truth presented covered the entire Fourfold Gospel, i.e., Christ as Saviour, Sanctifier, Healer and Coming King. Special stress was laid upon the Atonement covering both spiritual and physical needs."[27] Commendable aspects of Bosworth's ministry, according to Williams, included the thorough preparation of the workers who were ready to pray for those who came forward, as well as the preparation of the hearts of those who were so ready to receive.

Williams went on,

The meetings were generally very quiet, with few expressions of any kind from the audience....It was evident...that each message was taking deep root in hearts....There was no attempt upon the part of the Evangelist to produce an effect or to urge anyone to hasty decisions by emotional appeals. The total dependence

F. F. Bosworth

upon the Holy Spirit for all results was gratifying. In short, "They preached not themselves but Christ."[28]

There was a "holy joy" that pervaded the atmosphere at Bosworth's meetings. Because the man himself was joyful at what had been provided in Christ's atonement, he passed that same hope and joy on to his audiences. The men and women who came to the Bosworth revivals heard the good news of complete salvation in Christ!

Fred Bosworth was also acknowledged as a gifted teacher. P. S. Campbell, a professor of Greek from McMaster University, Toronto, said this of Bosworth:

> His addresses are thoroughly biblical. He believes in the Word of God, and his arguments are amply supported by quotations from the sacred Scriptures. His language is absolutely free from sensationalism, and is the acme of simplicity. And what is clear to himself, he never fails to make clear to his audience. His sermons show that he possesses in a marked degree the teaching gift. Hence his hearers never fail to be instructed by his presentation of the truth.[29]

Pioneer of Radio Evangelism

As the 1920s drew to a close, there was such a demand for Bosworth's time and ministry, yet so few resources, that he realized he needed a new means to reach people with the gospel. After ministering with Paul Rader in Chicago for a while, Bosworth had his answer: radio. Rader had already begun one of the first Christian radio programs in the nation. The first crude radios had been released for sale in 1926, and people had rushed to purchase them as a welcome addition to their homes.

F. F. Bosworth's first radio program was called *The Sunshine Hour*. Each morning at 9:00 a.m. on Chicago's station WJJD, Bosworth's theme song "Don't Forget to Pray" would fill the airwaves. Soon after, he established the nonprofit organization National Radio Revival Missionary Crusaders to reach the masses with the gospel of Jesus Christ.

The Bosworths settled in River Forest, Illinois, outside of Chicago, and Fred recorded his radio shows in a studio in his home. The message then traveled ten miles to Chicago by telephone wire and was put on the air from the radio station. Thousands heard the message and wrote to Bosworth requesting prayer for healings or praising God for their salvation. The successful reports of lives touched by the Holy Spirit poured into his home office. By the time he retired from radio ministry in the 1940s, Bosworth had received over 250,000 letters from those who had been touched or healed from his preaching.

Even though Bosworth's daily radio preaching enabled him to limit his travels, his healing meetings were not discontinued altogether. Thousands still flocked to hear him preach the Word of God with power and to receive their healings. But in the 1930s, the Great Depression made it very difficult to travel far from home, so most of his ministering was done in the Chicago area. In his years of radio ministry, Bosworth may have reached tens of thousands with the gospel message, but he was largely reserved when it came to his personal life.

During this time, Bosworth adopted a controversial view called British Israelism, a concept that gained popularity in the early twentieth century and continues to be accepted by some people today. British Israelism maintains that Western Europeans, particularly those from Great Britain, are direct descendants of the ten lost tribes of Israel who were taken into captivity by the Assyrians. (See 2 Kings 17:18.) The belief was most widely upheld in England and the United States. How strongly Bosworth embraced this idea is unknown, but he did resign from the Christian and Missionary Alliance denomination for several years because of it. By the mid-1940s, Bosworth had renounced his belief in British Israelism and was reinstated in the church.

Retirement Not in His Plans

By 1947, at seventy-one years of age, Fred Bosworth was ready for the next step in his life. He and Florence decided it was time to retire to Miami, Florida. But what would this dedicated man of God do with the remainder of his years?

But retirement was clearly was not in the Lord's plan for him. William Branham, an American evangelist from the Midwest, was beginning to move out in his healing ministry and had been invited to Miami,

Florida, to conduct a revival campaign. Curious, Fred and Florence attended the revival and were moved by the powerful presence of the Holy Spirit and the number of healings that had been recorded as a result of Branham's ministry. Bosworth introduced himself to the younger man and, after they'd spent some time fellowshipping together, offered to travel with him and minister as part of his team.

Branham jumped at the opportunity to be mentored by the older, wiser evangelist, who had forty years of experience in the healing ministry. Beginning in 1948, Fred Bosworth traveled with the Branham team and taught about faith for salvation and divine healing. He spoke at the daytime meetings so that Branham would have time to rest and have enough energy to conduct the larger healing meetings, which were held in the evening. Joining them in the ministry was W. Ern Baxter, a young evangelist from Canada, who served as Branham's traveling manager and preached daytime messages during the campaign, as well. The reports of Branham's successful healing meetings were written by Gordon Lindsay in the magazine *The Voice of Healing*. As a result, Branham's reputation as a Pentecostal grew rapidly.

Fred Bosworth was still very sharp-witted and solid in his biblical presentation of the Word. In 1950, Branham was challenged to a debate on divine healing by W. E. Best, the pastor of a large Baptist church in Houston, Texas. Best believed that miracles and divine healing had ceased, and that the healing evangelists were frauds. Branham declined the challenge, but seventy-three-year-old F. F. Bosworth accepted it enthusiastically. He was an adept apologist and welcomed the opportunity to spread the truth about God's healing promises in the atonement.

The debate was covered closely by the local newspapers. During the debate, Bosworth presented the scriptural evidence he had outlined years earlier in *Christ the Healer*, including healing in Christ's atonement and one of the redemptive names of God, Jehovah-Rapha. Then, he appealed to the "living witnesses" who were present, asking them to stand if they had been healed by God. The *Houston Press* reported, "When the Rev. Best made a point, the Rev. Bosworth would rush to the microphone on stage and dramatically ask those in the audience who had been cured through faith to stand. Each time hundreds would rise. 'How many of you are Baptists?' the Rev. Bosworth shouted. At least 100 stood up."[30]

✫✫✫✫✫

Bosworth was confident in the Word of God and the proof that God was still ministering healing power to His people.

Overseas Ministry Captures Bosworth's Heart

William Branham also ministered overseas. On November 25, 1951, F. F. Bosworth looked out incredulously at a vast crowd of people at the Grayville Race Course in Durban, South Africa. The police estimated the crowd at 75,000 people. In over forty years of ministry, Bosworth had never seen anything like the tens of thousands who sat there with open hearts to hear the Word of God.

In the morning service, Bosworth preached on the Holy Spirit's desire to heal and explained how to obtain the faith to receive that healing. Later that day, thirty-seven-year-old Ern Baxter gave a message of salvation through the blood of Jesus Christ. When Baxter invited those who wanted to receive Christ as Savior to stand, over ten thousand people stood to their feet. Turning to Bosworth, Baxter whispered in awe, "They must have misunderstood me. There couldn't be all these thousands who want to become Christians!"[31] Baxter repeated the message of commitment to Christ, and the people waved their hands in surrender to the Lord. Later that evening, William Branham brought forth the message, and thousands more were saved and healed by the grace of God. During the three services on that day alone, an estimated thirty thousand people gave their hearts to Christ! Bosworth was delighted to be a part of this move of God.

In those later days of ministry, nothing touched Fred Bosworth's heart like the overseas ministry he participated in. He was astounded by the sizes of the crowds and the open hearts of faith, the likes of which he had never experienced in the U.S. While he was traveling with the Branham team, they went on to hold overseas campaigns in Germany and Switzerland.

Bosworth was in his mid-seventies by this time, but he still carried a full load of responsibilities in these foreign fields, teaching every morning and bringing the Word of God to help build up the faith of those to whom he ministered. He also stayed at the evening meetings long after Branham left, exhausted, and prayed for the sick.

✷✷✷✷✷

F. F. BOSWORTH

F. F. Bosworth and William Branham in Germany in 1955

In 1952, Bosworth left the Branham campaigns, but he continued in the foreign mission field for several more years, conducting meetings in South Africa and Cuba, and taking two missionary visits to Japan, where his final meeting took place.

Praising as He Goes Home

One of Bosworth's biographers, who wrote in the *Herald of Faith* magazine in 1964, was Oscar Blomgren Jr., a young man who first met the healing evangelist as a boy. At five years of age, Oscar was walking precariously on the back of a park bench near Lake Forest, Illinois, when he fell. He was rushed to the hospital, where an X-ray revealed that his elbow had been shattered into several fragments. Doctors were concerned that his arm would be stiff for the rest of his life.

Oscar's father was a faithful Christian and a personal friend of Bosworth, so he called the evangelist at his home for prayer. He didn't ask him to come and lay hands on the child, just to pray in faith on the phone for Oscar in the name of Jesus. The next day, the little boy had several hours of surgery on his arm. The following morning, X-rays were taken again to determine whether the surgery had been successful. Puzzled, the doctors ordered a third X-ray. They called Oscar's parents into the therapy room to discuss the results. Both X-rays revealed no sign of a break. It was as if nothing had happened. Oscar's elbow was completely restored.

The rambunctious little boy hung from his arms on a crossbar in the hospital therapy room while his parents and the doctors discussed his miraculous recovery. His cast was removed immediately. In relating the story, Oscar Jr. always gratefully added that his once-shattered arm played in many successful football games in the years to follow!

In his biography of Bosworth, Oscar remembered the man with great affection:

Fred Bosworth gave me, and tens of thousands of others an unshakable faith in God that we will carry to our graves. He demonstrated again and again that the real benefits of Christianity are not just spiritual, but physical as well. And through him God gave the inquiring mind a granite-solid foundation for faith.... Those of us who were privileged to know him will remember him always. But more important, the Faith that he gave us will live on in our children and grandchildren for years to come.[32]

In 1958, when Bosworth returned to Florida, and to Florence, after his final campaign in Japan, he announced to his family that the Lord was about to take him home. At the age of eighty-one, he was not ill; he had asked the Lord to allow him to live his life without succumbing to any illness, and he simply believed that his time on earth was over.

Bosworth retired to his bed, and all of his children came home to say good-bye, getting together for the first time in over sixteen years. His son Bob wrote about the final weeks of his father's life:

About three weeks after he took to his bed, we were around the bed talking, laughing, singing. Suddenly Dad looked up; he never saw us again. He saw what was invisible to us. He began to greet people and hug people—he was enraptured. Every once in a while he would break off and look around saying, "Oh, it is so beautiful."[33]

For several hours, Fred remained in this state, between two worlds. Then, he quietly fell asleep. Sometime later, he passed from sleep to his eternal place in Christ. It was Thursday, January 23, 1958. After five decades of honoring and preaching about Jesus Christ, his Redeemer and Healer, Bosworth joined Him in heaven. It has been estimated that

✶✶✶✶✶

during his lifetime, Bosworth was instrumental in more than one million decisions for Christ. There would have been many joyful souls to greet him in heaven.

Just days before his death, Bosworth was quoted as saying, "All I have lived for, for the past sixty years, has been the Lord Jesus. And, any minute, I'm looking for Him to walk in the door and go with Him for eternity."[34]

ENDNOTES

1   Eunice M. Perkins, *Joybringer Bosworth: His Life's Story* (1921), 162.
2   *Exploits of Faith* magazine, 1928, 4.
3   Perkins, *Joybringer Bosworth,* 163.
4   Ibid.
5   Ibid., 25.
6   Ibid., 27.
7   Oscar Blomgren Jr., "Man of God, Fred F. Bosworth," Part IV: Bosworth Begins His Work, *Herald of Faith,* (June 1964), 16.
8   Ibid. (Citing Perkins, *Joybringer Bosworth,* 37.)
9   http://www.healingandrevival.com/BioBosworth.htm.
10 *Bosworth's Life Story: The Life Story of Evangelist F. F. Bosworth, as Told by Himself in the Alliance Tabernacle, Toronto* (Toronto, Ontario: Alliance Book Room), 3.
11 Perkins, *Joybringer Bosworth,* 53, 55.
12 Bosworth, *Life Story,* 22.
13 Perkins, *Joybringer Bosworth,* 129, 130.
14 Ibid., 89–90.
15 Ibid., 91.
16 Ibid., 99, 100.
17 *Exploits of Faith* magazine, 1928, 14.
18 Ibid., 15.
19 Ibid.
20 Ibid., 15.
21 Ibid.
22 F. F. Bosworth, *Christ the Healer* (New Kensington, PA: Whitaker House, 2000), 12.
23 Bosworth, *Life Story,* 43.
24 *Exploits of Faith,* 25.
25 Perkins, *Joybringer Bosworth,* 101.
26 Ibid., 94.
27 Ibid., 114.
28 Ibid., 115.
29 Ibid., 169.
30 Roscoe Barnes III, *F. F. Bosworth: The Man Behind "Christ the Healer"* (Newcastle upon Tyne, England: Cambridge Scholars Publishing, 2009), 52.
31 *The Voice of Healing* magazine (South Africa), March 1952.
32 Blomgren Jr., "Man of God," 15.
33 Barnes, *The Man Behind,* 15.
34 Ibid.

★★★★★
CHAPTER TWO

GEORGE JEFFREYS

"Great Britain's Pentecostal Apostle"

"Great Britain's Pentecostal Apostle"

On Good Friday in April 1928, tier upon tier of historic Royal Albert Hall in London was filled to overflowing, testing the capacity of the amphitheater, the arena, the boxes, and the orchestra pit. Several thousand people watched in anticipation, their faces beaming. They rose to their feet, rejoicing, and looked with rapt attention at the scene below.

In an area below the platform stood a long line of exuberant men and women who had changed from their street clothes. The women were dressed in long, white robes, the men in white shirts and trousers. They shouted "Hallelujah!" and "Praise the Lord!" as they waited their turns with joyful anticipation. Some of them sang hymns or waved enthusiastically at the crowd around them. One at a time, they descended the stairs into the sparkling water in the baptismal tank in the center of the hall, which was surrounded by beautiful hydrangea bushes.

A dark-haired man wearing a black robe stood waist-deep in the waters waiting to greet each candidate before plunging him or her into the waters of baptism.

In the specially designed iron tank, the water ran in a stream as a reminder of the Jordan River. As each candidate came forward, evangelist

George Jeffreys introduced him or her and asked for a brief testimony. The first to be baptized was Florence Munday of Southampton, who had been bedridden for fourteen years before being healed in the name of Jesus. One by one, each individual would emerge from the water and exit on the other side of the stage, full of the love of Christ and the power of His Holy Spirit.

Nearly one thousand candidates followed Miss Munday into those baptismal waters, and, by God's grace, Jeffreys and his team immersed each one of them.

Two days later, on Easter morning, the crowds lined up before dawn for the eleven o'clock service. Newspapers would later report that ten thousand people were in attendance, filling the hall with sounds of praise and thanksgiving to a risen Savior. The two-thousand-member Crusaders Choir, comprising vocalists from all over London, stood on both sides of the platform and sang songs of joyful praise to the Lord. There was a beautiful Communion service, and the congregation broke bread in memory of the death and resurrection of Christ.

The service that evening ended with hundreds raising their hands in surrender to the saving grace of Jesus. Hundreds more stood up to acknowledge that they had received a healing. Finally, thousands of voices rose together in glorifying praise to God. The meeting closed with the hymn "All Hail the Power of Jesus' Name," after which the redeemed and transformed filed out of the hallowed hall. For the next eleven years, Jeffreys would fill the Royal Albert Hall each Easter weekend, giving the praise to God for His work among the people of London.

George Jeffreys

An Apostle/Evangelist

George Jeffreys began his Spirit-filled ministry in the first half of the twentieth century as a healing evangelist. Thousands came to Christ as a result of the four-part gospel he preached: Jesus as Savior, Healer, Baptizer in the Holy Spirit, and coming King.

Jeffreys was a product of the Welsh Revival, which first brought him into the kingdom of

✶✶✶✶✶

God. Not only was the Welsh Revival responsible for his conversion, but it also influenced his vision of the body of Christ—and would do so for the rest of his life. In Jeffreys' concept of the kingdom of God, revival was not to be considered a mere hope for the future; it was available to the church today. Jeffreys knew that God moved in power to bring people to their knees in repentance and new life, and he wanted to see the flames of that revival ignite the hearts of men and women all over the globe.

God placed Jeffreys in the apostolic office according to Ephesians 4:11. This office signifies a servant whom God sends out with the message of the gospel of Christ to those who live in areas bereft of God's Word. Through signs, miracles, and wonders that accompany their teaching, they birth new churches. Jeffreys was a true apostle—he preached conversion and built churches.

> **Jeffreys knew that God moved in power to bring people to their knees in repentance and new life, and he wanted to see the flames of that revival ignite the hearts of men and women all over the globe.**

Today, conferences with numerous speakers may fill various halls and conference centers, but Jeffreys, with his apostolic mantle from the Lord and the power of the Holy Spirit, filled the Royal Albert Hall, the Crystal Palace, and Bingley Hall, among others—all by himself.

As such, George Jeffreys deserves to be recognized as one of God's generals who was used to birth the Pentecostal movement in Great Britain, as well as to help pioneer the healing revivals of the twentieth century.

A Small Beginning

In the late nineteenth century, to be poor in Wales often meant working in the coal pits and succumbing to lung disease before the age of fifty. Thomas Jeffreys and his wife, Kezia, lived in Maesteg, Wales, where Thomas performed backbreaking labor as a collier in the coal mines.

The couple had nine sons and three daughters, and they worked hard to eke out an existence in the small mining town.

Their seventh son, George, was born on February 28, 1889. Thirteen years earlier, his brother Stephen had been born. By the time George came into the world, Stephen had already been working with his father in the coal mines for a year. Stephen would continue to work in the mines for the next twenty-three years of his life, even while preaching the gospel.

Like many poor mothers in Wales, Kezia Jeffreys had suffered the heartbreak of losing two young children to illness. One of those children had been named George, and so she named her sixth son in memory of the child she had lost in November of 1888. The second George Jeffreys was small and sickly, yet Kezia was not about to lose another son. She determined never to let him join his father in the coal mines, for she wanted a different life for him. After finishing school at the age of twelve—as was the custom—George worked as a door boy in the mines for just a few years before his mother found him a job as a store clerk.

Every Sunday, the family attended the Siloh Independent (Congregational) Chapel in Nantyffyllon, Wales. As a young boy, George often thought he might become a preacher in the Congregational church one day. When he was just six years old, his father died of chronic lung disease at the age of forty-seven.

As George grew older, his own frailty became more pronounced. He had a speech impediment and a facial paralysis that began to creep down the left side of his body. This caused him distress, as he feared he would never be able to preach the gospel, and also that the paralysis could bring his life to an early end.

A Powerful Revival in Wales

When George was fifteen years old, his life changed radically, as did the life of his brother Stephen. A Spirit-filled young man named Evan Roberts began preaching throughout the Welsh countryside, bringing a powerful move of the Holy Spirit wherever he went.

✻✻✻✻✻

GEORGE JEFFREYS

From the age of thirteen, Roberts had cried out for a visit from God. For ten years, he had prayed for revival to come to Wales. Then, in 1903, at the age of twenty-five, he began to pray for a mighty movement of the Holy Spirit. That year, after hearing a message about surrendering to God, he fell to his knees and asked the Lord to bend him and use him for His glory. He felt the peace and power of God visit him, as well as a burning desire to bring the gospel of Christ to people throughout Wales.

Beginning in November 1904, as Roberts preached in churches and at outdoor meetings, the Holy Spirit was poured out. There was weeping and brokenness, confession of sin, and repentance at every meeting. The Welsh Revival had begun. Revival sessions were held wherever Roberts was led to minister. The crowds would come, and the Holy Spirit would move in waves upon the people's hearts. Singing and praise would go on, sometimes for hours, followed by confession of sin and holy repentance. Prayer was lifted in unison, and members of the congregation often interrupted the prayers with a word from the Lord. These meetings would go on into the early-morning hours, with the Spirit moving in people's hearts, even when there was little or no preaching.

Tens of thousands streamed to the daily sessions and were converted by the power of God. The effect on Wales was enormous. Bars and public houses were closed; liquor sales were down by 75 percent. Chapels were open, and church numbers were growing. During the course of the Welsh Revival, hundreds of thousands of people were converted.

The revival spread like wildfire, and one of the areas that was most affected was Maesteg, the hometown of George and Stephen Jeffreys. Roberts and his workers visited the area on three separate occasions and brought more than five thousand people into the kingdom of God.

On November 20, 1904, the Reverend Glasnant Jones stood before the Siloh congregation and preached a message of salvation. Prior to this date, George and Stephen had attended church on occasion. That morning, they experienced a dynamic conversion and were baptized in the Holy Spirit. Immediately afterward, they started serving the Lord at the church in any way they could. To the dismay of the Jeffreys brothers and much of Wales, the Welsh revival lasted only two years before it fell into decline.

★★★★★

Revival Must Go On

The Welsh Revival was fading, but a group of young men in Maesteg were not willing to let go of the power of God. They didn't believe He would birth such a sweeping revival, only to let it end so quickly. So, they formed a small prayer band and called themselves the "Children of the Revival." On their knees, they beseeched God to send His power. In the decades to come, their prayers would be answered in ways beyond anything they had imagined.

While the Welsh Revival was winding down, the Azusa Street Revival in Los Angeles, California, was moving forward at full speed. In addition to repentance, the Azusa Revival emphasized the experience of the baptism in the Holy Spirit with the evidence of speaking in tongues.

Soon, the work of the Holy Spirit that had begun in Azusa Street swept into Europe. A Norwegian pastor by the name of Thomas Ball (T. B.) Barratt sailed for the United States in 1905 to raise funds for his Methodist mission in Oslo. Though he stayed for over a year, the visit was a financial failure. As he prepared to return to Norway in Fall 1906, he heard about the Azusa Street Revival and read the first issue of their newspaper, *Apostolic Faith*. After corresponding with them, he attended a small meeting in New York and was baptized in the Holy Spirit.

On returning home in December, he shared his testimony with people there, resulting in a move of the Spirit that aroused great interest, as well as some opposition. Visitors arrived from many places.

One of them was an Anglican minister, Alexander Boddy, from Sunderland in the north of England. On his return home, he invited Barratt to hold meetings in Sunderland, testifying that what he had observed in Norway was greater than that which he had witnessed during the Welsh Revival.

On the last day of August 1907, Barratt arrived, and he stayed in Sunderland until early October. A number of people were baptized in the Holy Spirit and spoke in tongues, including Boddy's wife, Mary, and their young daughters, Mary and Jane. It was during the last few days of Barratt's meetings that the local newspaper took an interest in what was taking place. The news then spread to larger newspapers and Boddy soon found his home besieged by reporters. Boddy himself was not baptized in the Spirit until December, after Barratt had left. The following year, Boddy organized the first in a series of Annual Pentecostal conferences in Sunderland that continued until 1914 and the outbreak of World War I. It would be at these meetings that Boddy's path would intersect with that of Jeffreys.

Healed to Preach His Word

Some of the people of Wales welcomed this Pentecostal teaching. Early in 1910, George and Stephen Jeffreys began to attend Pentecostal meetings held by the Welsh Baptist minister, William George Hill. Previously, the brothers had been opposed to this teaching, but shortly thereafter, they had accepted the scriptural basis for this as a present-day experience, specifically, Matthew 3:11: *"I indeed baptize you with water unto repentance: but he that cometh after me is mightier than I, whose shoes I am not worthy to bear: he shall baptize you with the Holy Ghost, and with fire."*

The baptism in the Holy Spirit filled George with a passionate desire to preach the gospel. But there was a serious impediment barring his way: his weakness and facial paralysis were becoming more pronounced and would make preaching nearly impossible.

One Sunday morning in 1910, before the church service began, George was healed by the power of God. He would recount his experience to his congregation later:

> We were kneeling in prayer one Sunday morning and were interceding on the subject of the services of that day. It was exactly nine o'clock when the power of God came upon me, and I received such an inflow of Divine life that I can only liken the experience to being charged with electricity. It seemed as if my head were connected to a most powerful electric battery. My whole body from head to foot was quickened by the Spirit of God, and I was healed. From that day I have never had the least symptoms of the old trouble. Many times since then I have relied upon the Spirit's quickening power for my body.[35]

The opportunity to preach would come soon for George, but for Stephen, it was now. Even though he worked by day in the coal mines,

Stephen began to preach at night. He was an enthusiastic minister who walked up and down the aisles, calling the people to repentance. And they answered that call because of the anointing of the Word of God. Stephen wanted George to minister with him, but George wanted to attend Bible school first in order to become better prepared for what he thought would be a calling to the foreign mission field. Kezia Jeffreys had remarried by that time, and she agreed to send George to Bible school.

In the fall of 1912, George entered the Thomas Myerscough Bible School in Preston, Wales. There, by God's providence, he met several of the men with whom he would serve throughout his adult life, including William Burton, future founder of the Congo Evangelistic Mission, and Ernest John Phillips, who would serve as Secretary-General of the Elim movement for almost four decades.

The Emerald Isle

In early 1913, Stephen began preaching at an evangelistic crusade in Swansea, Wales, and the meetings quickly grew in frequency and size. Urgent for help, Stephen called George home from Bible school to help him.

The meetings went on for seven weeks and officially launched the ministries of both Jeffreys brothers. From there, they preached in other parts of Wales and had scores of converts. Their first healing miracle occurred when Edith M. Carr was healed of a diseased foot, which her doctors had planned to amputate. Stephen and George went to her home, anointed her with oil, laid hands on her, and prayed. God answered the prayer of faith and healed her completely. She later gave a testimony to the power of God that had touched her as the Jeffreys brothers prayed, saying, "A great light came around me, and filled me with great power, and I arose from the couch and stood on both feet and then walked gently round the room with scarcely any help."[36] People came from miles around to see for themselves the woman who had been healed and to hear the Jeffreys brothers preach.

In 1913, Boddy invited the Jeffreys brothers to attend his Annual Pentecostal conference in Sunderland, but only George accepted. Nearly all the men on the platform were Christian leaders in their forties and fifties who had served God for years. George was only twenty-four, but he made such an impression on the platform that Boddy invited him to remain in Sunderland and continue preaching even after the close of the convention. This confirmed his rising influence in England's Pentecostal movement, which had been birthed along an apostolic succession from Azusa to Barratt to Boddy, and now, to Jeffreys. Though he had believed that God's calling for his life would be as a foreign missionary, George soon discovered that his true mission field would be in Great Britain itself.

Stephen Jeffreys

It was at this point in the Jeffreys brothers' lives that the ministries of Stephen and George went in separate directions. Stephen was invited to pastor a church in Llanelli, Wales, while George moved into itinerant work and the eventual Elim movement. The brothers ministered together on occasion under the Elim umbrella in the following years, but the remainder of this chapter will focus on the ministry of George Jeffreys.

God's next call for George was to the Emerald Isle. William Gillespie, a Pentecostal pastor from Belfast, Ireland, had attended the Sunderland Convention and had been thoroughly impressed with George's preaching. He invited him to come to Belfast to conduct a series of meetings. George's decision to go to Ireland was a turning point in his ministry. Initially, things moved slowly, but, as he ministered throughout the countryside of Ireland, more converts were added to the church, and the fires of revival were stoked.

It was in Ireland that George first met Robert Ernest Darragh, a song leader who would be George's closest confidant for the next forty years. E. J. Phillips joined them in 1919 along with several others, including John Carter, brother of Howard Carter, and E. W. Hare, who had been the leader of the Christian Union at Cambridge University.

A Band of Brothers

The Lord brings people into the body of Christ to minister together for His purposes. By January 1915, George gathered with a group of six young men in Monaghan, Ireland, for what would become a momentous meeting. Records from the session reveal that the young men "came together for the purpose of discussing the best means of reaching Ireland with the Full Gospel on Pentecostal Lines."[37] They were committed that "George Jeffreys of South Wales who was present with us be invited to take up a permanent evangelistic work in Ireland,"[38] and that they would work with him to provide the place and support for his evangelistic efforts. The men choose the name "Elim Evangelistic Band" to represent their effort.

Why Elim? In the Old Testament, Elim was an oasis in the desert, a place where the children of Israel found refreshment shortly after they left Egypt for the Promised Land. (See Exodus 15:27.) The prayer band believed they would bring refreshment to the people of Ireland through the preaching of God's Word and the power of the Holy Spirit. Shortly

George Jeffreys

after this, Darragh became one of the first, along with Margaret Streight, to join with George Jeffreys and the Elim Evangelistic Band. He was ready to work beside his friend and see lives changed for Jesus Christ.

The Elim Band set up their first church, Elim Christ Church, in Belfast, and appointed George as pastor. In 1917, it became necessary to launch a formal organization. The group had inherited some property from an elderly parishioner, but, in order to receive the income from the sale of the property, they had to be a viable organization. Thus, the Elim Pentecostal Alliance Council was born. According to Pentecostal historian Desmond Cartwright, "it was at this point that what had started as a simple evangelistic effort by a small group anxious to win others for Christ now became a separate denomination."[39]

Within the Alliance, there formed a smaller group of men who would help Jeffreys directly in the evangelistic meetings. They were called the "Revival Party." These men would become Jeffreys' most steadfast supporters through the days of glory and persecution that lay ahead.

✦✦✦✦✦

GEORGE JEFFREYS
England for Jesus

In 1921, the Elim group decided to relocate the movement's headquarters to the Clapham district of London, where they opened a church that soon grew from a handful of people to five hundred members. George didn't want to desert their work in Ireland, but all of Great Britain was open before them. Everywhere he was invited to preach, he emphasized the fourfold gospel message, which, again, was that Jesus Christ is Savior, Healer, Baptizer in the Holy Spirit, and coming King. Over the next several years, the evangelistic campaigns gained momentum, slowly but surely, throughout the British Isles.

In 1924, the Elim movement acquired a printing press and opened a publishing house, another avenue to share the Word of God. They also planted a Bible college to train new laborers for the churches that were birthed following Jeffreys' evangelistic crusades. It was a small beginning, but things were starting to blossom.

That same year, a small group of men from the Elim Pentecostal Alliance, including the Jeffreys brothers and Darragh, traveled to the United States and Canada to observe the move of the Holy Spirit in those nations. While visiting the U.S., Jeffreys spent time at the five-thousand-seat Angelus Temple in Los Angeles, California, the central house of worship of the Foursquare Gospel Church, and met with Aimee Semple McPherson, who founded the denomination. Jeffreys was intrigued by her ministry and the dramatic way in which she presented the full gospel. After meeting her, his self-confidence as a revivalist seemed to increase.

Aimee Semple McPherson

At the outset of 1926, the Elim group launched a revival campaign in Town Hall in Portsmouth, England. Within a few days, the hall was no longer big enough to hold the crowds. Jeffreys sent a letter to E. J. Phillips, Secretary-General of the Elim Alliance, and excitedly informed him, "I am having the time of my life. Souls are continually flocking to Christ, most startling and marvelous healings, while yesterday hundreds were turned away from the Town Hall an hour before the starting time."[40]

Jeffreys' next campaign was in Liverpool, where he rented the Liverpool Boxing Stadium to hold the meetings. Understanding the need for

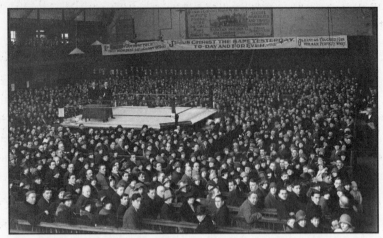

George Jeffreys and Robert Ernest Darragh in a Liverpool boxing ring

publicity to draw crowds to this new work, he preached from inside the boxing ring itself.

In the days before Easter 1926, the Elim team was getting ready for a convention at Liverpool's Surrey Tabernacle when Jeffreys received a surprise phone call from Aimee Semple McPherson. She told him that she was in France and wanted to travel to London to conduct a few meetings before going on to Palestine for ministry. The team was a little perplexed, but they invited her to participate at the Surrey Tabernacle meetings. She spent a few days ministering in London before she left for Palestine. On the way back from the Middle East, she planned to join Jeffreys for the Easter meetings.

Aimee Semple McPherson meets George Jeffreys.

The reservation at Surrey Tabernacle was cancelled, and the meetings were rescheduled for Royal Albert Hall in London to accommodate the crowds that Aimee Semple McPherson was expected to draw. She preached on the night of Easter Sunday and the next day. The British press had been thrilled by the opportunity to cover the meetings led by this well-known, flamboyant American preacher. Yet the crowds in Great Britain did not really warm to her, perhaps because the stereotypically sedate British personality was not accustomed to her dramatic, boisterous mannerisms.

✶✶✶✶✶

One month later, Jeffreys was grieved to receive the following telegram from Aimee's mother:

SISTER MCPHERSON DROWNED WHILE SWIMMING TUESDAY. SOUL GLORIFIED. SISTER HAD ANNOUNCED YOUR CAMPAIGN. WHOLE WORLD LOOKING TO ANGELUS TEMPLE. FOURSQUARE EVANGELIST IMPERATIVE. NEED YOU HERE IMMEDIATELY THIS CRISIS HOUR. CABLE EARLIEST POSSIBLE DATE YOU CAN LEAVE. MOTHER KENNEDY.[41]

On May 18, Aimee had taken a day trip with her secretary to Ocean Park Beach in Los Angeles. Soon after their arrival, she had disappeared from the area. The authorities were summoned, and they searched the beach frantically, yet there was no trace of the famous evangelist. Divers were called in for a search, which proved fruitless, and it was assumed that Aimee had gone into the water for a swim and drowned. Her supporters were fraught with grief and combed the beaches for days afterward for some sign of her.

Jeffreys' response to the cable was tentative. He informed Mother Kennedy that he was in the middle of a campaign in Belfast and could not travel to America, but he would pray about her request. His closest counselors urged caution because of the nature of the city of Hollywood and the dramatic flair of the ministry at Angelus Temple. Before there was time for much consideration, Aimee turned up on June 23 in the desert outside a Mexican town near the Arizona border. She explained that she had been kidnapped, tortured, and held for ransom. The authorities did not know what to make of her story, but she returned to minister at the Angelus Temple.

Although Jeffreys was never directly involved with Aimee's ministry, he did adopt the Foursquare designation, so that the Elim Pentecostal Alliance became the Elim Foursquare Gospel Alliance.

Revival and Healing Fires

The fires of revival burned brightly in 1927. That year, Jeffreys conducted a record nine crusades and saw thousands converted to Christ

✯✯✯✯✯

and healed in dramatic ways. He and his Revival Party moved from one large, successful campaign to the next. They began the year in Glasgow, where more than fifteen hundred were saved within one month's time.

> **In just two weeks, over two thousand people were saved, and many of them experienced God's miraculous hand.**

The most outstanding campaign of the year was in Leeds in March and April. It was Jeffreys' third campaign in Leeds, and the faith of the congregation there had been elevated to believe God for miracles. In just two weeks, over two thousand people were saved, and many of them experienced God's miraculous hand. An outstanding demonstration of God's love and power was the healing of James Gregson, a miracle that was long remembered by the people of England.

James Gregson was "an absolute cripple whose only way of getting around was to propel himself along the ground dragging his twisted legs behind him."[42]

James was an ironmaster by trade who had fallen in a serious accident at work that resulted in the displacement of many of the bones within his body. Doctors had not been able to do anything for his broken body, and he had become a helpless cripple. He could not sit, as it caused him excruciating pain, and so he had to lie down most of the time.

One evening, while reading the local newspaper, his wife learned of the Elim campaign and the ministry of George Jeffreys. The following Saturday, James went to the meeting. He arrived on his crutches, his legs dragging behind him. That night, the greatest miracle of all happened: he was saved, and his soul was redeemed for eternity. Overjoyed at the grace of God, he dragged himself back to the coliseum the next day. The campaign attendants carried him to the front and laid him before the platform, where Jeffreys prayed for him.

James later recalled, "When he laid his hands upon me I felt as if a dozen hands were placed all over my body, and I felt every bone going back into place. I was instantly released and I was completely healed."[43] Over the next two weeks, James gained strength and put on thirty-three

✶✶✶✶✶

pounds! Soon, he was able to return to work as an ironmaster. On Easter Monday, just a couple of weeks after his healing, he gave a testimony in Royal Albert Hall before thousands. The next morning, London's *Morning Post* printed a story about the meeting with a headline that read, "London Audience Mesmerized." Years later, James Gregson testified that he had never missed another day's work after his healing.

Miss Edith Scarth was also gloriously healed during the Leeds campaign. She suffered from tuberculosis of the spine and had to lie flat on her back and be wheeled around in a spinal carriage. For years, she had worn a spinal jacket and splint that came up behind her head and was fastened to her forehead by a strap. On first hearing about Jeffreys' meetings at Leeds, she was skeptical, but then, despairing, she determined to go and see for herself if God was really moving.

At the second meeting she attended, Edith embraced the message of salvation and was saved. Jeffreys called for prayer for those in need of healing, but there were too many for him to lay hands on individually. So, he asked them to stand for corporate prayer. By holding on to the seat in front of her, Edith managed to stand. Suddenly, the Holy Spirit moved in her body.

"Principal Jeffreys prayed and something happened. I felt as if someone lifted something right off me. My whole body was charged with new life and power. My head clicked back into place; I was healed! My mother looked on in amazement. I wanted to sing, to shout, to dance. When I reached home, I ran up the steps; I could not take the time to walk! I was healed on April 11, 1927. My doctor could find no trace of tuberculosis. My back was perfectly straight and I was quite well!"[44] Eighteen months after Edith was saved and healed, she received the baptism in the Holy Spirit with the power to witness to others about the marvelous thing God had done for her. She continued to spread the word, "When all others fail, He never fails!"[45]

A Miraculous Spring

Later in the spring of 1927, Jeffreys' campaign moved on to Southampton. At first, the meetings were small, but they soon grew in size and recorded numbers of salvations. Miss Florence Munday experienced an outstanding miracle at the Southampton meetings. She was raised from her wheelchair at a service in Wesleyan Central Hall in May 1927. Her stirring testimony increased the faith of many.

Fourteen years earlier, Florence had fallen and hurt her knee. Tuberculosis had settled into the injury, and she had been unable to stand or walk since that time. In addition, since early childhood, she had suffered from a skin disease that required her to cover her arms completely with bandages to protect the broken, bleeding skin. Doctors had designed a number of different casts for her knee, but to no avail; each one still left her writing in pain. They had finally decided that the only answer was to amputate her leg, and so completely that an artificial limb would be out of the question.

It was at this point that the Lord intervened. Florence's sisters attended a Jeffreys revival meeting and saw a woman receive healing and stand up from her wheelchair. Soon after this, Florence's sister Ivy urged her to attend a Jeffreys meeting. Florence was nervous, yet she agreed to go. On May 4, 1927, her mother and sister wheeled her to a meeting in her "invalid carriage." Jeffreys preached on Christian disappointments, a subject that touched Florence's aching heart. During the hymn "All Hail the Power of Jesus' Name," Florence felt the power of God begin to fall on her.

Before long, an intense Jeffreys approached Florence in her wheelchair. "How long have you been lying in this old carriage?" he asked her. Florence told him, "Fourteen years. I have not walked for fourteen years. The trouble is my knee. It is a wasting disease." "Do you believe the Lord

George Jeffreys baptizes Florence Munday at London's Royal Albert Hall in 1928.

✶✶✶✶✶

can heal you?" he asked. "Yes," Florence replied. Jeffreys then asked her to return the following afternoon for the healing meeting.

"The next afternoon, Jeffreys prayed over her, 'Oh, Lord, turn back the disease, and unlock these joints.' As he prayed the power of God surged through her body, shaking the carriage and she felt the knee bend in the splints."[46] Her testimony continued, "I was anointed with oil, and as he prayed, my whole body vibrated with life. I was under the power of God. My leg moved up and down three times in my splint, and soon I was able to sit up. All pain was gone. I was healed. I was on my feet for the first time after fourteen years! I walked around that big building three times....Jesus Thou art everything to me!"[47]

She slept through the night for the first time in years and awoke the next morning to find that all traces of her skin disease had disappeared. As mentioned at the beginning of this chapter, the following year, she was among one thousand converts who were baptized at Royal Albert Hall on Easter. For the next thirty years, Florence served as pastor of the Elim Church in Gosport, England, and she did not retire until she was in her seventies. The campaign in Southampton had been a tremendous success in salvations and healings. The Lord had moved in mercy and mighty power!

The Evangelist: Signs and Wonders Following

In May 1927, Jeffreys moved on to Brighton, where he held revival campaigns for ten weeks. The preaching of the Word continued to bring new converts to Christ with signs and wonders following. Mrs. Algernon Coffin, the wife of a Baptist minister, was miraculously healed of cancer and dropsy.[48] Mrs. Coffin had been diagnosed with cancer ten years earlier and had been told that she now had only months to live. God had spared her life, but she continued to suffer from pain and took the strongest drugs available to bring relief. Because of the fluid on her lungs, she had not been able to lie down for ten years, and she slept in elevated chairs.

Mrs. Coffin testified,

The doctors saw me again and again and told my dear husband there was no hope whatsoever. I was in utter despair; the doctors had done all that they could, and I was given up to die. But, praise God, man's extremity is God's opportunity.

Just at this time, God sent His dear servant Principal George Jeffreys to Brighton. I decided to go to the Divine Healing meeting on the afternoon of May 19th, 1927, in the Royal Pavilion. I was prayed for; I felt an inward thrill go right through my body, and was instantly met with healing! All my pain ceased, I was able to sleep and no longer needed the drugs.[49]

Less than a week later, when a doctor came to her home for a house call, he was astonished when his patient answered the door herself. "'What has happened, Mrs. Coffin?' he asked in amazement. 'Is it really you?' 'I am healed and quite well, after you told me there was no hope. In my helplessness and distress I appealed to a higher One, whose power is not limited. I did not appeal in vain.' The doctor's reply was, 'I cannot understand it, but I rejoice with you.'"[50]

The Apostle: Chosen to Plant Churches

During these years of great revival, George Jeffreys' apostolic mantle was revealed. Not only did he preach and prompt conversions by the hundreds or even thousands in each town, but he also planted new churches in every town where he preached. As a pioneer of the Pentecostal movement, Jeffreys was sent by the Lord to preach a full-gospel message. Those who were newly saved and baptized in the Holy Spirit wanted to fellowship in a church where the power of the Holy Spirit was welcomed and embraced. Jeffreys would campaign for several weeks in a city and find a group of believers who wanted to join the Elim movement. He would then appoint a pastor to handle the new Pentecostal church, the Elim Alliance would rent or purchase a building where the new congregation could meet, and the administration team would handle any remaining details.

The following year, the campaigns continued, although not as many as the year before. Jeffreys visited Croydon, Reading, Eastbourne, Bath, Exeter, and Bradford, adding thousands of converts to the body of Christ. In 1928, there were seventy Elim churches throughout the British Isles. By 1930, the number had risen to 100, and by 1933, the churches totaled 153.

In 1933, Jeffreys preached in towns such as Aberdeen, where 400 converts were added. Immediately, a new church was founded there.

Again, in his apostolic ministry, Jeffreys continually established new congregations to extend the kingdom of God on the earth. "His success can surely be the result of serving God with the ministry gifts he had received, namely those of apostle and evangelist."[51]

A few years later, in 1936, the Elim churches recognized Jeffreys' apostolic ministry and his twenty-five years of dedicated service to the Elim movement:

> As an Apostle, you have pioneered the Full Gospel message and established churches in the largest cities and towns of the British Isles. As an Evangelist, your ministry has been signally owned and blessed of God. Through your faithful proclamation of the old-fashioned gospel, you have led countless thousands to Christ.[52]

The Elim churches that Jeffreys had planted were governed by a set of rules that were revised to meet the changing needs of the growing denomination. Three forms of government were recognized by Elim churches: central government from Clapham, personal government by a minister, and local government from deacons. The ministers of the denomination were closely supervised from the London headquarters, and the whole work was divided into districts, each with a governing superintendent. As the campaigns expanded and the churches grew, so did a sense of restlessness among the people in regard to the governing policies. Yet the power of the Holy Spirit continued to move among the cities of the British Isles.

In his apostolic ministry, Jeffreys continually established new congregations to extend the kingdom of God on the earth.

Filling the Largest Halls in England

In the late 1920s and early 1930s, the increased momentum of the Elim movement was reflected in the huge crowds that flocked to the ministry meetings of the charismatic Jeffreys. In each city, the Revival Party found that it had to move from the scheduled hall to another, larger building that could accommodate the crowds. For example, Jeffreys began his 1930 campaign in Birmingham in a Congregational church in the city. Within five days, the church was filled to capacity, and so the meetings were moved to Town Hall, then to the Embassy Skating Rink, which sat eight thousand. In the final weeks of the campaign, they moved to the massive Bingley Hall Exhibition Centre, which had seating for fifteen thousand! Jeffreys preached twenty-six meetings in that hall, and the number of converts during the entire campaign was recorded at ten thousand.

At that time, the Revival Party consisted of R. E. Darragh, song leader; Albert W. Edsor, pianist; and James McWhirter, campaign organizer. These men were with Jeffreys almost constantly, offering him aid and support. They worked as a single unit and "took the city by storm."[53]

Car advertisements for Jeffreys at Bingley Hall

None of these men was married, as they all dedicated the sum of their time and energy to spreading the gospel of Jesus Christ. When James McWhirter married later in the 1930s, he stepped down from the Revival Party and helped in less time-consuming capacities. Fifty years after the Birmingham campaign was over, it was possible to still speak with people who had been converted during those days, or whose parents had given their lives to Christ at Jeffreys' meetings.

✷✷✷✷✷

GEORGE JEFFREYS

Jeffreys rented the huge Crystal Palace in London for the first time in 1930, and the crowds filled it to capacity. The building had been constructed for the Great Exhibition of 1851 and was used every year following by the Elim movement until it burned down in 1936.

Healing Rays

In 1932, Jeffreys wrote an in-depth book entitled *Healing Rays* on the healing power of Christ throughout the history of the Christian church. In the book, Jeffreys contended that while sin, sickness, and death compose a curse that came upon the earth through Adam's disobedience, the atoning and redeeming work of Jesus Christ is the answer to overcome the curse in its entirety. Healing and deliverance from sickness can be experienced now, according to Jeffreys, and the final deliverance from death will come when Christ returns to bring His own to glory.

In *Healing Rays*, Jeffreys also made a clear case for divine healing today based on the Word of God and the great cloud of witnesses who have testified to healing since the foundation of the Christian church. He shared the testimonies of the early church fathers, who spoke of God's healing power at work. Clement in the first century, Irenaeus in the second century, and Tertullian and Origen in the third century all spoke of "disciples in His name who still do miracles...others still heal the sick by laying their hands on them, and they are made whole."[54]

For members of mainline denominations who mistrusted claims of divine healing, Jeffreys included a quote from Martin Luther: "How often it has happened, and still does, that devils have been driven out in the name of Christ; also, by calling on His name and prayer that the sick have been healed."[55] John Wesley, the founder of the Methodist church, was healed from tuberculosis and wrote, "When I was about seven and twenty, I began spitting blood and continued for several years. Eleven years after, I was in the third stage of consumption; it pleased God in three months to remove this also. This God hath wrought."[56]

Jeffreys included the testimonies of other church leaders who testified to the effect of divine healing on their own bodies: George Fox, Quaker and founder of the Religious Society of Friends, who was beaten by a mob and then healed immediately of his injuries; Dr. E. Stanley

Jones, world-famous missionary, who experienced divine healing in India and was therefore able to continue his missionary work; A. B. Simpson, founder of the Christian and Missionary Alliance, who was completely healed from a lifelong sickness when he began to preach the fourfold gospel of Christ, including healing; and Andrew Murray, who entered a home for the sick, was taught about divine healing from the Word of God, and then was healed completely. Murray wrote, "This healing granted to faith has been the source of rich spiritual blessing to me. The Church possesses in Jesus, our Divine Healer, an inestimable treasure which she does not yet know how to appreciate."[57]

Whenever people scoffed at the idea of the power of God to heal today, Jeffreys would answer in his determined manner, "It is almost 2,000 years since the sacred canon of Scripture was closed, but the dispensation of the Holy Ghost, with its miracles, signs and wonders, continues to this present day."[58] He reminded believers that the same gospel message that brought men and women to Christ in the New Testament is still converting sinners today, and that the same Holy Spirit who convicted them of sin and healed them is also convicting and healing today.

Co-Laborers in Christ

By the mid-1930s, Jeffreys and E. J. Phillips had been ministering together for almost twenty years. Their ministry had started in 1919, when Jeffreys had asked Phillips to join the Elim Evangelistic Band in Ireland. Although Phillips had begun by pastoring an Elim church, his prior experience in business was helpful in addressing the administrative needs of the new denomination.

E. J. Phillips

Jeffreys and Phillips had had significantly different experiences growing up. Jeffreys had been raised in relative poverty, and he had been a part of a Congregationalist church where the congregation had input in the church's government. He'd surrendered to the Lord during the fiery days of the Welsh revival, when spontaneity and freedom in the Holy Spirit had been paramount, and was forever marked by the passion of that revival. To him, powerful, Spirit-led meetings were the benchmark of success in the church. He believed that revival was available to believers at all times because the Holy Spirit was always moving on the earth. If Jesus was the same yesterday, today, and forever (see Hebrews 13:8), then His power should be always moving to save, heal, and baptize in the Holy Spirit.

Phillips, on the other hand, had grown up in a family that had monetary experience. Among his father's side of the family was the first Jewish Lord Mayor of London, as well as others who had been financiers and businessmen in both Great Britain and South Africa. His father had become a Christian and had brought up his son in the church. Normal church life for Phillips would have been much calmer and more "ordinary" than the fire-filled, Spirit-led revival meetings Jeffreys had experienced. When Phillips received the baptism in the Holy Spirit at the age of sixteen, he believed it was "to empower him to live a life fully consecrated for God."[59]

Jeffreys and Phillips had worked in close harmony in the leadership of the Elim movement, writing letters to each other daily and exchanging ideas. They didn't make any decisions about the campaigns or the ministry without consulting each other. They certainly didn't agree on everything, but they had a close relationship built on years of trust. Together, they had faced fierce persecution against the early Pentecostal ministers in Britain. And, together, they had enjoyed the success of the ministry. They were, without question, the two leaders of the Elim movement.

A major change in the government of the Elim Foursquare Gospel Alliance occurred on April 10, 1934, with the adoption of new church legislation called the Deed Poll. Prior to this time, all decisions for the Elim movement had been made by Jeffreys and Phillips. With the adoption of the Deed Poll, an Executive Council of nine would have legislative authority in the denomination. The nine would consist of Jeffreys and Phillips, three people nominated by Jeffreys, and four others elected from within the denomination. With this decision, Jeffreys gave up his vote on the governing council. It was a decision he would come to regret in the years that followed.

★★★★★

World Revival Crusade

In 1934 and 1935, Jeffreys was invited to hold revival campaigns in Switzerland and Palestine, and the events were successful in converting thousands to Christ. The following year, Jeffreys founded an organization called the World Revival Crusade to handle the financial responsibilities of his overseas ministry. In actuality, he used it to manage the financial responsibilities of all of his crusades. The purpose of the organization was to invite international members who were believers in the fourfold gospel to support Jeffreys' ministry through prayer and financial giving. Jeffreys would be in control of the organization and appoint his own commissioners to administrate it. Through the Crusade, he would no longer need to receive all of his financial support from the Elim headquarters.

E. J. Phillips, however, was not pleased with the new arrangement. He felt that Jeffreys had placed a wedge between himself and the Elim movement. Because Jeffreys would no longer depend on the Elim Foursquare Gospel Alliance for his income or for direction in the campaign ministries, Phillips was certain that he was moving toward a split and developing the Crusade as an alternative organization. But Jeffreys insisted that he would continue to be an evangelist and the spiritual father of the Elim movement.

Generally, Jeffreys had kept himself separate from many of the administrative tasks of the denomination. He was always too busy conducting revival campaigns. That began to change in 1936, when he suddenly became involved in the denomination's finances. At the time, Phillips had just married and was battling tuberculosis, so he was not at the office headquarters.

Jeffreys discovered the mortgages for all of the churches they had planted and became deeply concerned about the financial situation of the denomination. Jeffreys and Phillips viewed these mortgages differently. Jeffreys, coming from a working-class background, saw them as a burden of dangerous debt obligations, while Phillips, coming from a middle-class business background, viewed them as proper business agreements. Jeffreys shared his concerns with all of the Elim congregations through the church magazine *Elim Evangel*, an act that publicly

*****

made Phillips appear to be a poor administrator. Jeffreys introduced a Jubilee Fund and asked readers to give money and help alleviate the debt on many of the Elim church buildings. After several months, the congregations had given what amounted to a small percentage of what Jeffreys had hoped to raise.

One unforeseen outcome of Jeffreys' concern over the finances was Phillips's strong personal reaction to it. Phillips felt that his abilities and judgments were being publicly questioned by Jeffreys. Because the church assets were worth more than the debt liabilities, and because all of the mortgage payments were being met, Phillips was certain that they were not in the midst of a financial crisis. He suggested that Jeffreys concentrate on raising money in his evangelistic efforts and leave the accounting work to the administrative staff. This argument put an additional strain on the relationship between Jeffreys and Phillips.

"Set Your House in Order"

Early in 1937, Jeffreys wrote a number of letters to Phillips voicing his concerns about church government reform in the Elim movement. "God had spoken to me in no uncertain sound, 'Set your house in order.'"[60] This was the same command that the prophet Isaiah brought to King Hezekiah in the Old Testament. (See 2 Kings 20:1.) To Jeffreys, it meant two things: He was to continue in his efforts to pay off the debts of the denomination, and he was to work diligently to reform Elim from being a church governed by centralized control to one with more power delegated to the local assemblies.

Jeffreys' efforts to make major reforms in the Elim church government were met with the stiffest resistance, first from Phillips and the Executive Council and later from the Ministerial Conference. For most of the ministers, the use of laity as elders to help govern the local assembly meant a loss of control over their churches. The ministers were appointed and paid by the Elim headquarters, which meant their allegiance lay with the denomination and not necessarily with the needs or the spiritual inclinations of their congregations. Jeffreys felt that this policy left out many people who might hear from the Lord but not have a voice in the congregation. Other Pentecostal denominations, such as the Assemblies of God, granted local churches a much greater degree of autonomy.

The majority of the Elim Executive Council was committed to keeping a centralized church government. As a result, Elim Trust Company owned over two hundred buildings in the denomination and carried an enormous amount of financial muscle. It was all controlled by a small group of men, of which Phillips was the head.

Jeffreys' desire to see the development of local church government for the Elim churches was further solidified in 1939, when he was invited by Lewi Pethrus to speak at the European Pentecostal Conference in Stockholm, Sweden. With more than five thousand members, Pethrus' Filadelphia Church was the largest Pentecostal church in the world at that time. In addition, the church supported a network of smaller churches, and Pethrus had granted each individual assembly the freedom to govern itself at the local level so that the individual gifts of the saints could be used. He believed that the autonomy of the local church was established by the pattern in the New Testament. "It was affirmed by Brother Pethrus that the Scriptures reveal no organization beyond the local assembly."[61]

Jeffreys was determined to bring this form of church government to the Elim movement in Great Britain. But he wasn't certain of how to accomplish that, and his various attempts to make the necessary changes, as well as his suggestions about how to do so, added strain to the relationship between Jeffreys and Phillips.

A Grave Distraction

Perhaps the issues regarding church government could have been worked out between Jeffreys and Phillips if there had not been another deeply divisive problem at hand. For some time, Jeffreys had been distracted by the doctrine of British Israelism, the belief that people from Western Europe, particularly Great Britain, are the direct descendants of the ten lost tribes of Israel. One of the earliest books on the subject, *The Rights of the Kingdom*, was published by John Sadler in 1649. British Israelism reached the height of its popularity in the early twentieth century and was embraced by many of the intellectual elite of European society.

GEORGE JEFFREYS

Jeffreys came into contact with some of those intellectuals and was swayed by the theory. He was also influenced by John Leech, a close friend and longtime Elim member and attorney for the movement. Leech became the General Commissioner of the British-Israel Federation in July 1926 and gave up all of his legal responsibilities in other areas to devote himself to that work. He remained a stalwart defender of the Israel connection throughout his lifetime.

Adherence to British Israelism was not unique to Jeffreys during the first half of the twentieth century, but he was very vocal about the theory at the Elim conferences. Phillips, on the other hand, was adamantly opposed to the doctrine. He saw it is as a grave distraction from more important matters, such as evangelism and building up the Elim movement.

While Jeffreys had strong personal convictions about British Israelism, he insisted that he would not force the doctrine on the denomination. One writer noted, "Jeffreys clearly believed that British Israelism was simply one supplementary belief, amongst many, which should not be prohibited."[62] Still, though it may not have been a major doctrine for Jeffreys, it *was* a formidable distraction. He fought persistently for the "freedom" of the ministers in the Elim movement to believe in this specific prophetic interpretation of the Old Testament. At several annual conferences, he promised to drop the subject, only to bring it up for consideration the following year.

Phillips remained opposed to British Israelism and did not want it to be associated with the Elim movement in any way. By opposing the controversial doctrine, he believed he was saving the denomination from going down a questionable path. Phillips found Jeffreys obsessive in his desire to establish British Israelism as a supplementary issue in the Elim movement, but Phillips became equally obsessive in putting a halt to any and all of Jeffreys' plans.

In the end, Phillips believed British Israelism to be behind Jeffreys' desire for local church government. He feared that Jeffreys would use his influence to prompt individual churches to accept that and other strange doctrines. However, there is no proof that Jeffreys ever intended to reform the denomination simply to spread the doctrine of British Israelism.

✦✦✦✦✦

"Having Begun in the Spirit..."

Starting in 1936, Jeffreys introduced legislation to the Elim Executive Council every year, asking them to give more authority to the lay leaders in the local churches. At the Elim Conference of 1938, he suggested that the Ministerial Conference include lay representation and have more authority than the Executive Council. But the ministers voted resoundingly against this measure.

For the next two years, the disagreement between Jeffreys and Phillips became increasingly heated. Both men wanted the support of the overall body of believers in the Elim movement. Phillips had slowly gained the support of the Ministerial Conference because his work at Headquarters paid their salaries and guaranteed their roles in the local churches. In their rivalry to win the hearts of the people, both Jeffreys and Phillips began sending out questionnaires to the pastors and laity to assess the type of church government most of them favored. By this time, they were trying to lead the Elim flock by public opinion polls rather than by the guidance of the Holy Spirit.

To aggravate the situation further, Phillips refused to allow Jeffreys to see the full results of the church questionnaires. "At this point, Phillips' power was all-embracing."[63] And Jeffreys came to the realization that his influence in the denomination he had founded was slipping away.

How could something begun in the power of the Holy Spirit be reduced to these actions in the flesh? As the apostle Paul admonished the church in Galatia, *"Are you so foolish? Having begun in the Spirit, are you now being made perfect by the flesh?...Therefore He who supplies the Spirit to you and works miracles among you, does He do it by the works of the law, or by the hearing of faith?"* (Galatians 3:3, 5).

To challenge Phillips' control, Jeffreys began sending out letters to individual churches to ask for support. What followed was a six-year period of devastating attacks and counterattacks between Jeffreys and Phillips through this correspondence.

Frankly, both of these men were guilty of immaturity in their handling of the leadership conflict. They had begun the Elim movement as

✳✳✳✳✳

young men who loved the Lord and desired nothing more than to see His kingdom increase in the world. But the rapid growth of the denomination, along with the popularity, influence, and power that came with their positions, would have affected any man. Jeffreys erred in looking primarily to the people in the Elim movement for counsel. As the apostolic leader of the denomination, he should have sought counsel for how to bring about change in the church government from his peers in ministry, such as T. B. Barratt of Norway and Lewi Pethrus of Sweden. And Phillips, though he was a diligent administrator, should have been willing to listen to the man whom God had used to bring so many into the kingdom of God and the Elim churches. In the end, both men leaned too much on their flesh and gave Satan a place to intensify the conflict.

"Spiritual Warfare over Europe"

It may seem odd that so little has been written about the Elim conflict in light of the state of warfare in Europe at the time. The Bible is clear to point out to believers, *"For we do not wrestle against flesh and blood, but against principalities, against powers, against the rulers of the darkness of this age, against spiritual hosts of wickedness in the heavenly places"* (Ephesians 6:12).

As Phillips and Jeffreys were on the brink of war over control of the Elim denomination, there was a nightmarish conflict brewing in Europe. As the evil forces of darkness working at that time through Hitler and the Nazis began the bloodshed of world war, it seems clear that spirits of conflict and desire for power were also attacking the church of Jesus Christ.

One of the ugliest parts of the Elim conflict came at the Conference of 1939, just as Hitler was preparing to enter Poland. Because of the caustic letters and questionnaires that had been circulating, Jeffreys initially refused to come to the 1939 Conference and instead stayed in a home just a few miles from the meeting location. He sent emissaries to the meeting to give his answers on the subjects that were brought up for discussion. Frustrated and angry over his lack of cooperation, Phillips used Jeffreys' absence as an opportunity to put the "nail in the coffin" of eroding support for Jeffreys.

Phillips opened the Conference by refuting all of the changes Jeffreys had again proposed for church government. He then ridiculed the number of changes Jeffreys had proposed for Elim church government over the years, including a couple of mistaken plans that had cost the denomination both time and money.[64]

Next, Phillips attacked the proposals having to do with British Israelism, arguing that the only reason Jeffreys wanted to empower the local church governments was to make it a possibility for them to teach British Israelism, which contradicted the spiritual guidance from Headquarters. Phillips ended the discourse by attacking Jeffreys' motivations and stating, "The fact is, he is not fighting for a principle, he is fighting for his own way—for every new scheme that comes into his head."[65] And Phillips' final conclusion was that George Jeffreys was to "have no more say in [Elim's] government than King George VI has to the government of this land."[66] "It was a devastating attack on Jeffreys' character and ability."[67]

It is tragic how far those attending the conference had fallen from their Spirit-filled desire to extend the gospel of Jesus Christ through the work of George Jeffreys, anointed evangelist, and their commitment to support his work throughout the British Isles. What a sad day it was for Christendom.

Astoundingly, after his discourse was over, Phillips suggested that Jeffreys continue to be the "spiritual father" of the denomination. To come to some sort of compromise, the Executive Council agreed to add a small number of lay representatives to the Ministerial Conference and to allow that Conference to be the governing body over the denomination, with the Executive Council taking a secondary role.

Jeffreys' response to the compromise was simply that he would discuss it with some of his lay advisers. At this point, all polite discourse ended. The Council members gave Jeffreys an ultimatum on the timing of his decisions and asked him to transfer all the properties in which he still held a trustee position back to the Elim Trust Corporation. In response, Jeffreys personally entered the Conference site and formally resigned from the Alliance and from the Elim Church.

In 1940, both Jeffreys and the Executive Council worked to reach some kind of compromise, but Jeffreys would never again return to the

Elim movement. He gave his final resignation, stating that the work of the movement was now upon the Executive Council's shoulders.

The Apostolic Spirit

This conflict in the Elim movement, which happened more than seventy years ago, is still a subject of discussion among some church leaders in Great Britain today. It is important to consider what the Scriptures have to say about the ministry gifts that were given by God to George Jeffreys and E. J. Phillips.

In 1 Corinthians 12:28, the apostle Paul reminded the Corinthian church that it is God who gives ministry gifts to His church: *"And God has appointed these in the church: first apostles, second prophets, third teachers, after that miracles, then gifts of healings, helps, administrations, varieties of tongues."* Paul, who often stated that he was called to be an apostle by the will of God, later reminded the church of his apostolic calling, saying, *"Truly the signs of an apostle were accomplished among you with all perseverance, in signs and wonders and mighty deeds"* (2 Corinthians 12:12).

George Jeffreys flowed in the anointing of the apostolic spirit. God had chosen him in the early days first as an evangelist to proclaim the fourfold message of Jesus as Savior, Healer, Baptizer in the Holy Spirit, and coming King. Within a few years of his ministry, the apostolic mantle became obvious to Jeffreys. In addition to the signs and wonders mentioned in the Scripture above, he was also successful in planting Pentecostal churches in the Elim Foursquare Gospel Alliance and building the church of Jesus Christ as it had been built in the New Testament days. As testament to his lasting legacy, every church that Jeffreys planted from 1925 to 1934 became successful except for two: a church in Leicester was closed after a few days because the congregation lacked a proper facility to hold meetings, and a church in Manchester closed months

> **As testament to his lasting legacy, every church that Jeffreys planted from 1925 to 1934 became successful except for two.**

afterward because a strong Assemblies of God congregation already existed nearby.

Once this apostolic calling was revealed, it remained the main office that Jeffreys functioned in for the rest of his life. As we can see in the apostle Paul's ministry, the apostolic office is one in which all five ministry gifts (see Ephesians 4:11) become evident from time to time. Therefore, we see Jeffreys functioning in the different ministry gifts at different times throughout his ministry. These gifts were joyfully recognized in the commemorative address given to Jeffreys in 1934.

E. J. Phillips was a skilled administrator who took the task of administering and consolidating the Elim movement very seriously.[68] He was also, for many years, a close personal friend and confidant of Jeffreys. He even prepared Jeffreys' taxes each year. As Jeffreys gained notoriety and attracted the spotlight of success, their close friendship dissolved into a power struggle over the organization they led. What Phillips failed to realize was that his skills as an administrator were given to him to serve alongside Jeffreys as a ministry of helps. The sheer workload of the ministry makes the work of administration and helps a vital service. While Phillips was a dedicated worker in building the kingdom of God, sacrificing years of his life to the Elim movement, his skills in the areas of administration and helps were service gifts intended to build up the body of Christ. Administrative skills are needed to facilitate a movement of God once it starts, but they are never to be equal to or take precedence over the fivefold ministry gifts as found in Ephesians 4:11. I believe that this is where the Elim collision took place. Administrators thrive on order and precision; apostolic leaders must step out in faith and will occasionally make mistakes. In some ways, it is inevitable that these two temperaments would have found it hard to coexist.

One writer noted, "Phillips believed that his task was to protect the churches from the force of Jeffreys' personality."[69] The Holy Spirit had moved powerfully through Jeffreys for decades. Was Jeffreys' appeal now just the power of human personality, as Phillips suggested? It is hard to believe that that was so. The healings that took place under Jeffreys' ministry could never have been performed by simple human personality or will. In fact, it would have been difficult for Jeffreys' personality to command any special attention on its own, as he was known to be "painfully shy" when not preaching from the platform.

The power of the Holy Spirit had moved freely in Jeffreys in the 1920s. Had his power turned into a force of his personality just because of his newfound desire to reform the Elim church? Or, had Phillips simply ceased to recognize the power of an anointed leader because of the mounting administrative responsibilities of such a large organization? We may never know the full answer to those puzzling questions. However, it certainly seems of Jeffreys, and if Jeffreys had released his commitment to the supplementary doctrine of British Israelism and submitted himself to the counsel of some of his peers in other countries, such as Barratt and Pethrus, then this tragic fracture in the body of Christ might never have occurred.

The Conflict Escalates

After Jeffreys' resignation, the Executive Council put a small paragraph in the *Elim Evangel* stating that Jeffreys had resigned from the Executive Council and was released from the "business side of the work" to be free to conduct his spiritual ministry.[70] However, Jeffreys wanted the members of the Elim Alliance to know that the separation had been due to quarrels. He wrote and circulated a pamphlet entitled *Why I Resigned from the Elim Movement.* In response, the Executive Council published *A Reply*, which announced some of the opposing views of the Executive Council. Letters of this nature from both sides were sent to the churches for the next six years, demoralizing many of its members.

Jeffreys wanted to bring his plea for local church government to the people, but he was no longer permitted to speak in any Elim churches. So, he set up meetings in other churches to inform the Elim congregations of his side of the story.

A New Home; A New Ministry

In the early 1920s, the pastor of Horbury Chapel in Kensington had invited Stephen Jeffreys to hold a campaign there. It was so successful that local newspapers referred to it as "Bethesda of the West End" due to the miracles that occurred. Soon afterward, however, Horbury's pastor wrote against Pentecostalism, especially speaking in tongues, which caused Stephen not to return there. By 1930, the congregation at Horbury had declined markedly and was in disarray. George put up the money for a third party to buy the church, afraid they would not sell to one named Jeffreys. By putting up his own money, he kept the building in a separate trust, apart from the Elim movement. Jeffreys and several other members of the Revival Party were appointed trustees of the building, including Darragh, McWhirter, and Robert Tweed.

After his departure from the Elim movement, Jeffreys began a new denomination that he called Bible Pattern Church Fellowship. He did this primarily for two reasons: (1) to keep some of his young ministers out of the war; and (2) to continue to build a platform on which to formulate a better church government. Between 1940 and 1941, twenty-five of the 161 Elim ministers left the Elim movement to join Jeffreys. Most brought their congregations with them. At first, some of these congregations remained in their church buildings. However, the Executive Council took a forceful position on the ownership of all church property.

In a decision that would later be seen as extremely reactionary, a group of Elim leaders, including Phillips, traveled to the Portsmouth Elim Church, led by Pastor Robert Mercer, who was present at the first Elim organizational meeting in 1915. The Elim leaders marched into the church early one Sunday morning as the service was beginning and demanded that the pastor and congregation leave the building. One of the Elim leaders walked to the pulpit and began to conduct a church service. Pastor Mercer "ran down the church aisle shouting, 'These men have come to disturb our worship, follow me!'"[71] and led the congregation out of the building.

What was the date of this unusual decision to interrupt a service meant to honor Jesus Christ? It was Sunday morning, December 7, 1941, just a few short hours before the bombing of Pearl Harbor and the escalation of the war throughout the world. Surely, Satan was celebrating a victory on the earth that day. This was another clear demonstration of how ridiculous the entire conflict had become, and of how spiritual warfare had become a dominant force in this tragic denominational split. As the entire world faced the horrible reality of a looming world war, these men of God were fighting over the control of a denomination of believers.

Jeffreys and his closest supporters, including Darragh, McWhirter, and Edsor, as well as John Leech, moved their headquarters to Kensington Temple. Because he and McWhirter were still trustees of the building, Jeffreys was able to establish his headquarters there and preached in that building until his death. The Bible Pattern denomination never became a large one; in fact, there are less than five churches in operation today with connections to the denomination.

In 1956, Jeffreys wrote an article entitled "Elim—Then and Now," in which he stated, "The sum and substance of the reason for my resignation from Elim was the refusal of the majority of my fellow-governors in the Executive Council to move with me towards establishing the sovereignty of the local church in all Elim Foursquare Gospel Alliance Churches....In 1940 I called a conference of Elim Ministers and Church Officers who shared my conviction. At this gathering the Bible Pattern Church Fellowship was founded on the basis of the sovereignty of the local church."[72]

Jeffreys concluded, "It was then—back in 1915—that we in Elim made the big mistake that shaped the destiny of the Movement. We did not establish the Scriptural sovereignty of the local church in the first Elim Church."[73]

During his twenty-plus years as the leader of the Bible Pattern movement, Jeffreys made it clear that he regarded British Israelism as a nonfundamental doctrine open entirely to the individual and not the major focus that Phillips had feared.

Still Preaching to Thousands

From 1933 to 1950, Jeffreys conducted a number of healing revivals abroad, especially in Switzerland and France. Thousands came to Christ, and many were healed. Once again, Jeffreys preached before maximum-capacity crowds in Geneva and Paris. In Nice, France, he preached in a casino, walking among the gambling tables and sharing the message of Christ's salvation.

One writer commented on a campaign in France: "The two largest churches in La Chaux-Fonds, France, were packed to suffocation and over 1,000 souls were saved. Surely this must be the greatest revival ever witnessed in this lovely land."[74]

Dr. Emile Lanz, one of Jeffreys' interpreters, wrote about the healing revivals on the Continent, saying, "A mighty wave of Foursquare Revival has just rolled over Switzerland sweeping thousands of precious souls into the kingdom of heaven and bringing encouragement and bodily healing of all kinds of disease and infirmity to thousands of stricken folk."[75]

Jeffreys remained close friends with Rev. Lewis Pethrus of Sweden and T. B. Barratt of Norway because they were the leaders of the Pentecostal movements within their countries, but also because of their firm belief in the sovereignty of the local church and their continual support during his fight to reform the Elim movement.

As late as 1960, Jeffreys received a telegram from Pastor A. Hunziker in Geneva acknowledging his role in the founding of his church in Geneva twenty-five years earlier: "For its 25th anniversary our church remembers and sends you, dear Principal, our gratitude and love.... (Signed) Hunziker."[76]

In May 1960, Jeffreys' teachings were instrumental in the healing of Mrs. Margery Stevens of England, who was in critical condition—paralyzed, confined to a wheelchair, and fed every meal by her parents. The teachings the family had received for years from Jeffreys had strengthened the faith in her heart. While in prayer one day, she received a vision of her healing. Five months later, the Lord brought it to pass exactly as she had envisioned it. She gave the testimony of her healing to "an enthralled audience" the following Sunday in the People's Church in Clapham, London, with Jeffreys as the presiding minister.

Serving the Lord to the End

On Sunday night, January 14, 1962, Jeffreys ministered at Kensington Temple, London, still preaching the Word with power. At the close of the service, he made a passionate plea for the lost to accept the call of Christ. The service concluded with a Welsh song about Christ's free forgiveness.

✵✵✵✵✵

The next Tuesday, Jeffreys visited the homes of people with needs and laid hands on the sick. That Friday night, January 25, he traveled around London with Albert Edsor, posting notices for the annual Easter Monday meetings that would be held at Westminster Central Hall. The following morning, by nine o'clock, a friend entered Jeffreys' bedroom and found he had gone home to be with the Lord. On January 26, 1962, one month before his seventy-third birthday, the beloved founder of the Elim movement had finished his course on this earth.

Just five weeks earlier, E. J. Phillips and his wife, Molly, had paid Jeffreys a visit. It was the first time they had spoken in years. Some attempts at reconciliation were made by both sides. After Jeffreys' death, Phillips wrote a tribute to him in the *Elim Evangel* entitled, "A Tribute to One of Britain's Greatest Evangelists."

Jeffreys' funeral service was held on February 1, 1962, at Kensington Temple. Over a thousand people came from all over the British Isles to pay tribute to this apostle of the Lord. Members of the Bible Pattern Church Fellowship were joined by believers from Elim, the Assemblies of God, and other denominations from around the country, as well as by envoys from churches in Sweden, Switzerland, and France.

The reverent congregation shed tears as Pastor R. G. Tweed, Secretary of the Bible Pattern Fellowship, read the Scriptures, and Jeffreys' close friend, Albert Edsor, played the piano for Jeffreys one last time. Missing was Jeffreys' dearest Revival Party associate, R. E. Darragh, who had died three years earlier, on Jeffreys' seventieth birthday.

In his tribute to the beloved Principal, Edsor shared the following: "Jeffreys was a faithful man of God, a fearless man of God and a foremost fisher of men for God....He was first and foremost an outstanding soul-winner and ranks as one of the greatest Evangelists of this century, being active in his God-honored service for lost souls and the sick in body right up to the last."[77]

After the service, the congregation moved toward the cemetery, and "crowds lined the steps; crowds filled the forecourt; crowds thronged the streets; with many cars and taxis engaged for the occasion."[78] One participant commented nostalgically that it was "the funeral of a Prince," Prince being the nickname used for Jeffreys by those closest to him.[79]

✴✴✴✴✴

Serving Together Once Again

After Jeffreys resigned from Elim, E. J. Phillips remained the Secretary-General of the denomination for nearly thirty more years. During that time, he remained wholly committed to the work of the Elim movement. After a few years of illness, Phillips died on September 5, 1973, at the age of seventy-nine. He had served in the Elim movement for more than fifty years. While Phillips remained at the helm, no one made an attempt to challenge his authority. Through the 1950s, Phillips served on no fewer than ten of the thirteen committees that had been formed to run various aspects of the denomination. Believing it was in the best interests of the Elim churches, he had personally maintained the central control.

Since he was an administrator without the five-fold ministry gifts, Phillips' leadership was one of maintenance, not one marked by aggressive evangelism and church planting. The question remains: When Phillips took control of the Elim movement, did it result in a stable church or a stagnant one? David Neil Hudson notes in his thesis on the Elim schism that "by 1973, Elim had not essentially changed since 1940."[80] During his time as the senior pastor of Kensington Temple, Wynne Lewis made a personal observation concerning the Elim conflict: "They kicked out the apostolic spirit and took the dead hand of the administrative spirit to lead the denomination."[81]

> Today, the Elim movement continues to grow and flourish with five hundred fifty churches in the United Kingdom and their work in more than forty nations around the world.

In 1984, the nine-member Advisory Committee of the Bible Pattern Church Fellowship joined with the Elim Foursquare Gospel Alliance. Twenty-two years after Jeffreys' death and eleven years after Phillips', the two Pentecostal denominations came together once again to serve the Lord. Many of the things that George Jeffreys wanted are now a part of the Elim churches.

Today, the Elim movement continues to grow and flourish with five hundred fifty

✫✫✫✫✫

churches in the United Kingdom and their work in more than forty nations around the world.

The Apostolic Anointing on Kensington Temple

George Jeffreys left a legacy for the body of Christ. He moved in a dynamic apostolic ministry throughout Great Britain, and a great portion of his apostolic mantle now rests on Kensington Temple in Notting Hill in London's West End. In the years directly following Jeffreys' death, Kensington Temple stood empty, with no congregation to call it home. The Elim Trust Corporation had purchased the property rights from the one remaining trustee, but they had no one to fill the pulpit.

In 1965, the Elim Executive Council asked Eldin Corsie, an Elim pastor, to take his small congregation of fifty members to the impressive Kensington Temple to start a new work. Corsie's parents had been converted through Jeffreys' campaign in Birmingham years before. After the long-neglected building had been thoroughly cleaned, the services began in earnest. Within a year, the congregation grew considerably. Corsie and his volunteers began to clean out the basement for expansion, and what they discovered ignited within them a passion for the miraculous for years to come. Stored under the floor of the main church were numerous crutches, wheelchairs, and leg braces that had been discarded following miraculous healings in the revival meetings held there. Faith for the miraculous and an assurance of God's power coursed through the pastor's spirit. Over the next fifteen years, Corsie built a church where freedom of the Spirit was welcomed, along with prophetic ministry and revivalist worship.

Kensington Temple continued to grow in its evangelistic efforts and miraculous results under the ministry of senior pastor Wynne Lewis from 1980 until 1991. A visionary and a skilled organizer who was also sensitive to the Holy Spirit, Lewis welcomed the opportunity to minister to the internationals who called London home. Through its outreach, Kensington Temple became a tremendous cross-cultural center for believers in Christ, growing from five hundred members to as many as five thousand. By allowing the individual cultures to meet in separate church fellowships and preach the gospel in their own languages, the

Kensington congregation promoted a work that flourished. As he was led by the Spirit, Lewis would call for healing meetings in the church services, and people would be made whole.

In the 1980s, a young pastor named Colin Dye joined Kensington Temple. He founded a Bible school to train men and women for the work of the ministry and to release them to serve God around the world. Today, the International Bible Institute of London (I.B.I.O.L.) continues to train students and send them out into God's harvest.

According to its Web site, "IBIOL operates under an Apostolic and Prophetic mantle, with a mandate to prepare His people to the ministry of the apostle, prophet, evangelist, pastor and teacher and to see them fulfill their purpose and destiny as radical disciples of Jesus."[82]

When Wynne Lewis resigned in 1991 to take on a new leadership role with Elim, Colin Dye became the Senior Minister of Kensington Temple. Under his leadership, the congregation has grown from five thousand to twenty-five thousand members, with more than ten thousand members involved in church cell groups.

Today, Kensington Temple is appreciative of their history and is following in the steps of their founder. While they have always revered their history, today they are able to discuss it openly without fearing it. Their Web site speaks freely of Jeffreys' role as the founder of the Elim movement:

> We at KT recognise the apostolic foundations of our ministry today. More than any movement or modern spiritual trend our future is tied up with foundations dug at KT by the apostolic work of George Jeffreys. Salvation, healings, miracles, missionary work, church planting, releasing ministries and revival—this was the vision of George Jeffreys that launched the ministry of KT and it is the same vision that will launch us into [the future].[83]

An Evangelist's Legacy

At the end of 1961, a young German Bible student named Reinhard Bonnke was walking in the streets of Clapham, London, with a few hours to pass before his trip home. He was en route to Germany from the

Bible College of Wales in Swansea, where he was training for the ministry. Looking at the homes around him, Bonnke suddenly recognized the name of George Jeffreys posted outside of a castle-like house.

Bonnke knocked excitedly on the door and inquired whether he might see Jeffreys, whom he knew to be the greatest English evangelist since John Wesley. The housekeeper was about to turn Bonnke away when Jeffreys came to the door himself and invited him in. Bonnke felt he had been "transported to the abode of an apostle."[84] They spoke for some time about the lost world and the widespread need for the gospel of Jesus Christ, and then Jeffreys reached out and laid hands on the young man's head. He prayed for his ministry and for the empowerment of God for evangelism. To this day, Bonnke believes that that was when he received his mighty anointing. "I now realise that was God's true ordination for me as an evangelist."[85]

In the latter half of the twentieth century and into the twenty-first, Bonnke proved to be a world evangelist, indeed, especially in Africa, where his open-air gospel campaigns attracted crowds as large as 1.5 million.[86] And signs and wonders of the healing evangelist have followed.

And so, George Jeffreys' mantle remains most active through the anointing of Kensington Temple and the ministry of evangelist Reinhard Bonnke who spreads the powerful gospel message as Jeffreys did in the first half of the twentieth century.

Jeffreys' lifelong friend and Revival Party associate Albert Edsor said of Jeffreys after his death,

> To the end of his earthly pilgrimage he was engaged in seeking those who were sick in soul and praying for the sick in body. Time alone will reveal the magnitude of his mission and the extent of his powerful influence for God, and history will be kinder to him than those of his critics and contemporaries who misjudged him and what he stood for. As time rolls on, *his spiritual stature will be enhanced*, and the stamp of his integrity and sincerity in *his God-given and God-honored ministry will be appreciated the more.*"[87]

And that is how George Jeffreys is remembered today.

✶✶✶✶✶

ENDNOTES

35 George Jeffreys, *Healing Rays* (London: Elim Publishing Company, 1932), 56.

36 Desmond Cartwright, *The Great Evangelists: The Remarkable Lives of George and Stephen Jeffreys* (Hants, England: Marshall Pickering, 1986), 33.

37 Elim Evangelistic Minute Book. See Albert Edsor, *George Jeffreys: Man of God* (London: Ludgate Press, 1964), 23. The original Minute Book is now held in the Donald Gee Centre at Mattersey Hall College and Graduate School, Doncaster, England.

38 Ibid.

39 Cartwright, *The Great Evangelists*, 47.

40 Ibid., 76.

41 Ibid., 82.

42 Jeffreys, *Healing Rays*, 180.

43 Ibid., 181.

44 Ibid., 203.

45 Ibid., 205.

46 Cartwright, *The Great Evangelists*, 90.

47 Jeffreys, *Healing Rays*, 180.

48 Dropsy is known today as *edema*.

49 Jeffreys, 188.

50 Ibid., 189.

51 David Neil Hudson, "A Schism and Its Aftermath: An Historical Analysis of Denominational Discerption in the Elim Pentecostal Church, 1939–1940" (Ph.D. diss., King's College, 1999), 98.

52 Albert W. Edsor, *George Jeffreys: Man of God* (London: Ludgate Press Limited, 1964), 95.

53 Hudson, "A Schism and Its Aftermath," 131.

54 Jeffreys, *Healing Rays*, 116.

55 Ibid., 121.

56 Ibid., 126.

57 Ibid., 134.

58 Ibid., 111.

59 Hudson, "A Schism and Its Aftermath," 71.

60 Ibid., 249.

61   Edsor, *Man of God*, 81.

62   Hudson, "A Schism and Its Aftermath," 186.

63   Ibid., 259.

64   Ibid., 267.

65   Ibid.

66   Ibid., 268.

67   Ibid.

68   Ibid., 138.

69   Ibid., 97.

70   Cartwright, *The Great Evangelists*, 155.

71   Hudson, "A Schism and Its Aftermath," 305.

72   Edsor, *Man of God*, 83.

73   Ibid.

74   Cartwright, *The Great Evangelists,* 128.

75   Edsor, *Man of God,* 46.

76   Ibid., 48.

77   Ibid., 140.

78   Ibid., 142.

79   Ibid.

80   Hudson, "A Schism and Its Aftermath," 150.

81   Ibid.

82   http://www.kt.org/ibiol/.

83   http://www.kt.org/apostolicfoundation/.

84   Reinhard Bonnke, "My Jubilee—50 Years of Evangelism," November 10, 2009, http://uk.cfan.org/article.aspx?id=10655&page=2.

85   Ibid.

86   http://us.cfan.org/Reinhard-Bonnke-Biography.aspx.

87   Edsor, *Man of God*, 144.

LESTER SUMRALL

"Running with a Heavenly Vision"

"Running with a Heavenly Vision"

It was the morning of his seventeenth birthday, and Lester Sumrall was dying. After months of lying in a sickbed with tuberculosis, he had reached his end. Everyone agreed that his life was ending. The coughing that racked his lungs was out of control. His pillow, splattered with blood from his spasms throughout the long night, was a witness to his shattered life.

This fateful day, February 15, 1930, was a day of days. The ninety-three-pound, emaciated young man began to cough up blobs of tissue that the doctor declared were part of his lungs. Shaking his head in defeat, the doctor entered Lester's room for the last time.

"In two hours, your boy will be dead," he said gravely to George and Betty Sumrall. "That's the death rattle in his throat right now, and that bluishness in his face means he's not getting enough blood to his brain for his body to live. He's going to die tonight."[88]

The doctor left the Sumrall house and went back to his office to write out Lester's death certificate. He left the exact time of death blank, knowing it was just an administrative detail easy to attend to. George Sumrall would need to pick up the death certificate first thing in the morning so that he could go and buy a burial plot for his son.

✶✶✶✶✶

George Sumrall was a rough man who hardly believed in God and definitely didn't believe in the power of prayer. He left his son's deathbed with a mixture of grief and anger. Betty Sumrall was the opposite. A firm believer in the power of Jesus Christ to save and heal, she was not ready to give up her son. She stayed by Lester's bedside, crying and praying for God to intervene and save her boy's life.

As the night grew darker, Lester became more frightened. Was this the end of his life at just seventeen years of age? O God, he didn't want to die. Lying in pain on the bed, Lester turned to face the wall. Suddenly, he blinked his eyes and found himself staring at a vision of a coffin suspended in midair, open, and leaning toward him. The inside walls were lined with a white, silky material prepared for a body just his size. He knew that the coffin was meant for him.

> **After Lester spoke his willingness to submit, something opened up inside of his heart. He turned to God, cried for the forgiveness of his sins, and asked Jesus Christ to save him.**

Turning his head the other way in fear, Lester saw another vision, this one of practically the biggest Bible imaginable. It stretched from the ceiling to the floor with huge letters on its pages. As Lester stared in amazement, he heard God speak to his heart, *"Tonight, you will choose that coffin or that book. I want you to preach My Word or tonight you will die."*[89]

Lester had run from the thought of being a preacher his entire young life, but there was no way that he wanted to die. So, he took God at His word and agreed, saying, "God, if the only way in the world for me to live is to preach, then I'll preach." After Lester spoke his willingness to submit, something opened up inside of his heart. He turned to God, cried for the forgiveness of his sins, and asked Jesus Christ to save him.

As his mother slept fitfully on a chair near the bottom of his bed, Lester Sumrall became a new creation in Christ. He was still a boy full of questions and quarrels, but he now belonged to the King of Kings. He fell asleep a terminally sick teenager and woke up the next morning completely healed!

"Mama, please get me some breakfast," were Lester's first words the next morning. His mother could hardly believe her ears and tried to talk him out of eating. Then, thinking she was giving him his last meal, Mama Sumrall went and filled a breakfast plate for Lester. He cleaned his plate with no problem and startled his mother with his next statement: "Mama, you don't need that doctor no more. I'm healed, and I'm going to be a preacher."[90] With eyes full of tears and a heart full of joy, Lester's mother praised the living God. Her heart's desires had been answered. Her boy was saved, miraculously healed, and called to preach!

God's Missionary Giant

For this poor, Southern boy growing up near the beaches of Pensacola, Florida, the dramatic summons to preach would become a resounding call that would reach around the world with the message of Jesus Christ. Lester Sumrall's ministry would span almost the entire twentieth century. He became a missionary who was sold out to Jesus and the salvation message alone, and his compassionate journeys took him to 110 countries and a thousand cities to spread the life-changing gospel of salvation through Jesus Christ.

Through his years of ministry, Lester saw the Lord move in powerful ways and touch the world with His Holy Spirit.

He wrote,

I have been in every move of God throughout the entire twentieth century. I grew up in the aftermath of the Pentecostal move of God [beginning with the Azusa Street revival]. After World War II, I saw the Latter Rain movement....After that the Healing revival [with the huge tent ministries] of which I was very much a part. Then I saw the Charismatic revival and the Word of Faith movement that followed. I endorsed it and became a part of that flow of the Spirit of God. I am now ready for the last outpouring of God on the face of the earth![91]

More than a voice to the multitudes, Lester Sumrall was a genuine father of the faith to many young preachers of the gospel—including this author when I was a young pastor. I first saw Lester Sumrall in Tulsa, Oklahoma, at one of Billy Joe Daugherty's Word Explosion conferences. Years later, I finally met him face-to-face while traveling in Europe. At that meeting, he gruffly said, "I'm eating breakfast at 7:30; you should be there." The next morning, after breakfast, he blurted out, "I live in South Bend. You should come visit me." I really didn't know if this was a serious invitation or merely polite conversation. Six weeks later, however, I received a call from Sumrall's secretary, who said, "We were wondering where you were. Dr. Sumrall had said you would be visiting." I told her of my impression that Dr. Sumrall was only being polite. She replied, "Dr. Sumrall doesn't say polite things." Thus began my relationship with this great hero of the faith. He was my spiritual father and mentor for many years, always providing bold words of encouragement and strength as I grew in service to the Lord. His story and life stand as a shining example of Christian leadership, sacrifice, and devotion.

The Prayers of a Spiritual Powerhouse

As a boy, Lester Sumrall was the last kid on the block whom you would have expected to become a preacher. His father was a rough, fighting man, brawny and blustery, and Lester wanted to be just like him. Betty Sumrall was a courageous Christian woman who had been saved and filled with the Holy Spirit long before she married her husband. She abandoned the call to be a missionary to marry George Sumrall, her sister's widowed husband, and take care of his four children. She spent her days praying that her children would pick up the gauntlet and take the gospel to the lost.

Lester Frank Sumrall was born on February 15, 1913, the sixth child in a home that already seemed to have too many children. His father told him on more than one occasion that he really wasn't wanted. Still, there were three more children born to his parents after he was.

In spite of his father's cold attitude, Lester longed to be strong and mean, just like he was. If there was a brawl in the school yard, Lester was in the middle of it. If there was a financial need in the family, Lester would find something to sell or someone to bully in order to get the money. If there was a pastor's kid who needed to be "taught a lesson," Lester was happy to oblige with all the scorn he felt for preachers *and* their families. And throughout each reckless activity, Mama Sumrall prayed faithfully for God to use her hardheaded son to preach His message of salvation to the ends of the earth.

Prayer Warriors

When he walked into the living room every morning, Lester would find the Ladies' Prayer Group that met in his home each day. These long-skirted women with modest hairstyles and no makeup were firebrands of the faith. They called down the blessings of heaven as they prayed for the needs of the church, their families, their neighbors, and the world. It was through their faith and prayers that Lester Sumrall first saw the power of the Holy Spirit to heal.

As a boy, Lester had a vitamin deficiency disease called pellagra. Once thought to be a kind of leprosy, the condition caused burning lesions, first on his skin and then throughout his digestive system, making it nearly impossible for him to eat. His skin was excruciatingly painful to the touch. The doctor declared the disease fatal, but the Ladies' Prayer Group had something to say about that! After they laid hands on Lester and lifted their cries to heaven daily, Lester was completely healed.[92]

A couple of years later, Mama Sumrall was diagnosed with an open, bleeding cancer in her breast. Medical help was very limited, and the doctors were unsure what to do, but nothing limited the hand of God. Mama knew the answer—she was an "unrelenting prayer warrior," and so she prayed to a powerful God who answers the cries of His children.

One night, as she was praying, she had a vision of Jesus entering her bedroom and touching her. At the breakfast table the next morning, she announced, "Jesus came into my room last night, and I am healed."[93] Lester's father grunted in disapproval, but, just three days later, Mama came out of her bedroom with a glob of human tissue sitting on her bandages. Lester never forgot what it looked like. It had a round center and tendrils extending from it. It was the cancerous tumor, and it was out of her body!

★★★★★

Mama Sumrall had gone to the Lord with her childlike faith, and He had answered her with a tremendous healing. She served the Lord for forty-five more years before joining Him in heaven!

A Dropout with an Attitude

In spite of his mother's prayers and the miraculous deliverances he saw around him, Lester determined to avoid God. Even though he attended church services with his mother, he shared his father's opinion that all preachers were parasites who lived off of others.

Lester dropped out of high school at age sixteen and spent his days fishing and looking for ways to make easy money. It was then that the tuberculosis struck with a vengeance. After months of trying to fight the disease, Lester neared his untimely end. At the brink of death and discovery, he experienced the visions of the coffin and the huge Bible and made the choice that would change his life forever. Lester's instantaneous and complete healing from tuberculosis firmly established his belief in a God who heals today.

George Sumrall was happy that his son was healed but not certain how it had come about. He was excited about Lester's natural ability to do well in business and assumed that he would resume earning money for the family's needs. Yet, three weeks after his miraculous healing, Lester heard the Lord say once again, "You need to preach My Word!"

> **With determination, Lester went to his strong-willed father and explained that he would be leaving home to preach the gospel.**

With determination, Lester went to his strong-willed father and explained that he would be leaving home to preach the gospel. He believed that obeying God was the only thing that would keep him alive! Furious, his father roared at his "stupidity," forbade him to leave, and stomped out of the house. With tears in his eyes, Lester ran up to his room and pleaded with the Lord for an answer to this conflict. Should he obey his earthly father or follow the call from God? The Lord answered Lester's prayer with a Scripture.

It would be the first of hundreds of times throughout his life that the Lord would use His direct Word to give Lester Sumrall guidance and direction.

Isaiah 41:10 made a lasting impression on Lester's heart. It reads, *"Fear thou not; for I am with thee; be not dismayed, for I am thy God: I will strengthen thee; yea, I will help thee; yea, I will uphold thee with the right hand of my righteousness."* "Okay, Lord," Lester replied. "If You're with me, I'm ready to go."[94] With God's clear assurance, Lester packed a small bag of his belongings and prepared to leave.

Kissing his tearful mother good-bye was difficult, but he knew that he had to go. "You prayed for years that I'd be a preacher. Now that I'm going to do it, you're still crying," he told her.[95] He let his mother know with grim determination that he would not return to his home. He was going out to preach for God and would stay out there, doing God's will, for the rest of his life.

Nothing could have prepared that skinny, seventeen-year-old boy for the adventures that God had in store for him over the next sixty-six years of his life!

Indifferent toward the Lost

Remember how Jonah refused to go to Nineveh because he didn't want the people of that city to be saved? Even though Lester was moving out in God's call, he didn't really care about the lost people of the world. He was willing to preach the Word, as he had heard men of God do since he was a small boy, but whether the people responded or not hardly meant a thing to him.

Lester left town with only a suitcase. He was accompanied by a friend from church who wanted to come along for the adventure. This young man would also help to lead the praise services before Lester preached. *Where should we go?* they wondered.

After their first day of driving along northern Florida's rural roads, they saw an old, empty schoolhouse in a field. Searching the fields

*Lester Sumrall
as a teenage evangelist*

nearby for anyone who knew something about the building, Lester found the farmer who owned it. He asked the man for the use of the schoolhouse to preach. Reluctantly, the farmer reached into his dirty overalls and pulled out a set of keys. With a grin, Lester informed the man that he would be preaching there that evening, and he invited him to come.

Lester was on a mission to satisfy God's commission to him. Exactly eight farmers arrived at the schoolhouse that first night to hear the skinny, teenaged boy preach the gospel. But the farmers came for sport and ridicule; they laughed at the testimony of his healing and thought he was making up the stories![96] *What am I doing here?* Lester asked himself.

Surprisingly, the second night, forty people arrived early at the schoolhouse and waited outside the door. They wanted to hear the entertaining, storytelling preacher. So, for several nights, Lester kept telling his story of salvation and healing, and, each night, more people came to hear it. Soon, they stopped laughing at his message and started listening to the gospel of salvation from the Word of God.

Although Lester still cared very little about them, people were coming to the altar each night to receive Jesus Christ as Lord and Savior. In his indifference toward the lost, Lester would give the altar call and then walk out the door, not waiting to pray with any person or even to see who had come to the altar to repent. He was preaching to stay alive—it was merely part of his agreement with God. And, as far as he was concerned, the consequences of his preaching were totally up to God.

After Lester had conducted six weeks of revival services, the newly saved began asking for water baptism. More than sixty people walked to the local creek and were baptized by the skinny "Little Preacher," as they called him.[97] Recalling what he had seen other ministers do in the past, Lester baptized these people in the name of the Father, the Son, and the Holy Spirit, and they began to walk in the newness of life. Still, for this now eighteen-year-old preacher, it was as though he performed on a stage, somehow separated from the reality of the hearts and lives changing around him. He just watched as God took care of the people who were drawn to the gospel.

Traveling throughout Florida, Louisiana, and Tennessee, Lester continued to preach with ferocious zeal in every church that invited him but felt no compassion for those who came to hear. He was angry and disgusted with them more often than he was friendly and warm.

The Roadway to Hell

Then, one night, all of that changed.

A full-scale revival was going on in a small schoolhouse in rural Tennessee, where Lester was preaching. The service began, and joyful praises were rising to the Lord in swinging harmony. Suddenly, the scene in front of Lester dramatically changed. He was no longer sitting in the schoolroom or aware of anyone or anything around him.

Lester was receiving his second vision from God, and it was even more dramatic than the first. It was a vision that he would share with millions of people around the globe for the rest of his life.

With his eyes wide open, Lester saw a great highway filled with the peoples of the world. Every nation was represented. He saw them dressed in the colorful, native costumes of their individual countries, walking in one stream of humanity. Japanese, Chinese, Africans, Europeans, Americans, and others all were walking quickly along the road together. Lester realized that he was seeing the highway of life.

In the vision, he rose with the Holy Spirit above the crowded highway and traveled to the end of it. What he saw next was fearful and life changing. Before him was a "raging, bottomless inferno that looked like a blazing volcano. This vast procession of people marched to the edge and then fell screaming into the eternal flames. As they neared the pit and saw their fate, they struggled in vain, trying to push back against the unrelenting march of those behind them. The great surging river of humanity swept them over into the abyss."[98]

You Are to Blame!

What a horrifying scene! Lester saw the screaming masses tearing their faces and clawing the air as they tried to save themselves from their fate. He saw the world descending into hell. God's words came clearly into Lester's mind and shocked him to his very core.

"You are responsible for those who are lost," the Lord said to him. "Me, Lord? I don't know these people. I'm not to blame," he answered hastily.[99]

The Lord's response to Lester was quick and sure; once again, it was a Scripture verse—Ezekiel 3:18: *When I say unto the wicked, Thou shalt surely die; and thou givest him not warning, nor speakest to warn the wicked from his wicked way, to save his life; the same wicked man shall die in his iniquity; but his blood will I require at your hand.*[100]

Protesting his innocence to the Lord, Lester looked down to see an image of blood running through his fingers in a continual flow. God was serious. There were millions lost for all eternity throughout the world, and Lester Sumrall's call from the Lord was to go and tell them the amazing truth of God's love.

As suddenly as it began, the vision ended, and Lester was sitting all alone in the old, dark schoolhouse. Standing up and peering around, he struggled to get his bearings. How long had he been sitting there watching humanity plunge into the flames of hell? Everyone had quietly left him, adjourning the meeting and leaving him alone to communicate with God. They had taken their lanterns with them, and the only thing lighting the schoolhouse was the moon.[101]

Dropping to his knees in that country schoolhouse, Lester began to weep and wail from the depths of his soul for himself and for the people of the world. "I asked forgiveness for not loving the lost, the last and the least of this world," he later declared.[102] He pleaded with God to forgive him for his sins and for not loving those around him who were lost and dying.

With the light of God's Spirit burning in his heart, this young preacher from the Deep South asked the Lord to reveal Himself. Lester travailed in prayer all night, agonizing before the Lord until the early morning sun shone through the schoolhouse windows.[103]

The vision was so vivid and yet so terrifying that Lester kept it to himself for several years. Yet, he never forgot it, and, from that day forward, he proclaimed the gospel of Jesus Christ to every soul who would listen. The entire earth became his congregation, and he sought opportunities to preach wherever he went.

✱✱✱✱✱

LESTER SUMRALL

"I Have Anointed You"

The Lord has many different ways of speaking to His servants. For Lester Sumrall, as mentioned earlier, in times of decision or difficulty, God answered his prayers by placing Scripture verses on his heart. In his bedroom two years earlier, when Lester had been struggling to leave his family to preach, God had encouraged him with Isaiah 41:10: *"Fear thou not; for I am with thee."* When Lester had argued that he was not to blame for the lost souls plunging into eternal fire, God had convicted him with Ezekiel 3:18.

Now, Lester went before the Lord again, wondering how he was to travel around the world to reach the lost. He was alone and without resources. Once again, God spoke through Scripture, saying, "Read John 15:16." Looking it up, Lester read, *"Ye have not chosen me, but I have chosen you, and ordained you, that ye should go."*[104]

God chooses men and women to serve Him as He sees fit. Whom He chooses, He anoints; whom He anoints, He sets aside as ones consecrated to fulfill His purposes. Lester wasn't working for any other ministry or church, but God nonetheless had ordained him to serve Him. Although Lester had no formal training at the time, he found that "church planting" became a natural outflow of his ministry.

As Lester traveled from town to town, there were often so many people saved and filled with the Holy Spirit that they would establish a new church in order to continue growing together in the Lord. Once a church had been built by local hands and established, Lester would call on the Assemblies of God to send a pastor to lead the flock. Then, he would move on to the next God-appointed town.

The young traveling preacher

As the numbers of people responding to the gospel grew, Lester was pleased when his younger sister, Leona, joined him. She had a beautiful voice, and she led the worship services, as well as preached a powerful message of salvation. Their dear mother had been well rewarded for her prayers, as most of her children were now actively serving the Lord as ministers of the gospel. The effectual, fervent prayer of Betty Sumrall had accomplished much! (See James 5:16.)

Listening to Leona preach God's Word, Lester realized she had a gift of power that he did not. Although he had preached on the baptism of the Holy Spirit and the power of God for a renewed life, he had never received it himself. Somehow, the tradition of travailing at the altar had not brought him any results. As Lester watched others receive the baptism of the Holy Spirit with the evidence of speaking in tongues, he asked in anguish, "What's wrong with me, Father?"

Finally, one evening, after a revival meeting, he cried out to God again concerning his failure to receive the baptism of the Holy Spirit. The Lord spoke to his heart and admonished him that there was no formula for receiving His gifts and blessings. God would simply give the infilling of the Holy Spirit to Lester as a gift of His love. That night, in a room far from the bustle of church services or the "travailing altar," God gloriously baptized Lester Sumrall in His Holy Spirit, and Lester began to speak in a new, heavenly language.[105]

"I Will Send a Companion"

It had been over a year since Lester had received the terrifying vision of the roadway to hell. In the Sumrall revivals, many people had been saved, healed, and filled with the Holy Spirit. Yet, as much as the Lord was doing through his life, Lester could not begin to imagine the plans God was preparing for him in another part of the world.

The same night that Lester had seen a vision of hell, Howard Carter had been praying on the other side of the Atlantic Ocean. At the time, he was the president of Hampstead Bible College in London, chairman of a large British denomination, and a strong believer in the Pentecostal power of God. While seeking new direction in his ministry to Christ, Carter was impressed with an unusual prophetic word from the Lord. It went as follows:

I have found a companion for thee: I have called a worker to stand beside thee. He hath heard my call, he respondeth and he joineth thee in the work to which I have called thee….He is called and chosen and shalt join thee.[106]

✶✶✶✶✶

The Lord reassured Howard that he would recognize this companion by the words he would say to him upon their first meeting:

Wherever you go, I will go. Over the high mountains, over the temptuous waves of the sea, into the deep valleys, into the plains. I will succor you, I will assist you, I will strengthen you, I will help you, and in every time of need I shall be with you. When you are old I will strengthen you and assist you and help you. I will succor you in your old age, and you shall be unto me as a father.[107]

This was not the first time that Howard Carter had received a prophecy from the Lord, but it was certainly the most puzzling word he had heard. Standing before the Hampstead Bible College faculty and student body, Howard read the prophecy aloud. "This is a prophecy," he told them. "If I am a false prophet, mark me as one and discard me—but, if this comes true, then you will know that I am a prophet of God."[108]

God's "Coincidental" Hand

Nothing happened concerning that prophecy for eighteen months. Howard Carter was expecting to leave for a long missionary trip to the Far East when he received an unexpected invitation to preach in Eureka Springs, Arkansas. When he inquired of the Lord, he was amazed that God actually wanted him to accept the invitation to the United States.

At the same time, led by the "coincidental" hand of God, Lester Sumrall was impressed to leave a revival he was preaching in Oklahoma and drive 150 miles to Eureka Springs, Arkansas, for a Bible conference. Unsure of why the Lord wanted him to go there, he asked his sister, Leona, to pack up their things so they could be on their way.[109]

On the day of Lester's arrival, Howard Carter lectured on the nine gifts of the Holy Spirit, according to 1 Corinthians 12:7–10. Lester was fascinated by the depth of Howard's understanding of the gifts of the Spirit—he was speaking of things Lester had never considered before.

After the lecture, Lester followed the Bible teacher outside to discuss the Scripture passage with him further. To his own amazement, after just a few polite words, Lester Sumrall began to speak prophetically to Howard Carter. He talked of things he had never considered, using language that was not in his Southern vocabulary. His prophecy began like this: *"Wherever you go, I will go. Over the highest mountains, over the temptuous waves of the sea into the deep valleys, into the plains...."* On and on, Lester spoke the exact words of prophecy that Howard Carter had received eighteen months earlier! His statement ended with, *"...and you shall be unto me as a father."* Immediately after he had finished, Lester apologized for the unusual words, especially as they had been spoken to a stranger, and began to walk away, shaking his head.[110]

With a bemused smile, Howard invited Lester to come to his hotel room to talk for a few minutes. They were accompanied by Stanley Frodsham, a Christian editor and friend of Howard's. In the hotel room, Howard opened his prayer journal to reveal the prophetic words recorded a year and a half earlier over three thousand miles away on the other side of the Atlantic Ocean.

Dumbfounded, Lester listened as Howard questioned him about his interest in missions. When he asked Lester which country he was most interested in, Lester replied, "All of them."[111] Lester shared his vision from eighteen months earlier and the passionate call on his life to take the gospel message to the lost around the world. Thoughtfully, Howard asked him, "Are you willing to travel with me?" When Lester agreed, Howard responded immediately, "Then you're the one!"[112]

The prophecy had proven true. Lester was more than willing to go and thus formed a godly bond of friendship that would last for the next forty-one years.

Although they began with a simple plan that Lester would be the evangelist and Howard would be the teacher, God had so much more in store for them. He established a Paul-and-Timothy type of relationship that benefited both of them personally and spiritually throughout the rough and glorious parts of ministry alike.

Start at the Bottom

Before departing on a journey that would be long and uncertain, Lester decided to pay a visit to his parents in Pensacola. George and Betty Sumrall welcomed their son home with great joy. During the years of Lester's absence, his father had finally surrendered his life to Christ.

With his years of anger and fighting behind him, George Sumrall spent the remainder of his days preaching the Word of God to anyone who would listen.

Over the next few weeks, a series of small financial miracles eventually brought Lester to California. Unfortunately, Howard had been very vague about their exact plans for departure. When Lester arrived in San Francisco, he searched for some message or letter left behind by Howard at the Assemblies of God church there, yet he found no directions of any kind. Every person who had seen him before he'd sailed gave Lester a different answer as to where Brother Carter had gone.

Quite concerned about his next step, Lester finally inquired of the Lord. What he heard in response was, *"Start at the bottom."* When Lester asked, "What is the bottom?" the answer in his spirit was, *"Australia."* Howard had left the United States without Lester, possessing an amazing faith that Sumrall would somehow know what to do and where to go to follow him. With a firm belief that God was leading him each day of his journey, Lester made plans to cross the vast Pacific Ocean to meet this mysterious man of God somewhere on the continent "down under."

Ready to set sail aboard the R.M.S. Makura in San Francisco in 1934

Lester Sumrall had always been a brave and blustery young man, but embarking by himself on a trip to the other side of the world still brought tears to his eyes as he settled into his cabin. It was November 21, 1934, when Lester embarked on the *R.M.S. Makura* for Australia. He was learning firsthand what it meant to be completely obedient to God's call.

The Dynamic Duo

Who was Howard Carter, and what role did this powerful man of God have in Lester Sumrall's early ministry? Lester often called the years he spent traveling the world with Brother Carter the "highlight of his life."[113] The heartfelt love of a father had been tragically missing from Lester's early relationship with his natural father, and the Lord saw fit to restore that affection to him through Howard. At the time of their miraculous meeting in Arkansas, Howard was in his early forties, and Lester was barely twenty.

Howard was a true British aristocrat, in every sense of the word—refined, well-educated, and wealthy. Beyond that, he was a vibrant man of God, sold out to the gospel of Jesus Christ. Instead of using his wealth and position for leisure, though, he dedicated it all to the work of the kingdom of God. His inheritance was willingly invested in the Hampstead Bible College, with much of the money providing free tuition for ministry students in need.[114]

During World War I, Howard had been arrested and imprisoned for a time as a conscientious objector. As other powerhouse believers of the past, Howard had used his time in prison to meditate deeply on God's Word. He'd yearned to grasp the contemporary purpose and place of the gifts of the Holy Spirit. After studying at great length, he wrote an important book, *Questions and Answers on Spiritual Gifts*, about the nine gifts of the Holy Spirit. This work became a foundation for the early twentieth-century Pentecostal movement and is still the basis of much of our understanding of the gifts of the Spirit today.

It was to this humble, dedicated teacher of the Word that God entrusted the formation of Lester's ministry heart.

"Mystery! Wonder! Providence!"

"Mystery! Wonder! Providence! Here I was on my way to Australia to meet and travel around the world with a man I had only met once. How strange."[115] This excerpt is from Lester's diary entry on the first day sailing on the *R.M.S. Makura* for Australia. Lester was reflecting with amazement on how the Lord had brought him to the place where he was. Although he had only twelve dollars to his name, he had faith to believe God would make a way. The pastor who had driven him to the docked ship had expressed concern, saying, "Lester, you will starve." The young man's response had been to suggest that if that happened, his tombstone should be inscribed: "Here lies Lester Sumrall—starved to death trusting Jesus."[116]

No church or mission society was backing or supporting Lester and Howard on their journey. However, Howard had told Lester that they needed to travel by faith and never ask for help or even mention to anyone but the Lord that they had a need.[117] As the ship sailed out of the San Francisco Harbor and into the vast Pacific, Lester resolved that he would spend his lifetime adventuring for Christ. He looked at his finances and declared, "If God could feed Elijah by the brook of Cherith, He can supply our needs." (See 1 Kings 17:2–4.)

The first great challenge to his faith for God's provision came as the ship entered the port in Sydney, Australia, seven weeks later. The Australian government informed the passengers that they couldn't disembark unless they had the equivalent of 200 English pounds to bring with them into the country. The Australians wanted tourists, not beggars!

Two hundred pounds! As they lined up to meet with the customs officers, a young man just ahead of Lester was refused entrance to Australia because he had only seventy-five American dollars. He was to be sent back to the United States on the next boat!

When it was Lester's turn, the customs officer asked Lester how much money he had, and his vague reply was that he didn't have much. Then, under the influence of the Holy Spirit, Lester humbly replied, "I am going around the world to preach the gospel to those who have never accepted Christ as their Savior. I am going to Java, Singapore, China, Manchuria, Korea, and Japan, and the Lord will provide."[118]

While Lester prayed silently, the officers spoke among themselves and then made their decision. They were going to let him enter the country. What rejoicing—God's hand was supernaturally present in his circumstances! After docking, Lester was met by the pastor of Richmond Temple, who had a much-awaited letter from Howard Carter for him.

> **As the ship sailed out of the San Francisco Harbor and into the vast Pacific, Lester resolved that he would spend his lifetime adventuring for Christ. He looked at his finances and declared, "If God could feed Elijah by the brook of Cherith, He can supply our needs."**

Lester was to meet Howard there in Sydney, Australia, a few days later. It had been five months since their only meeting in Arkansas! On January 1, 1935, Lester watched as Howard's ship sailed into the harbor and docked. Looking for the somewhat familiar face, Lester finally found him in the customs office. Lester looked forward to beginning their ministry adventure!

Adventuring with Christ

They called it the "Canvas Tabernacle." Lester and Howard set up the large tent in Brisbane, Australia, for their first outreach to the lost

Howard Carter and Lester Sumrall in Sydney, Australia

in their travels together. Night after night, Lester preached the gospel, speaking of the saving power of the blood of Christ, and hundreds of people came to the altar to receive salvation for their souls and healing for their bodies. What an exciting way to begin the new ministry!

One night, a man approached the altar in a great deal of pain and with many questions concerning supernatural healing. The pain in this man's side and back had confounded his doctors for years. When Lester explained God's healing power, the man reacted with fear and uneasiness.

"The pain may appear to be gone, but it will return tonight," was the gentleman's response, revealing his inner conflict of faith versus fear. With conviction, Lester reassured him that God had done a complete healing.

The next evening, the same man arrived at the revival meeting, grinning from ear to ear. "Preacher, I am healed! I have not had a pain in my body since last night!" he announced.[119] As a result of this and other healing testimonies, the faith of the people grew each day. A young woman with a cancerous sore on her nose approached the altar for prayer; within days, the sore was healed completely.

The time seemed to pass swiftly, and Lester and Howard's last evening in Australia was filled with praises to God for His blessings on their ministry there.

The Land of Perpetual Summer

Lester and Howard were eager to bring the good news of Jesus to the scores of human beings lost in spiritual darkness at their next destination: Java, Indonesia, the most densely populated island in the world.

Lester was overwhelmed by the beauty of this hot, humid tropical paradise, where luscious flowers were in bloom all around him. But he was not so overcome that he didn't immediately sense the spiritual barrenness of this garden paradise. Java was an island where numerous false religions and superstitions had kept the people in spiritual bondage for generations.

For weeks, Lester and Howard preached about the power of God to save and heal. Lester preached the salvation message to the lost, and Howard taught the established believers on the island, leading them to develop deeper walks with Christ. He prayed for many to receive the baptism of the Holy Spirit and God's power.

One lasting spiritual lesson came on a pleasure trip to Dieng, a volcanic mountain on the island. Lester and Howard had accepted a friend's invitation to visit a live volcanic crater. As they reached the summit of the mountain, they looked south to the Indian Ocean and then north to the Java Sea. It was a breathtakingly beautiful sight.

As they descended into the crater pit, the beauty was replaced by large sulfur springs "vomiting a nauseous cloud of smoke, and about a dozen small springs bubbling up a muddy substance."[120] The ground beneath their feet was hot to the touch because the volcanic activity was simmering just below the surface. Wanting to show them more of this powerful, dangerous mountain, their friend asked if the men would like to visit Death Valley, which was a short distance away.

They rounded a curve on the mountain path and discovered a sign engraved with sinister skull and crossbones above large, black letters that read, "DEATH VALLEY." Beside it was the tombstone of a German scientist who had scoffed at the warning and descended into the valley by rope to prove it was just a native superstition. He was pulled back up from his descent a dead man.

The mysterious Death Valley was filled with enticingly beautiful foliage that resembled a tropical paradise. But one more sign decorated the top of the ravine; it was a final warning of impending doom: "Danger! Stop!"[121]

How much like the "Death Valleys" of life this is, thought Lester. While some valleys of death are obviously dark and gloomy, many are apparently beautiful, fascinating, and glamorous. They may be filled with the enticements of fame, wealth, and education—yet, when we worship them and place them above the Lord, they become our own valleys of death.[122]

Whatever may entice us into the death valleys of life, there are warning signs given by a loving Father all along the way. They come from His Word and from believers who share the gospel with those around them. Never ignore the "Danger! Stop!" signs along the way of life! They can save you from the highway of sin, pain, and destruction.

Demonic Confrontation

Traveling through a land of spiritual darkness like Java, it was inevitable that Lester would face demonic spirits protesting the message of Jesus Christ. Still a young man, he really wasn't prepared for such intense spiritual warfare.

Acts 10:38 says, *"Jesus...went about doing good, and healing all that were oppressed of the devil."* At a revival service one evening in Java, Lester had his first encounter with demon possession.

As the song service proceeded, a young girl about twelve years old slipped away from the front pew, where she had been sitting with her family, got on the floor, laid on her belly, and "began to writhe on the floor like a snake foaming at the mouth."[123] Her tongue would flick in and out like a serpent's as she slithered back and forth in the front of the church. Lester was horrified at what he saw, but the Javanese pastor continued on with worship as though nothing unusual was happening.

Lester had never been a shy man. When he stood in the pulpit to speak, righteous anger rose up in his spirit. He pointed at the young lady, who understood no English, and commanded her, "Get back in your seat!" Immediately, she sat back in her seat and remained there, sitting as still as a statue, for the entire sermon.

✲✲✲✲✲

As Lester preached, he was also having a private conversation with the Lord. He asked God to take care of the problem of the little, demon-possessed girl. He didn't know what to do with her. The Lord answered him clearly, "This is your problem. You take care of it!"[124] Never having dealt with the occult before, but knowing that, in Christ, he had authority, Lester finished his sermon. Immediately afterward, he leaned over the pulpit, looked at the young girl sitting rigidly before him, and shouted at the top of his lungs, "Now come out of her!"[125]

Lester never touched the little girl or had any conversation with the demons wrestling within her. But, in a moment, the Spirit of the Lord descended on her. Her eyes became clear, and a sweet smile lit up her face. She was unaware of where she was or what had happened. As the Javanese pastor explained to her that she had just been freed from an evil spirit, she danced around with joy.

As if on cue, hundreds of people in the congregation stood up and streamed to the altar, trusting in the God of power for salvation, healing, and deliverance. For hours, Lester prayed with those at the altar, but he was still shaken by what had happened.[126]

Howard Carter had been teaching at another church and had not been present at Lester's meeting. Back in Lester's room later that night, Howard reassured him that he had handled the entire situation well, according to the Word of God. Just the same, Lester hoped with all his heart that it would never happen again!

Unfortunately for him, there were other demonic conflicts in Java before they left. Lester remarked afterward, "The greatest thing I learned was that I was not personally in the conflict. It was *Christ in me*. Also, it was not the *person* who caused the battle, but the *devil* within him or her."[127]

When Lester and Howard ministered together in Java, the results were powerful. Thousands of Javanese were saved and received the baptism of the Holy Spirit through the laying on of Howard's hands. When Lester ministered to them, many would be instantly healed of their diseases and would give their hearts to Christ. Like Paul and Timothy, this duo of ministers made an impression for Christ wherever they walked.[128]

★★★★★

Pastor F. Van Abkoude summed up the success of Lester and Howard's three months of ministry in Java, saying, "We prayed God to send a messenger, and Brother Carter came to Java with Brother Sumrall.... Souls have been saved, healed, and baptized with the Holy Spirit. The result of their ministry will be seen in eternity."[129]

Fraught with Danger

Lester and Howard spent a few weeks preaching and visiting the Christians in Singapore and Hong Kong before entering the nation of China. During their time in Hong Kong, the Christians there gave financially to the ministry so that they would be able to travel 3,500 miles in mainland China, along the borders of Burma and Tibet.

Ministering in China was extremely unnerving. The Chinese people did not have a long attention span. Often, after a few minutes of listening to the interpreter, groups of Chinese people would stand up in the middle of the message and walk out, simply finished giving their time. At other times, people would talk loudly about one point of the sermon while the message was still being presented.

Traveling in China in 1934 was fraught with danger. Lester's life was almost lost on more than one occasion. One time, after drinking water that had not been boiled long enough, he became deathly ill with dysentery and fever. As his conditioned worsened, he began to hemorrhage from his intestines, racked with pain and an ever-rising fever. Lester wasn't a complainer, though, so Howard had no idea how ill he really was.[130]

The next morning, when the caravan began to move, with Lester's mule last in line, the hours of diarrhea and lack of food made Lester faint, and he fell off of his mule. Crawling to a bush, he fastened the mule's rope and then passed into unconsciousness. No one in his party was aware of what had happened. He was left on the road in China to die.

Hours later, Lester woke up alone but was astonished to discover that he was completely well! His fever was gone; his strength was returning. God had healed him as he had slept. Lester remained in that spot until someone from his caravan returned and found him. He then continued on in the journey, rejoicing in God's faithfulness.[131]

✴✴✴✴✴

A few years later, while preaching in Mobile, Alabama, Lester discovered what had really happened in the heavenlies that day. The pastor of the church in Mobile, who was also a longtime friend, and his wife shared a strange story. They had been warned by the Holy Spirit one evening that Lester was dying somewhere on the other side of the world. They had fallen on their knees, crying out to the Lord, "Save him. Save him. Don't let him die."[132] Later that evening, when Lester checked his diary, he discovered that their prayers on his behalf had been offered at the exact time he had been struggling for his life. He shared this with his friends, and God's faithfulness once again brought them to their knees in thanksgiving!

Bandits and Brutality

The mortal dangers in China came from outside sources, as well. The Communist Chinese were creating havoc throughout the nation as they "persuaded" people to accept their Communist doctrine—using brutal tactics. Just a few weeks before Lester and Howard arrived in China, two young missionaries, John and Betty Stam, had been martyred for their faith, with only their infant daughter surviving. Lester and Howard were now traveling in the same area near the Tibetan border by mule, going from village to village to preach salvation through Christ.

Traveling by mule caravan through the mountain villages of Tibet

On more than one occasion, the fact that Lester's life was in God's hands became immediately obvious. Once, Lester's mule panicked and ran away from the caravan, stranding Lester fifteen hundred miles away from Hong Kong in the midst of a crowd of laughing Chinese people with no interpreter and no idea where Howard had gone. Lester gave a frantic plea to the Lord for direction and assistance. By God's grace, an older Chinese man approached him, speaking in words incomprehensible to the young missionary. The gentleman simply led the mule in the opposite direction and gave him a quick kick in the behind. What a relief to Lester when, a few hours later, the mule caught up with the Christian caravan.[133]

✶✶✶✶✶

Determined to preach the gospel to the poor Chinese far away from the big cities and Christian ministries, Lester and Howard traveled even where they had been warned not to go. One day, they had dinner at an inn where two men had just been murdered. Their soldier guards became so frightened of the danger that they left the two men of God to finish their journey without their protection. They traveled past cities that were mere heaps of smoking rubble after the Chinese soldiers had burned them down. But each day passed without confrontation from soldiers or bandits.

Finally, one morning, as they were traveling through a bandit-infested area, they were met by three tough-looking, burly men brandishing rifles. The men joined the small caravan and walked silently and menacingly behind them. Lester and Howard had heard reports that these same robbers had recently killed twenty-five men. After the caravan had walked in fear for one hour, one of the burly men finally requested money from them. Through the interpreter, Howard understood what the man wanted and handed him the money they had. After giving a high-pitched scream to a fellow bandit on the next mountain, the robbers left them without another word. God had kept the missionary travelers in safety "from a desperate, ungoverned, bandit-ridden land, in peace."[134]

Asia's Far Eastern Nations

According to Howard's original plans, they had three more Far Eastern nations to visit before beginning their cross-continental journey toward Europe. Leaving China and sailing a short distance to Japan, they found a much more civilized nation, judging from appearances. But, how cold and closed Japan was to the gospel message!

It was 1934, and Japan was preparing her military might for the invasion of mainland China, which would occur three years later. It appeared that Western civilization had given Japan a social gospel with schools and hospitals and orphanages, which they had eagerly accepted. But nowhere did Lester and Howard find where the true power of the message of Jesus Christ had made an impact on the Japanese.[135] How well Lester remembered the Japanese faces in his vision of hell, screaming and clawing as they fell into a flaming pit. The church was failing to rescue those lost ones from eternal destruction.

✴✴✴✴✴

Sailing on to Korea, Lester and Howard found a much different spiritual climate. The Korean nation was not yet divided by Communism, and the Christian faith was strong there. As a result, many miraculous events took place. Salvations abounded; healings were occurring almost daily.

One man who had great difficulty walking and could not even leave his yard was healed completely. Another man approached the altar at a meeting, crying about a life filled with emotional and mental illness. As Lester laid hands on him for prayer, a sense of well-being began to fill the man's mind and heart. Within days, he was declared completely well and was reinstated in his old job.[136] Hundreds of dedicated Christians came forward after Howard's preaching to receive the baptism of the Holy Spirit.

The healings and miracles continued as Lester and Howard entered the country of Manchuria. On the day after their arrival, Lester noticed the terrible diseases that seemed to abound throughout this poor country. The next day, he and Howard announced a special healing service, and many people came forward to be healed of all sorts of diseases. One woman approached the altar walking with a crutch because of a badly deformed leg. After prayer, she was able to jump up and leave her crutch at the altar. She walked about the church with a faster and faster gait and went home praising God and His healing power.[137]

In Manchuria, Lester and Howard stayed with Brother Kvamme, the missionary in charge of the region. Brother Kvamme had been quite ill before they arrived and could eat only a limited amount of foods, due to his strict diet. As brother Kvamme interpreted the message during their first service, he felt the Lord's healing power touch him, and all of his intestinal pains vanished completely.

While the blessings of God were marvelous to behold, the wretchedness of Manchuria was often hard for Lester to fathom. In the city of Harbin, people died throughout the winter from the piercingly cold temperatures. Their naked bodies were left strewn about the city, having been stripped of their clothes by other beggars. The bodies would be removed when the spring thaw hit the nation.[138] Each time Lester saw human depravity and suffering, he pushed himself harder to reach the lost with the gospel of Jesus Christ.

✯✯✯✯✯

Through Communism to Freedom

When it was time for Lester and Howard to begin their journey across the vast wasteland of Siberia and eastern Russia toward Europe, they had to apply for special permission to cross through Russia as ministers of the gospel. One condition of their permission forbade them to share the gospel in any way during their journey. The train they traveled on was full of suspicious-looking policemen and unhappy citizens. It was a long, cold look at the results of communism in that part of the world.

Finally, they crossed the border into Poland, more than a year after they'd left Australia for the shores of Asia. What an astonishing year of victory they'd had! The message of Christ's love on the cross and in the empty tomb had been shared with so many.

In Poland, Lester and Howard found a greater thirst for the good news of Jesus Christ than they'd seen in any other nation they had visited. The Polish government frowned on the established church, so they were not permitted to conduct any large meetings. But, with each meeting held in a small church, people came from miles around to hear them. At one Bible conference, some believers had walked sixty-five miles in frigid temperatures to hear the message of encouragement and hope from the Word. More than a hundred of them slept on the mission floor that night on a thin layer of straw. They were hungering for the fresh Word of God and the move of the Holy Spirit, as in the days of Pentecost.[139]

Throughout the cities of Poland, Lester took note of how many Jewish people were living and working in the country—some in menial jobs as street sweepers, others as owners of the largest factories in town. They were usually dressed in orthodox clothing and were established in small communities of their own. Little could he have imagined the horrific fate that awaited many of these Polish Jews in the next few years at the hands of the Nazis.

Berlin, 1936

Early in winter 1936, Lester and Howard crossed the Polish border into the German Third Reich. They traveled directly to Berlin, where preparations were well underway for the summer Olympics. Everywhere were signs of Nazi control, from flags decorated with the swastika to signs that read "No Jews Allowed" in shop windows.

Lester could preach only in certain churches designated by the government. He had been warned not to preach on the supernatural power of the Holy Spirit in believers' lives or on the covenant of divine healing available today. Still, he and Howard were blessed to be able to share about the life, death, and resurrection power of a saving Lord.

Nazi influence surrounded the men like a dark, heavy cloak. Gestapo agents attended each meeting where they preached, taking notes in their little black books. While the churches were still open to some gospel preaching, many of the Christian pastors in Germany had become enamored of Adolf Hitler. Some of them spoke with admiration about his policies against the Jews. However, it wasn't long after Lester and Howard left Germany that the very churches in which they had ministered were closed by the Nazi government. Many of the pastors were imprisoned and eventually sent on to concentration camps.[140]

The very pastors who had not defended the Jews or listened to the cries of the Catholics became those who were persecuted. Although they had sympathized with Hitler, they soon found themselves suffering his hatred for all religion except the worship of himself and the Third Reich. Among the pastors he had met in Germany, Lester heard of none who survived that hatred.

Like many, these pastors were deceived by the policies of a government that attempted to bring prosperity and convenience to its people at the price of the destruction of their souls.

The Final Leg

Leaving the oppression of Germany behind, the team of Lester and Howard headed far north to finish their trip around the world for Christ. In Norway in late spring, the men were refreshed in their hearts and spirits by the depth of Christian love and fervor among the brethren they met. They found the love of God and the power of the Holy Spirit a rainstorm to cleanse them from the sinister hatred of Communism and Nazism in Russia, Poland, and Germany. In this atmosphere of God's presence, the Lord could move mightily.

✷✷✷✷✷

During their year-and-a-half-long missionary journey, Lester and Howard had traveled over sixty thousand miles, mostly in the interior of Asia; had used twenty-one different means of transportation, from airplanes to mules; and had preached through sixty-four different interpreters in twenty-six different languages and dialects!

Crossing the border into Sweden, Lester and Howard were continually blessed by the strong Christians they met. Pastor Lewi Pethrus was the father of the Pentecostal church in the Scandinavian countries. For twenty-five years, he had spread the gospel of Jesus and the power of the Holy Spirit throughout the area. A revival fire had burned in the church for so many years that decisions for Christ were being made every week.

The men basked in the sweet presence of Christ's love and power shown to them by the Swedish Christians. It was a powerful and fitting end to a glorious journey!

During their year-and-a-half-long missionary journey, Lester and Howard had traveled over sixty thousand miles, mostly in the interior of Asia; had used twenty-one different means of transportation, from airplanes to mules; and had preached through sixty-four different interpreters in twenty-six different languages and dialects![141]

Even though that particular phase of their journey had come to an end, the men were still on fire to spread the gospel to the unreached of the world. After a quick trip back to London, Lester and Howard returned to America. At twenty-three years of age, Lester had already ministered more in three years than many men do in a lifetime. But his amazing work in the kingdom of God had only just begun.

He and Howard next ventured to South America, ministering in Brazil and elsewhere across the continent. Then, it was back to Europe to visit Spain and France before finally settling for a time to teach in England.

Wigglesworth: Apostle of Faith and Power

After their first travels together, Howard Carter had a great deal of administrative work to catch up on at Hampstead Bible College, and God had another divine appointment awaiting Lester Sumrall.

A Pentecostal leader recognized throughout Great Britain, Howard had organized a teaching conference in Wales. He honored young Lester with an invitation to be the featured evening speaker. In accordance with Pentecostal conference tradition, Howard chose a man with a teaching ministry to speak at the afternoon session. This man was none other than Smith Wigglesworth, fondly referred to for years as the Apostle of Faith. Lester was speechless with excitement to know that he would be ministering on the same platform as Smith Wigglesworth.

To Lester's delight, Smith Wigglesworth had read some articles he had written for a Pentecostal journal. Wigglesworth listened to Lester preach the gospel that evening and then invited him to a visit at his home in Bradford, England.

What an exciting honor! Just one week later, Lester walked up to Smith Wigglesworth's front door and entered a new spiritual training ground in God's presence. The Apostle of Faith was totally sold out to the kingdom of God and spreading God's Word. He had little time for, or interest in, the cares of the world and concentrated only on knowing more of the presence and power of God. He even refused to allow Lester to bring a newspaper into his home, declaring that it was full of Hitler's lies.[142]

During their visits, Wigglesworth would read chapters of the Bible aloud to Lester; then, they would spend serious time storming the gates of heaven in prayer. When Smith Wigglesworth prayed, the Holy Spirit's anointing was always heavy in the room. After prayer, Wigglesworth would share testimonies from his many years of walking with the Lord, and Lester would sit and listen, overwhelmed and weeping, as Wigglesworth spoke of the blessings and miracles of God.

For nearly two years, Lester visited Wigglesworth regularly at his home. The eighty-year-old man could pray longer and stronger than Lester, though more than fifty years his senior! Later in life, Lester spoke of Smith Wigglesworth as an unconventional man who was abrupt, at times, in his dealings with others but had a heart full of the power of the

Holy Ghost. Wigglesworth believed God for divine health, and he spoke cheerfully of his morning ritual, saying, "I jump out of bed! I dance before the Lord at least ten or twelve minutes—high-speed dancing. I jump up and down and run around my room telling God how great He is, how wonderful He is, how glad I am to be associated with Him and to be His child."[143]

Passing on the Anointing

Lester's faith grew stronger as he spent time with Smith Wigglesworth, and he longed to be solely focused on God, just like Wigglesworth. Unfortunately, this special time would not last. The year was 1939, and Hitler's aggression in Czechoslovakia and Poland had erupted into World War II. Because Lester was on a temporary visa during a time of war, the British government informed him that he had just ten days to leave England.

With a heavy heart, Lester prepared to leave Howard Carter and Smith Wigglesworth. He said his good-byes to Smith Wigglesworth first. Lester never forgot the day that he and this mighty Apostle of Faith met for the last time on this earth. As he sat in Wigglesworth's familiar parlor, Lester spoke tearfully of his gratitude. He thanked Wigglesworth for the blessed times of prayer in God's presence and the rich inheritance he had shared on the blessings of faith. As they ended their visit, Wigglesworth asked Lester to stand because he wanted to bless him.

Lester described the extraordinary moment thusly:

He laid his hand on me and pulled me close to him, and I let my head go in closer to him. Tears flowed from his eyes and ran down his face and dropped off onto my forehead and ran down my face.

As he cried, he said, "Oh, God, let all of the faith that is within my heart be in his heart. Let the knowledge of God that resides in me also reside in him. Let all the gifts that function in my ministry function in his life."[144]

As the men stood there weeping and praying, Lester felt the tremendous anointing of God flow from Wigglesworth into his own spirit. He was quickly reminded of the prophets of the Old Testament and how Elijah's anointing was passed on to Elisha in the book of 2 Kings. (See 2 Kings 2:9–15.) Lester felt a special unction from the Holy Spirit and a new authority to serve God stir in his innermost being. Smith Wigglesworth had passed his spiritual blessing on to Lester Sumrall—glory to God for the great way in which He uses His mighty ones to minister in His kingdom!

When Lester said good-bye to Howard Carter just a few days later, he somehow knew that they would see each other and resume ministering together when the war was over.

South America's Call

Lester returned to America, determined to continue to travel the world with the gospel message. He no longer had Howard Carter as his companion, but the desire to minister to the lost now burned even more brightly in his soul. Hearing of a great need for God's ministry in Alaska, Lester crossed the United States and headed to the cold, barren frontier of America. He ministered there for several months, saddened that there were so few churches and so many saloons. In Alaska, he met many who were independent-minded and hardened to the good news of Christ.

Lester also traveled briefly through several provinces of Canada. For the first time, he heard of the work of a young missionary woman, Louise Layman, who had just left her native Canada to work in South America. His curiosity was piqued, but they had no opportunity to meet.

When the United States entered the war after the attack on Pearl Harbor, Lester attempted to enlist as a chaplain in the army, but to no avail—there were no openings. He determined instead to continue to fight the spiritual war for men's souls as he traveled throughout Mexico, Central America, and South America. Avoiding many of the larger cities filled with anti-American sentiment, Lester ministered to the impoverished Indians in the rural areas of each country. He loved them with the compassion of Christ, and they responded favorably to a gospel of hope.

In Central America, Lester encountered much superstition and witchcraft as a result of a mixture of paganism and Catholicism. He preached the gospel with power and saw men and women set free and

✯✯✯✯✯

healed of various diseases. Winding his way through South America in 1942, Lester found himself at the tip of Argentina. In two years, he had traveled from the northernmost parts of North America to the southern-most tip of South America, bringing the light of Christ to all nations. Now, God had a new path to reveal to Lester on his road of ministry.

"Changed My Life Forever"

At nearly thirty years old, Lester had spent the last thirteen years of his life concentrating on the power of God to save the lost. He had pat-terned his life after Howard Carter's, which he described by saying, "He had no time for sweethearts. Neither had I—until now!"[145] Just as Lester was contemplating a lifetime ministry as a bachelor, he had a "chance encounter" that changed his life. At a wedding in Buenos Aires, Argen-tina, Lester Sumrall finally met Louise Layman, the Canadian mission-ary he had heard about in Canada and throughout South America.

Lester often shared about that day, "At a wedding in Buenos Aires, we came face-to-face. She smiled, and I smiled. That encounter was to change my life forever."[146] Louise was playing the piano at the wedding and apparently had heard a great deal about Lester as well. After those smiles and an introduction, the young couple spent the rest of the day becoming acquainted.[147]

Soon after this, they met again on Christmas Day, 1942, in Lou-ise's host home in Argentina. Knowing Lester was coming, Louise had placed a surprise gift for him under the Christmas tree in her pastor's home. From that time, they began to correspond as they traveled sepa-rately and ministered for the Lord in South America.

A little over a year later, Lester proposed to Louise through the mail. It took over a month for him to receive her reply letter saying yes. They had met only those two brief times, but they had fallen in love while sharing about their ministry desires through their letters. Louise left the mission field in South America and returned home to Canada, and they were married in her home in British Columbia later that year, in Septem-ber 1944. The thirty-two-year-old newlyweds were ready to set the world on fire with the good news of Jesus Christ!

✶✶✶✶✶

A 50,000-Mile Honeymoon

There was nothing ordinary about these newlyweds. After a brief honeymoon in Niagara Falls, Canada, Lester and Louise planned their first missionary journey together. The rest of the world was still wrapped up in the battles of World War II, so the Sumralls headed back to South America. For Lester and Louise, this time was an extended honeymoon of 50,000 miles of preaching and singing about the Lord around the continent where they had met and fallen in love. Through their crusade ministry, they saw souls come to salvation and delivered from the occult, and countless people in South America were healed of their diseases.

An especially important healing prayer for Lester took place in Puerto Rico. There, in dirty living conditions, his young bride contracted a fatal form of malaria. The American doctor gave up all hope of seeing Louise rise from her sickbed, and Lester was devastated. His beautiful bride was more precious to him than he had imagined, and he was about to lose her so early in their life together.[148]

Throwing himself on his knees in prayer, he reminded God of His covenant of healing with His people. Then, he laid hands on Louise and prayed for her divine recovery from malaria. Within days, her fever broke, and she was soon well again! How that miracle stirred their faith for the healing message of Christ! They preached with a renewed fervor for God's power and His goodness toward those who believe.

Reaching Cities for Christ

Shortly after the one-year honeymoon/mission trip, Louise discovered that she was expecting her first child. Even though missionary work would always be their hearts' desire, the Sumralls decided to settle down in the United States for a while. They moved to Springfield, Missouri, where their first son, Frank, was born in 1946.

Because the war in Europe was finally over, Lester made a much-welcomed trip back to England. There, he was joyously reunited with Howard Carter and personally viewed the devastation of the bombed countries of England and France. It was while ministering in Europe that he heard the Lord begin to speak to him about a new work of ministry.

★★★★★

> **The Lord gave Lester a clear vision of reaching countries with evangelistic centers set up in cities like Buenos Aires, Argentina, and Manila, Philippines.**

Lester realized that the way to reach most countries for Christ was through their large cities. In many countries, 60 percent of the population resided in the major metropolitan areas. The Lord gave Lester a clear vision of reaching countries with evangelistic centers set up in cities like Buenos Aires, Argentina, and Manila, Philippines.

When he returned home back to Louise and Frank in the United States, he excitedly shared his ideas with the mission boards of several denominations, but none of them thought that his vision was possible. They deemed the task too large and far-reaching and therefore withheld their support.

Not possible?! What is not possible with God? Lester was amazed and frustrated by the lack of faith in those who could not catch his vision. Perhaps, it just wasn't God's time yet....

Why South Bend, Indiana?

There was a burning in Lester's heart to reach the lost of the world, but the Lord's call came loud and clear from an unexpected place. A small church in South Bend, Indiana, prayed and believed that God had called Lester Sumrall to pastor their congregation.

At first, Lester wasn't going to take the request seriously. A small church in Indiana? What about the billions of lost souls in the cities of the world? But the Lord began to speak in the quiet of Lester's heart, saying, "You'll never understand My heart if you don't pastor...a pastor gets into the sorrows of the family....He understands what it means to be a shepherd because I am a shepherd."[149]

It was a hard decision, but Lester knew he had to obey. When he arrived at the church, he found the building to be too old and confining for use. After convincing the congregation to sell it, he soon chose a new location in the center of town. The new, larger building that would house

Calvary Temple was built nearly debt-free because of the miraculous offerings that poured in. The Lord brought well-known evangelists like Oral Roberts to the new church to preach. Within months, the small congregation was averaging 2,500 participants in Sunday school, and all of the people were growing in the knowledge of Jesus Christ. There were salvations and healings regularly at Calvary Temple as God moved among His people. The Sumrall family grew there, as well, with the birth of a second son, Stephen.

In the midst of all of these marvelous blessings, the call to the mission field continued to burn in Lester's heart.

The Cry of God's Heart

During a short-term mission trip to Asia in 1950, Lester conducted a three-day crusade in Manila, Philippines. Even though it had been five years since World War II, the country was still shrouded in a spirit of gloom.[150] During the crusade, hundreds of people responded to the hope and joy found in the gospel of Christ. When Lester left the city, he despaired that there was no shepherd to guide these new sheep in his absence.

To Lester's great joy, not long after he returned to South Bend, the Lord called to him as before, saying, *"Lester, will you go to Manila for Me?"* Remembering his long-ago vision of the lost on the roadway to hell, Lester responded enthusiastically with a yes.

Calvary Temple was a thriving congregation. With Lester's success, another pastor might have felt a certain sense of pride in remaining there. But Lester Sumrall knew that the call of God was ever fresh in his life. It was time to move back into the mission field. He confidently parted with his Indiana congregation, trusting that God would equip and appoint a new leader for the church. Calvary Temple belonged to the Lord and not to Lester Sumrall.

Twenty-two days after sailing from San Francisco, Lester and Louise arrived in Manila with Frank, a toddler, and Stephen, a baby. Starting at an early age, the Sumrall boys would always be a part of Lester's ministry, learning about and witnessing with their own eyes the power of God to save and heal. God had promised Lester and Louise great miracles on the Philippine Islands, and Lester couldn't wait to experience them firsthand!

★★★★★

Breaking through the Barrier

Imagine Louise's disappointment when they first walked through Tondo, one of the dirtiest slum areas of Manila. The stench around the abandoned warehouse that would serve as their new church was so bad that they could not stay in the building for more than a few minutes. Tondo was too far from the center of Manila to reach the millions that Lester had on his heart. What could the Lord ever do in such a destitute place to offer the Filipino people freedom in Christ?

God had called a man of great prayer to Manila. As disappointed as he was with the first church building, Lester knew that his answer would be found in fervent prayer that the God of the universe would provide a location for them in the center of the city. The vision of Lester's heart was to build not just a church but also an evangelistic center to continually bring the message of salvation to an ever-growing audience of "the untold" of this world.

After some weeks of prayer, Lester was led by the Lord to a bombed-out lot near the center of town. It had remained vacant since the end of the war. Letters sent to Christians in the United States were answered with donations totaling $20,000 to purchase the property. Not long after this, Lester was able to purchase a disassembled airplane hangar. He wanted to reassemble it for the church building on the bombed-out property. There are so many things that God can use for His glory when people think outside the "church box," as Lester Sumrall did.

Bitten by Devils

Lester and Louise had received miraculous provision to purchase the land and the airplane hangar, but months dragged by with red tape and inefficient city authorities making it impossible to obtain the necessary building permits. Then, in the strangest of circumstances, the Lord flung the door wide open to the city of Manila.

The name of Clarita Villanueva, an eighteen-year-old girl, suddenly became the best known in all of Manila. Radio shows throughout the city reported the gruesome story of a young girl who had been arrested for vagrancy. She was locked up in Bilibid Prison, screaming about two unseen monsters who were biting her throughout the day.

*****

To the amazement of the police, guards, and prison doctors, there were indeed bite marks on her skin with red welts and bleeding every time she screamed. Over twenty-five people, including a Catholic prison chaplain, said that they saw evidence of her being bitten by two unseen beings.

Through her tears, Clarita described the creatures, saying, "One tall, evil-looking, dark, and garbed in black, and the other short and cherubic, with snow-white hair. The latter did most of the biting."[151]

Lester was listening to one of those radio shows, and as the program continued, he heard the screaming girl's horrible torture by unseen beings. Greatly affected, he turned to Louise and cried, "The girl is not sick, and the doctors are helpless against such an enemy. Her cry is the cry of the doomed; that girl is demon-possessed."[152]

Lester couldn't sleep the night he heard the radio broadcast. He prayed continually for the Lord's deliverance for Clarita. During that time of prayer, he sensed the Lord speaking to his heart, *If you will go to the jail and pray for her, I will deliver her.*[153] Lester was very reluctant to go into such a chaotic situation. The doctors, prison authorities, and reporters had already created a news story filled with sensationalism. Yet, in the end, Lester knew he would obey the Lord.

Raging Battles

It wasn't possible for Lester to gain entrance to the prison and see Clarita without some government assistance. He went to visit Leopoldo Coronel, the architect who had drawn the plans for the new church building. Because Coronel knew the mayor of Manila well, they were able to get an appointment with him. Although it took some persuading, the mayor and the prison doctor in charge gave their permission for Lester to visit Clarita. The doctor, Dr. Mariano Lara, begrudgingly admitted to Lester that, through all his years of practice, he had never believed in the existence of a supernatural force in the world. However, he said, "Reverend, I am humble enough to admit that I am a frightened man."[154]

Lester took the Word of God very seriously. He knew Jesus' words from Mark 9:29: that some demons come out only by prayer and fasting.

Since first hearing the horrific radio broadcast, he had been in prayer for Clarita's deliverance. On the day that he was to visit her for the first time, he had already been fasting for twenty-four hours and had spent many hours alone in his prayer closet.

Walking into Bilibid Prison, Lester knew he was entering a battle of epic proportions to be waged in the heavenlies. He remembered the confrontation between Elijah and the prophets of Baal in 1 Kings, chapter eighteen. Just like that spiritual battle of old, Lester knew that the observers in Manila would see the power of God move and would proclaim that the Lord he served was truly God! (See 1 Kings 18:39.)

As Lester and Dr. Lara walked into the prison that morning, newspaper reporters, doctors, and assorted onlookers followed him to the small chapel designated for female inmates. The enemy taunted him that he was about to make a fool of himself. But Lester knew it was time to set this young woman free from her tormentors.

As soon as Lester came face-to-face with Clarita, she began to curse him, God, and the blood of Jesus. She said all this in English, even though she didn't speak the language.[155] The devils within her were speaking to him every foul thing they could think to say.

"Clarita, I have come to deliver you from these devils in the name of Jesus Christ, the Son of God," he stated. "No! No!" she screamed in response. "They will kill me!"[156] Ignoring her fear, Lester cried out for the devils to come out of her in the name of Jesus. Immediately, Clarita screamed because the devils had bitten her in response to Lester's first command.

A holy boldness came upon him, and, instead of shrinking back in fear, he charged into the fight in the name of Jesus. As the devils continued to curse God, Lester used the Scriptures to speak of God's holiness and His power over them in Jesus' precious name.

Eventually, Clarita calmed down, and the warfare subsided. The bystanders had tears in their eyes, believing that the deliverance had been completed.[157] But Lester knew that it was not yet finished. He also knew that more prayer and fasting would be needed before the final battle was accomplished.

✳✳✳✳✳

Complete Deliverance

Lester was exhausted. One more day of battle would be necessary to win this fight. He spent the rest of the day fasting and in communion with the Lord, sensing His presence and reassurance that there was nothing to fear.[158] The newspapers, perhaps misreading his strained appearance, declared that Pastor Sumrall had been defeated by the devils. However, Lester knew that God's victory was at hand!

Good news greeted him at the Bilibid Prison the next morning. Clarita had not been bitten anymore overnight. There were onlookers in the chapel again that day, and Lester asked them all to kneel in prayer—newspaper reporters, doctors, and officials alike. They humbly obliged.

Once again, Lester commanded that the demons leave in the name of Jesus, and, this time, Clarita relaxed completely. They were gone. When questioned, Clarita responded that they had gone out the window. The newspaper reporters and officials who had crowded into the room were weeping in amazement at what the Lord had done.

One more time, Satan attempted to have his way. Clarita screamed, and the demons seemed to have reappeared. They declared that Clarita had not asked them to go. Once again, they were commanded to leave in the name of Jesus. Then, Lester explained to Clarita that she had the power in the blood of Jesus to refuse to allow them entrance again. That night, when they tried one last time to torment her, the guard reminded her of the power of the blood of Jesus. She commanded them to leave, and they left, never to return again! The victory was won!

Clarita left the prison shortly after this and moved in with a Christian family arranged by the Sumralls. A year later, she moved away from Manila to a small Philippine village, married, had children, and lived in Christian peace.

Opening Doors No Man Can Close

God had much ministering in store for Manila through the deliverance of that one young woman. The mayor was so grateful for this miracle of God that he offered Lester any help he needed with his new church. Within hours, Lester had the building permits necessary

★★★★★

to erect the airplane hangar as their evangelistic center—and free of charge!

The deliverance of Clarita Villanueva was headlined in all of the local newspapers and on the radio. The people of Manila were so excited to hear of God's power working in her life that they were ripe for receiving the gospel of Christ. Wanting to make a huge impact during this time, Lester made an unusual request. He asked for permission to hold a six-week evangelistic crusade in the beautiful gardens of Roxas Park in the center of Manila. The mayor was puzzled, but he granted Lester's request.

During the crusade, with the help of evangelist Clifton Erickson, thousands of Filipinos came to hear the Word of God. In one single night, five thousand men came forward for the prayer of salvation. As the weeks passed, the crowds grew to as many as sixty thousand per night. In addition to bringing salvation, the hand of God moved with healing among the Filipino people.

The most popular movie star in the country came to the crusade in a wheelchair and received a healing. After prayer in the name of Jesus, he was able to walk again! The people went wild with joy, and their faith in Christ grew to new heights. A well-known lawyer in the downtown courthouse had walked with the aid of two crutches for twelve years. He was healed by the power of God and walked unassisted for the first time in years! Miracle after miracle occurred as the people received the Word of God with open hearts.

Lester Sumrall (left) and Oral Roberts (in black bow tie)
meet with President Magsaysay of the Philippines in 1953.

✵✵✵✵✵

Oral Roberts visited the Philippines and held a revival in Lester's church. President Magsaysay of the Philippines received Oral and Lester for a visit to his office with open arms. During their meeting, he stated emphatically, "In this country, we have learned that Christ is the answer!"[159]

Thusly was Bethel Temple born as a church and evangelistic center in the heart of Manila, Philippines. Lester's initial vision had been fulfilled. He pastored the church for two years, and it grew in numbers and spiritual strength. As it grew, branch churches were begun in other Filipino cities.[160] The Sumrall family grew, as well—their third son, Peter, was born in Manila in 1953.

Everything was going so well, but, once again, God's call came to Lester's heart: *It is time to go home. America needs you. If you stay here, they will worship you and not Me.*[161]

And, so, once again, this pilgrim of God, with tears and joy, said good-bye to a work he had birthed by the Holy Spirit and moved on to God's next assignment. In Acts 20:37–38, the apostle Paul left Ephesus while the Ephesians hung on him, shedding many tears. In the same way, thousands of Christians crowded the airport in Manila to bid the Sumralls a tearful farewell, many crying inconsolably. Lester promised to visit them every year, and he kept that promise until he was in his eighties.

There are millions of people living in the Philippines today who are saved because of the deliverance of Clarita from the power of the enemy. That one act opened doors to the gospel very quickly. After that experience, Lester often reminded others, "God can do more in one minute that we can do in fifty years!"[162] Twenty years after Lester left

> **Thousands of Christians crowded the airport in Manila to bid the Sumralls a tearful farewell, many crying inconsolably. Lester promised to visit them every year, and he kept that promise until he was in his eighties.**

Manila, his great-nephew, David Sumrall, became the pastor of Bethel Temple. It is still a thriving church in the Philippines under David's ministry today.

South Bend and Beyond

For the next ten years, Lester Sumrall split his ministry time between his renewed pastorate in South Bend, Indiana, and his unquenchable call to minister to the lost overseas. In 1956, Lester felt a call to Israel and moved his family to Jerusalem. In that same year, the Sinai War was waged between Israel and Arab nations. Lester believed his family was in the middle of God's will, and they remained in Jerusalem. Lester's love for the Holy Land led to another ministry, and, over the next three decades, he led thousands of Christians on visits to Israel through his annual trip there.

In 1957, Lester followed the call of God to Hong Kong. While he was away from the South Bend church, Morris Cerullo became the interim pastor to lead the flock in Indiana.[163] Lester was excited to return to Hong Kong. It had been over twenty years since he had ministered with Howard Carter in that thriving city. He knew in his heart that it was another city God had chosen to be an evangelistic center. Thus, Lester began New Life Temple on the fourth floor of a downtown office building. The Chinese came to him in scores to hear the good news of salvation and healing through the blood of Jesus Christ.

There was so much to tell the thousands of people who had been blessed by Lester Sumrall's ministry. So, Louise and Lester began *World Harvest Magazine* to share the gospel through the written word. Lester had started writing books in the 1930s, beginning with *Adventuring in Christ*, about his trip around the world with Howard Carter. The Sumralls continued to produce books, knowing that doing so was another way to reach the lost with God's message.

The next evangelistic center to be built was in Brasilia, Brazil. The heartbeat of the people could be reached from these large evangelistic centers. Evangelism brought people in to hear the Word, and biblical teaching and the power of the Holy Spirit kept them growing in Christ. Ministering in these centers, Lester laid hands on the sick and saw them healed in the mighty name of Jesus.

Finished with Ministry at Fifty?!

There were few things in life that Lester Sumrall enjoyed more than a challenge. When he returned to the United States from his overseas work, he was uncertain of the direction in which he was to go next. It was the turbulent decade of the 1960s, but Lester knew that the Lord wanted to do great things in the United States and beyond to reach others with the gospel message.

A fellow pastor who did not possess the same vision for victory greeted Lester with these words: "Sumrall, you're over fifty, and you're finished."[164] But Lester didn't believe it. He went straight to the Lord to ask His opinion on the subject.

The Lord reminded Lester of the vision He had given him several years earlier before the Sumrall family left Manila. When Lester returned to the U.S., he was to get the message of Christ out to America through television. Although Lester had little idea where to even begin, he knew it was God's voice, and so he began to move. At the time, all he owned was a small house and ten acres of land in South Bend.

Lester and Louise Sumrall break ground for WHME-FM, the first 24-hour radio station in South Bend, Indiana.

A series of miracles provided the loan and other necessary funds to build a world evangelism building on his property. A little overwhelmed by the idea of a television station, Lester began by purchasing an FM radio channel and went on the air with the gospel. In addition, he organized a new church in South Bend, called Bethel Temple. It was an independent, full-gospel congregation of about three hundred members.

Next, the Sumralls began a ministry called World Harvest Homes to orphanages in different parts of the world. Shortly after this, Lester launched World Harvest Bible College to prepare young ministers for missionary work around the world. Rather than marking an end to Lester's ministry, the 1960s were years filled with the growth of the gospel of Jesus Christ.

★★★★★

Also during those years, Howard Carter returned to the United States. He had retired from the Bible college and had come to America, married a widow, and continued to travel, teaching of the power and baptism of the Holy Spirit. The Sumralls had the pleasure of visits and ministry with Howard Carter and his wife until Carter's death in 1971.

Television Power

In 1972, Lester attended the National Religious Broadcasters Convention in Washington, D.C. While he was there, a man approached him about buying a bankrupt one-million-watt television station in Indiana. Although Lester still felt inadequate, in his spirit, he heard the Lord say a loud and clear, "Yes!"[165] So, he signed the contract to pay one million dollars once the station purchase was approved by the FCC. One million dollars—had God really said yes?

Soon after he'd taken that step of faith and signed the contract, money began to pour in from unusual sources. Checks for amounts well over $50,000 came to the newly formed LeSea (Lester Sumrall Evangelistic Association) Broadcasting from people Lester did not even know. By the time the FCC gave their final approval of the purchase, all the money for the television station had been raised.

In 1972, World Harvest Missionary Broadcasting was born in Indianapolis.

Although Pat Robertson had begun his Christian Broadcasting Network ten years earlier, Lester Sumrall has often been referred to as the "father" of Christian television. He was the first person approved by the FCC to provide 24-7 Christian television broadcasting.

On November 3, 1972, World Harvest Missionary Broadcasting introduced its first family gospel programming. It was a call-in talk show initially called *Today with Lester Sumrall* but later changed to *World Harvest*, which still airs today. WHMB-TV Channel 40 has been broadcasting for over thirty-five years spreading the gospel of Christ in the Midwest.

✫✫✫✫✫

Reaching around the Globe

There was nothing more important to Lester Sumrall than preaching to the lost in places that had never heard Jesus' name. For years, Lester pursued the call to win one million souls to Christ. But, as broadcast technology grew throughout the world, his vision was enlarged. Deep in his heart, Lester believed that he was to win not just one million souls but *one million souls a day* to Jesus Christ. His radio and television broadcasts were reaching out to millions, but how to reach the billions in China, Japan, and Indonesia?

> **Deep in his heart, Lester believed that he was to win not just one million souls but *one million souls a day* to Jesus Christ.**

Convinced that he was living in the last days, Lester knew that God wanted him to reach *entire nations* for Christ. Lester couldn't reach the lost billions on the other side of the world with his television or radio stations in the United States, but he could reach many of them through shortwave radio!

Most people in China own shortwave radios. When Lester applied to the U.S. government to broadcast into China, he received a permit for 12.5 million watts; the station was set up on an island in the middle of the Pacific Ocean and can reach over three billion people in the Far East.[166] With the eventual addition of four other shortwave stations, LeSea Broadcasting had the strongest broadcasting voice in the world.

As the driving force for the ministry, Lester had never forgotten his vision of doomed people from all the nations of the world screaming and clawing as they fell into the pit of hell. He was forever reminded of God's word to him that their blood would be on his hands if he did not bring them the message of salvation through Christ. From the earliest time in his ministry, Lester would beseech the Lord for help, saying, "I hear

On Christmas, 1985, Lester Sumrall read the Word of God on WHRI Shortwave.

the cry of a billion souls!"[167] As Lester was faithful, God continued to give him inventive ways to reach the lost.

Broadcasting to the Whole World

Throughout the 1970s, Lester's ministry continued to purchase additional television stations across the U.S. God's initial word to Lester was to have not just a Christian station but also a network, so that people could be reached far and wide.

In the 1980s, an earth station was constructed on the grounds of WHME-TV, and LeSea was able to broadcast via satellite 24-7.[168] The 1980s also saw the first of the shortwave radio stations set up to minister to listeners in Europe and South America.

By the time LeSea Broadcasting entered the twenty-first century, it had grown to include thirteen television stations across the U.S.; two satellite channels covering the entire continents of Africa, Asia, and Europe; five powerful shortwave stations; and three FM radio stations. Through the media of LeSea Broadcasting, over 90 percent of the world's population can be reached with the gospel of Jesus Christ! One man with a vision from God, and the body of Christ walking beside him in faith, can bring the message of salvation through Jesus Christ to the ends of the earth!

One More Branch!

The year was 1987. Lester Sumrall was seventy-four years old. He had a blessed marriage of forty-three years with Louise, the love of his life. His sons and their families were in ministry alongside him. Frank was his copastor at the newly constructed, 3,500-seat Christian Center. Stephen handled all of the administrative details of the ministry. His youngest son, Peter, had oversight of the broadcasting division.

Lester was still preaching around the world, reaching 20,000 cell group leaders at Yoido Full Gospel Church in Seoul, Korea; four million people through World Harvest Broadcast from South Bend, Indiana; and hundreds more through yearly tours of the Holy Land. His life was rich and full...but God wasn't finished with him yet!

✭✭✭✭✭

Lester Sumrall preaching the Word in South Korea

Lester traveled to Denver, Colorado, to speak to a group of pastors about the new LeSea television station that would soon be on the air. As the evening drew to a close, a gentleman approached Lester from the back of the room. Quietly, the man stated that he had a message for Lester from the Lord. Lester's response was not very warm. He was more than accustomed to hearing from the Lord for himself!

However, the gentleman continued on with a prophetic word:

Your life is like a tree planted in God. Your life is a tree, and there are branches on your tree. Your first evangelism as a young man is a branch on your tree...your missionary branches bore much fruit and still do. Your church is a branch. Your television ministry is a branch. Your radio ministry is a branch.

Taking a deep breath, he continued:

Thus saith the Lord, a new branch will spring forth upon your tree of life. It will be larger than all of the other branches. It will bear so much fruit that you will be amazed.[169]

Unsure of the message's meaning, Lester was certain that he was too old for any new branches! What could it mean?

✫✫✫✫✫

Revelation in Jerusalem

A few weeks later, Lester was in Jerusalem conducting his annual Holy Land tour with a large group of believers. The Lord woke him up just before midnight one night with a new ministry vision.

Lester heard the voice of God in his heart, saying, *One of my greatest concerns is that My own people, part of My church, do not suffer death by starvation before I return. Will you feed them? To them it will be an angelic food supply! To them it will be a miracle!*[170]

> **There was so much ravaging hunger in the world, especially in the war-torn areas. If Lester would obey, God would provide the means for him to transport the desperately needed food into the interiors of many countries.**

For five hours, Lester heard the heart of God as He spoke of the suffering among much of His church throughout the world. There was so much ravaging hunger in the world, especially in the war-torn areas. If Lester would obey, God would provide the means for him to transport the desperately needed food into the interiors of many countries. The purpose was to bypass the government bureaucracy of third-world nations and to get the food and relief supplies directly into the hands of God's people through local pastors.

God spoke, "You will distribute the food through My churches only. Around the world I want you to feed My people who are hungry."[171] When Lester asked the Lord why He'd chosen him, God's answer was clear: "You've preached in 110 nations, and you love all those people. I want to use you to feed them."[172] At five o'clock that morning, in the Holy City, Lester answered God's call once again: "I am willing, Lord."

Over the next year, an unbelievable series of miracles occurred to bring the first load of food to a starving people. Lester realized that the ministry needed to have its own airplane to reach the interiors of countries, where the greatest food shortages occurred. He discovered that the best type of airplane for that mission was the C-130, a military transport plane. But Lester was laughed at when he declared that they were going to find a used C-130 to purchase for the ministry.

Miracle number one was finding a used airplane in excellent condition. Once that was accomplished, the 1.5-million-dollar asking price had to be raised. Finally, both the United States Department of State and the Federal Aviation Commission had to approve the purchase of a C-130 by a Christian ministry. No one thought that the last hurdle could be cleared. But with an extra stamp of approval from the White House administration, both applications were accepted! Within months, the first load of food was flown into Guatemala and delivered directly to a local missionary. The plane was able to land on a dirt airstrip in the mountains where food was desperately needed.

The C-130, nicknamed "Mercy Plane Zoe," was even used for more than two months to bring relief supplies to the suffering Kurds after Desert Storm.[173]

Lester Sumrall with Feed the Hungry in the African nation of Zaire

The mission was a success. Quickly, the Lord multiplied the work. God brought a Christian businessman named Don Tipton into Lester's path. Tipton owned a large cargo ship, which he named "Spirit" and dedicated to the work of bringing food, clothing, and medicine to those in need under Sumrall's direction. Where there were friendly ports and places where food could be distributed from the cargo ship, Don was there.

For Lester, this became the greatest step in his ministry: LeSea Global Feed the Hungry. This last branch on Lester Sumrall's tree of life was to feed the hungry around the world as the Lord supplied the need, mostly through donations collected from churches in the U.S. He worked on this last project with great passion until the end of his life. He was delighted that "God's people in a place of plenty had become an answer to the prayer of His people in places of need."[174]

A Legacy for Young Pastors

In his later years, Lester became a prolific author, writing many books for the benefit of young pastors. He would generously give of his time to preach anywhere in the world whenever he was asked by another pastor. It didn't matter if there were thirty people or three thousand people to hear him. He wasn't there for the audience; he was there for the benefit of that pastor. When he would arrive someplace, he would insist on being picked up by the local pastor; he had no interest in spending time with anybody else.

Mentored by Lester Sumrall

In those final years, I was privileged to be able to meet with Dr. Sumrall on a regular basis. In the beginning, he would ask me, "What questions do you have?" The first time, I told him that I didn't have any questions. He gruffly replied, "Don't ever come to me without questions. Don't waste my time. I'm busy." I made it a point to never waste his time ever again. I soon discovered that he had an amazing ability to answer complex questions with a few words of precious wisdom.

In one of our sessions, he warned, "As a pastor, you'll have few real friends in the community. If your church is smaller than those of other pastors, they will do anything to help you. If your church is the same size as theirs, they will begin to talk about your faults. When your church is bigger than theirs, they will collect information to use against you."

Whenever we were done, Dr. Sumrall would say, "Come here. I'll bless you before you leave." Then, he would put his hand on my head and, with an authoritative voice, give a two-word announcement: "Be blessed!" He did that every time I was with him. That was his way. He would tell you when to come and when to leave.

He once referred to 2 Corinthians 4:7: *"We have this treasure in earthen vessels."* He told me that pastors often focus on the treasure and ignore the vessel. He warned me that if the gift and the vessel do not cooperate, ministries will end in disasters such as divorce, sickness, or moral failure. Then, he would ask me if I was preaching for money or for souls—for faces or for dollar signs. "If you're not preaching for souls," he would say, "you've sold yourself to mammon."

After leaving our sessions, I often felt uncomfortable. I soon discovered, however, that our time together was much like a process described in Scripture: *"Iron sharpeneth iron; so a man sharpeneth the countenance of his friend"* (Proverbs 27:17). The Lord spoke to me and suggested that the places in which I felt insecure were my places of weakness—places that need sharpening. Dr. Sumrall taught me that being in the presence of authority and greatness will bring out your insecurities, not because of anything he was doing to me, but because these were areas in my life that I needed to address and strengthen. It wasn't long before I fell in love with his directness.

A Life of Obedience

From the time of his dramatic conversion and healing from tuberculosis at the age of seventeen until he went home to be with the Lord at the age of eighty-three, Lester Sumrall lived a life of obedience. He spent hours seeking the Lord's will and learned to hear His voice with surety.

To Lester Sumrall, "faith was a pilgrimage with God—just breaking loose from everything and saying, 'Lord, have Your way. I'm walking with You.'"[175] When he left his

Years later, Lester wrote that if God asked him to leave once again— his television stations, his great church, and his international headquarters— he would do it without losing one night's sleep.

pastorate to go to minister in Manila, he spoke of the pain of leaving those he had led to Christ. Yet, he did it out of obedience to God's calling. Years later, he wrote that if God asked him to leave once again—his television stations, his great church, and his international headquarters—he would do it without losing one night's sleep.[176]

Why? Because, to Lester Sumrall, faith was a walk of life itself. Was he willing to go with God? Abraham was, and he became the father of the greatest nation that ever lived—the nation of God's people. Lester was determined that he would walk in faith, as well.

Lester Sumrall was always ready to move to a new place in God. He was never afraid of the Holy Spirit leading in some new direction, as long as it was confirmed in the Word of God. When he studied all of the powerful moves of God in Christian history, he concluded emphatically:

- If I had lived during the time of Martin Luther, I would have become a Lutheran, because they were the ones who were carrying the banner of God.

- If I had been living in the days of John Knox, I would have joined the Presbyterians, because they were carrying the flames of revival.

- If I had lived in the days of John Wesley, I would have joined the Methodists, because that was where God was moving.

- If I had been living in the time when the Salvation Army was founded by William Booth, I would have joined that group, gone to the street corners, and "tooted a horn" for Jesus, because they were getting people saved.

- I want to be where the blessing of God is being poured out...where the anointing is on people.[177]

On my last visit with Dr. Sumrall, he told me, "You were the only one who ever asked me about the great old preachers I have known who have been forgotten over time. You asked me about their stories and their lives. This is important, Roberts. It is your anointing. You need to keep these stories alive. They are important for the 'unknown ones.' These stories will inspire the unknown great ones of future generations. Even now, there are great but unknown preachers who are agonizing over the decision-making process. They are struggling with whether or not to enter the ministry and put to death a career in business or medicine or law. They need to hear these stories. They need to know that a life of faith works!"

Near the end, Lester Sumrall awoke after lying in a coma for several days. As an old-school healer, he was never quite comfortable in the presence of doctors and hospitals. From his heavenly vision on his deathbed so many years before, he had known that he had to keep preaching to stay alive. Ever faithful to his calling, he had preached right up to his final week. On April 28, 1996—only a few days later—Lester Sumrall went home to be with the Lord Jesus Christ, leaving behind a powerful ministry that is still bringing lost souls into God's kingdom today.

CHAPTER THREE

ENDNOTES

88   Lester Sumrall, *The Life Story of Lester Sumrall* (Green Forest, AR: New Leaf Press, 1993), 28.
89   Ibid., 29.
90   Ibid., 31.
91   Lester Sumrall, *Pioneers of Faith* (South Bend, IN: LeSea Publishing, 1995), 16.
92   Sumrall, *Life Story*, 20.
93   Ibid., 26.
94   Ibid., 33.
95   Ibid., 34.
96   Ibid., 40.
97   Ibid., 43.
98   Ibid., 50.
99   Ibid.
100 Ibid., 51.
101 Ibid., 52.
102 Lester Sumrall, *Legacy of Faith* (South Bend, IN: LeSea Publishing, 1993), 17.
103 Sumrall, *Life Story*, 53.
104 Ibid., 55.
105 Ibid., 69.
106 Sumrall, *Legacy*, 24.
107 Sumrall, *Life Story*, 71.
108 Ibid., 72.
109 Ibid., 74.
110 Sumrall, *Pioneers*, 58.
111 Ibid., 59.
112 Sumrall, *Life Story*, 76.
113 Sumrall, *Pioneers*, 51.
114 Ibid.
115 Lester Sumrall, *Adventuring with Christ* (South Bend, IN: LeSea Publishing, 1988), 17.
116 Sumrall, *Life Story*, 81.
117 Sumrall, *Legacy*, 24.
118 Sumrall, *Adventuring*, 23.

[119] Sumrall, *Adventuring*, 27.
[120] Ibid., 37.
[121] Lester Sumrall, *Lester Sumrall's Short Stories* (South Bend, IN: LeSea Publishing, 2005), 101.
[122] Ibid., 102.
[123] Lester Sumrall, *Demons: The Answer Book* (New Kensington, PA: Whitaker House, 1979), 46.
[124] Sumrall, *Life Story*, 98.
[125] Ibid.
[126] Ibid., 99.
[127] Sumrall, *Demons*, 47.
[128] Sumrall, *Life Story*, 102.
[129] Sumrall, *Adventuring*, 50.
[130] Sumrall, *Life Story*, 106.
[131] Ibid., 107.
[132] Ibid.
[133] Sumrall, *Adventuring*, 80.
[134] Ibid., 89.
[135] Ibid., 107.
[136] Ibid., 117.
[137] Ibid., 122.
[138] Ibid., 123–124.
[139] Ibid., 137.
[140] Sumrall, *Life Story*, 113.
[141] Sumrall, *Legacy*, 33.
[142] Sumrall, *Pioneers*, 166.
[143] Ibid., 168.
[144] Ibid., 172.
[145] Sumrall, *Life Story*, 127.
[146] Sumrall, *Legacy*, 56.
[147] Ibid., 52.
[148] Sumrall, *Life Story*, 134.
[149] Ibid., 143.
[150] Ibid., 149.
[151] Lester Sumrall, *Bitten by Devils* (South Bend, IN: LeSea Publishing, 1987), 9.
[152] Ibid., 32.
[153] Ibid., 33.
[154] Ibid., 34.
[155] Ibid., 38.
[156] Ibid., 39.
[157] Ibid., 40.
[158] Ibid.
[159] Sumrall, *Legacy*, 72.

★★★★★

[160] Sumrall, *Legacy*, 70.
[161] Sumrall, *Life Story*, 181.
[162] Ibid., 176.
[163] Sumrall, *Legacy*, 76.
[164] Sumrall, *Life Story*, 181.
[165] Ibid., 183.
[166] Ibid., 185.
[167] Sumrall, *Legacy*, 154.
[168] Ibid., 123.
[169] Sumrall, *Life Story*, 196–197.
[170] Sumrall, *Legacy*, 129.
[171] Ibid.
[172] Sumrall, *Life Story*, 211.
[173] Ibid., 208.
[174] www.feedthehungry.org.
[175] Lester Sumrall, *Faith Can Change Your World* (South Bend, IN: Sumrall Publishing, 1999), 123.
[176] Ibid., 122.
[177] Sumrall, *Pioneers*, 16.

★★★★★

CHAPTER FOUR

ORAL ROBERTS

"Expect a Miracle!"

"Expect a Miracle!"

Rain fell in drenching torrents, blowing leaves and debris across the cold, farm landscape. The sun setting below the horizon made the dark, ominous clouds seem even more threatening. Thunder crashed; the following lightning revealed the barren fields. It was early in winter of 1917, and a half-Cherokee woman was walking determinedly across the farmland of southeastern Oklahoma. Claudius Roberts had been called out of her home by a panic-stricken neighbor because the doctor had announced that his ailing son was close to death. "Please, come pray for my boy, Sister Roberts," he'd pleaded. House calls had become a burden of her faith.

Claudius Roberts believed firmly in the power of prayer to a God who heals the sick. She went out on that cold, rain-swept night seven months pregnant with her fourth child, believing in a God who would keep her safe, in a God who is the Healer. As Claudius approached the heavy, barbed-wire fence that separated her home from the neighbors, she prayed that she would reach the young boy in time. The gate was broken, and it stuck tight. Even though heavy with child, she lifted up a piece of barbed wire, pressed her foot down on the wire below it, and crawled through the fence.

As suddenly as it had begun, the storm stopped raging, and, in the quiet night, Claudius "felt the Spirit of the Lord hovering hear." God was speaking to her: the child she carried in her womb "was a special child that would have God's anointing upon him."[178] On that dark night, as she made her way to the neighbor's home, Claudius made a promise to God. If He would heal the neighbor's sick child, she would dedicate the baby in her womb to the Lord as Hannah had dedicated Samuel. (See 1 Samuel 1:11.)

As she neared the sick child's bed in a spirit of prayer, Claudius felt the power of the Holy Spirit fall upon that small room. Claudius prayed for healing, and the little boy was healed instantly and completely! From that day forward, she knew that God had anointed her unborn child, who would be dedicated in service to Him.[179]

God's Anointed Man

Claudius Roberts had prayed that her last child would be tall and strong and would show features of his Indian heritage. She'd asked God for a blue-eyed boy, even though all of her other children had dark brown eyes. When the baby boy was born, Claudius rejoiced that God had answered every one of her prayers.

What she couldn't fully realize at the time was that this baby—Granville Oral Roberts—would become one of God's most anointed men in the second half of the twentieth century. Are there enough words to do justice to Roberts's powerful preaching and healing tent ministry to tens of thousands in the 1950s? Can we explain his inspirational call to build the largest Christian university in the world in the 1960s, the wisdom of his trendsetting television ministry to millions in the 1970s, the controversies and personal tragedy that surrounded his ministry in the 1980s, or the place that Oral Roberts holds in the church today?

I was the first baby born in Oral Roberts's school of medicine. In fact, Oral was such a hero to my family that I was named Kenneth Roberts Liardon, but I chose to go by Roberts. As a child, I remember being in Tulsa at a Partner's Weekend—a gathering of his financial supporters— where Oral began to pray for everyone in the room. At one point, he went over to a line of partners who were in wheelchairs. He went down the line, laying hands on each one and praying. One after another, they got up out of their chairs. I had never seen anything like it. Oh, there was the rare, occasional healing in my home church, but nothing like the sight of a line of people rising from their wheelchairs and walking.

It is essentially impossible to describe in detail a global ministry that has spanned seventy-plus years. Oral Roberts brought Pentecostalism to the right side of the tracks. He gave it respectability and dignity. My desire in this edition of *God's Generals* is to highlight specific areas of this anointed man's life: from his humble beginnings to the position of leadership and power he held in the latter half of the twentieth century, to the unfortunate scandals that pursued him, and, finally, to the place his ministry holds today. This is the amazing story of how God used one fallible human being who was willing to surrender his entire life in obedience to the call of an *infallible* God.

> **Oral began to pray for everyone in the room. At one point, he went over to a line of partners who were in wheelchairs. He went down the line, laying hands on each one and praying. One after another, they got up out of their chairs.**

Anointed from the Womb

It is remarkable how many of America's most powerful leaders, political and spiritual alike, were born to humble beginnings, and that was the case with Granville Oral Roberts. He was born on January 24, 1918, in a rustic, log farmhouse in Pontotoc County, Oklahoma, the fourth and last child of Ellis and Claudius Roberts. His parents were Spirit-filled Christians who preached the Word of God to anyone who would listen. Ellis Roberts was a dedicated Pentecostal Holiness preacher who knew the Word and was steadfast in his pursuit of God.

Claudius Roberts, or Mama Roberts, as I was privileged to call her, was a little firebrand of faith. She was an old-time Pentecostal woman, full of the Holy Spirit and the anointing of God—with faith to believe God for the impossible. She was descended from a proud, Native American tribe; her mother had been a full-blooded Cherokee, and she touched everyone she met with her determination to believe God for answered prayer. It was from Mama Roberts that Oral inherited his dramatic personality, his perseverance in the face of hardship, and his ability to capture and hold a congregation's attention. Mama Roberts instilled in her family the firm belief in the healing power of God.

The Roberts family was painfully poor. Perhaps Oral's drive to succeed in every endeavor of his life and ministry came from the sting of having been destitute as a child. Oral's clothes were hand-me-downs from the poor church deacons' children. Meals were simple and, at times, forgone for "fasting." Often, Oral and his brother, Vaden, would play outside until late in the afternoon and then come home to find that neighbors had left food behind the door for the family's dinner.

Despite his humble beginning, Oral was popular with his classmates. He vividly recalls when he was elected the "King of the School" before his elementary graduation. As "King," he was expected to wear new clothes for the school assembly. His parents, however, could not afford anything new, least of all a new "King" wardrobe. Undaunted, a determined Oral earned the money himself to buy a new pair of denim overalls.

When "King" Oral arrived at school to escort the "Queen" (the daughter of a rich family), he found her wearing a beautiful, white satin evening gown. The contrast of denim with white, lacey satin would have thrown most individuals for a loop. However, the young farm boy from the poor Pentecostal family extended his arm to that young lady, held his head high, and escorted her into the school assembly, looking every bit a king. It was a foreshadowing of the strength Oral would need in many difficult times throughout his life.

Stutterer to Preacher

Not all of Oral's early memories were as pleasant as being crowned king of the school. As a young man, he was greatly afflicted with stuttering. Although he was extremely bright, he could seldom do his school recitations without stammering so excessively that he ended up in tears. His uncles, who never believed he would amount to much, criticized him unmercifully. When Oral's father would speak of him being used by God one day, Oral's uncle would answer, "Why, Ellis, have you lost your mind? Oral can't even talk."[180] But Papa Roberts was persistent. "This boy, this is the one." Oral was taunted by his classmates and relatives alike. The godly influence of his parents, inspired by God's promises, became his greatest hope.

Mama Roberts was a short, stout woman, but she was a spiritual powerhouse. She would pull her growing boy onto her lap and boldly proclaim God's promises to him: "Oral, I gave you to God when you were a baby. You are God's property. Someday, he's going to heal your tongue, and you will talk. Son, you will preach the gospel!"[181]

During those years, Ellis Roberts also prophesied over his son in words that Oral had not forgotten through seventy years of ministry. Understanding his shy, skinny son who struggled to communicate, Ellis looked into his eyes and proclaimed, "Oral, someday, you will be a preacher. God will give you the largest meetings of your day. They will be so large others will go before you and prepare the way. All you will have to do is go preach and minister to the people."[182]

These prophecies and words of faith eventually led to Oral's complete healing from a stuttering tongue. Parents reading the histories of God's anointed generals should never forget the Holy Spirit-breathed power of speaking the word of faith—the word of blessing, the word of favor—over their children daily!

Rebellion and Forgiveness

Declaring yourself a Pentecostal in the 1920s and 1930s meant ridicule and shunning from most other Christian denominations. For Oral and his brother, Vaden, it made the teenage years particularly difficult. Ashamed of being poor and cringing from the label "holy roller," Oral moved eagerly into the worldly side of school life as a six-foot-tall, broadshouldered, handsome young man. He excelled at athletics, especially basketball and baseball. These sports became the most important things in life to him, as, through them, he found the acceptance he so longed for.

Oral always knew there was a call on his life and a burning in his heart to achieve great things. Finding success for the first time on the

Oral always knew there was a call on his life and a burning in his heart to achieve great things.

baseball field and the basketball court, he believed he had found his answer. He envisioned a great future. He saw athletics as his ticket to college, law school, and the glamour of a life in Oklahoma politics. As a young teenager, he owned a set of old law books. His dream was to someday be Oklahoma's governor—his golden plan to escape from his poor, shabby childhood.

When Oral was fifteen, an unexpected opportunity came for him to escape the poor, Pentecostal surroundings he resented. His coach, Herman Hamilton, took a job as the new basketball coach in Atoka, Oklahoma, a school fifty miles south of Oral's home. When the coach invited Oral to come along, he jumped at the chance to leave his impoverished home life and move anyplace that wasn't Ada, Oklahoma.

Ellis and Claudius begged Oral to stay at home and cried out to the Lord to keep their son from his pursuit of the world. Claudius told him with tears in her eyes, "Oral, you will never be able to go beyond our prayers. Each day we will pray and ask God to send you home."[183] But Oral ignored their cries and prayers and eagerly left for Atoka.

In his new surroundings, Oral's leadership skills emerged. During the following year, he was elected class president and became editor of the school paper. He worked three part-time jobs and was academically at the top of his class. The tall, dark-haired, blue-eyed basketball star became a popular young man with the sports fans and the pretty young ladies. The large, competitive high school gave him a chance to "try the world on for size." He learned to drive—and drive fast—and even began to drink alcohol as a way of breaking completely from the Pentecostal past that now shamed him. His Pentecostal roots forgotten, Oral now aimed to "live" in the world and escape from God.

Stopped Dead in His Tracks

On a brightly lit basketball court, more than a year after he moved away from home, young Granville Oral Roberts came to the end of

✭✭✭✭✭

himself. It was February 1935, and the final night of the Southern Oklahoma basketball tournament. Oral recalled, "Suddenly, I collapsed and was carried off the gymnasium floor. Blood was spurting from my mouth, and I was coughing with every breath."[184]

All of the fast living—pushing himself so hard to be the best at everything—apparently had an equally quick reward. Coach Hamilton carried Oral to his car and said, "Oral, you're going home," because he feared for his player's life. When they arrived at the Roberts residence, Coach Hamilton helped Oral out of the car and faced his father, saying gravely, "Reverend Roberts, I've brought your boy home."[185]

That episode began the heartache and pain of fighting a deadly illness. From that night on, Oral lay in bed for 163 days, not knowing if he would ever have the strength to get up again. His weight dropped from 160 to 120 pounds, and his friends hardly recognized him. Fighting to breathe and feeling like there was a knife in his chest, Oral cried out to his father, "Papa, what does this awful pain in my lungs mean? Why do I keep spitting up blood and coughing all the time?" The words he heard next were unforgettable: "Oral, you have tuberculosis in both lungs."[186]

In 1935, a diagnosis of tuberculosis was nearly equivalent to a death sentence. Oral turned his face from his father and gave up hope. He wailed and cried until he could no longer stand the pain he was causing to his lungs. "Papa," he sobbed, "when people take tuberculosis, they don't get well. This medicine isn't going to help me now. If I am going to die, then I will just die."[187]

In the midst of his agony and feelings of hopelessness, Oral learned his first lessons about sickness and the results of a lack of healing faith in the body of Christ. A leading pastor of the city came to see Oral, but he had no faith for his recovery. The man merely prayed that Oral would have patience with his disease and then went quietly away.

Some well-intentioned Christians who visited their home told the family that God had given the terrible disease to Oral for a purpose. Sunday afternoons were the most miserable for Oral as scripturally ineffective neighbors came over to talk about his disease and how God had "put" tuberculosis on him. All of Oral's hope was crushed by their predictions of woe. He cried out in revolt against the ideas they believed.

"If God put this on me," he shouted to his parents, "I don't want to serve Him."[188]

"God Is Going to Heal You!"

In His faithfulness, the Lord always sends someone into our lives at our moments of desperation. Just as when Oral was a small, stuttering boy, God used his mother to prophesy over him once again. Mama Roberts was a woman of incredible vision and the spiritual strength to believe. She spoke with the assurance of her faith, "Oral, God didn't' afflict you...the devil did! When God calls someone, son, the devil always tries to destroy him, but if you will give your heart to Jesus and have faith in the Lord, He will raise you up from this bed and heal you."[189]

Healing! How his heart leaped with joy. This was the first time Oral had a glimmer of hope for his own healing! It was the devil who had caused his illness. It was the devil who was stealing his life! God hadn't put this sickness on him! This was a new revelation to Oral and the hint of things to come.

There is often a turning point in our lives—that moment when a word is spoken or an act occurs and revelation becomes reality. Jewel Roberts Faust, Oral's older, married sister, was used by God to speak a revelation to him. As she had grown up in the Roberts family, the truth of God's healing power that had been planted in her heart had matured and blossomed.

One day, Jewel was at home, and she felt something stirring in her heart. Oral had lain in bed for nearly six months. Prompted by the Holy Spirit, Jewel believed it was time for Oral to be healed, and she felt he needed to know about it right away. She was certain that God had spoken to her that He not only was *able* to heal Oral, but also was planning on *doing it soon!*[190]

Jewel arrived at her parents' home and ran straight to Oral's sickbed. With the anointing of the Holy Spirit heavy upon her, she spoke these seven words: "Oral, God is going to heal you!"[191]

Instantly, Oral went from having an overwhelming fear that he would never get well to a God-given faith that he would get up from his sickbed and be completely healed. Faith leapt inside of his heart, and the presence of God's power fell upon the room. Jewel had delivered the good news, and Oral had the faith to believe it from the bottom of his heart! He didn't know when he would be healed, but he was certain that God had spoken through his sister—and that his healing was coming!

"I Saw the Face of Jesus!"

God's deliverance moved rapidly in Oral's life from that night, both spiritually and physically. The very next evening, his father came to his bedroom and declared, "Oral, I'm going to kneel beside your bed and pray and not stop until you give your heart to God and get saved."[192] For several hours, Ellis prayed fervently for the Lord to save his son's soul. Suddenly, it seemed to Oral that his father's face began to glow. As Oral watched in amazement, the loving countenance of Jesus appeared on Ellis Roberts's face.

> There, just as clear as anything, I saw the face of Jesus in Papa's face. Now, I had never wanted to be saved before....But when I saw His face in Papa's countenance, I began to cry....My heart was broken into a thousand pieces, and pretty soon I was asking God to save my soul.[193]

Oral felt the presence of God flood his soul and faith fill his heart. For the first time in years, Oral Roberts stopped running away from the God of his father and cried out to Jesus to save his soul!

Oral remembers,

> I felt as light as a feather and so happy, I wanted to shout at the top of my voice....I found myself standing up in the bed with my hands upraised, praising and magnifying God and saying, "I am saved! I am saved! I am saved!"[194]

A special destiny in God was set on fire that fateful evening in that young man's healing room.

Healing Power for a Generation

Our God is not a God of coincidence! Oral had finally reached the place where he'd stopped running from God, and so God began to "run" toward him with one personal miracle after another. During the same time that Oral was saved, a healing evangelist named Brother George W. Moncey came to Ada, Oklahoma, and set up a tent revival meeting. Brother Moncey is an enigmatic figure in history, as not much is known about him. A business card in the Oral Roberts University (ORU) archives is one of the only records about him, and it reads: "Geo. W. Moncey— evangelist, divine healer."[195] He seems to have been one of the scores of roving evangelists who thrived in the post-depression era. According to interviews with those who remember him, few Pentecostals had never heard of Moncey before the meeting, nor did he return to the city again; rumors even persisted that he left town under a cloud.[196] Nevertheless, hundreds of people filled the tent each night, including Oral's oldest brother, Elmer.

At each meeting, as the word of faith came forth, the power of the Holy Spirit fell upon the people, and many were healed. Elmer Roberts didn't own a car, and Oral now lived eighteen miles away with his parents, but Elmer knew that he had to get Oral into those healing meetings. Elmer borrowed a friend's car and used his last thirty-five cents to buy enough gas so that he could get his younger brother to the meeting.

Elmer entered his parents' house through the front door, walked straight down the hall to Oral's bedroom and said, "Oral, get up. God is going to heal you!" Oral was too weak to stand up on his own, so Elmer and Ellis lifted Oral's emaciated body—bed mattress, and all—and laid it in the backseat of the car. Ellis and Claudius excitedly climbed up front with Elmer, believing that God was going to do another miracle for Oral that night. As Oral lay in the backseat listening to Elmer tell of the healings he had seen, his own faith for healing began to grow.

At that moment, Oral understood not just that he would be healed, but also why God desired to heal him: he was to reveal the truth of God's healing power to a generation of people.

Gradually, the voices in the front seat seemed to fade away, and Oral heard a new voice as clearly as he had heard his brother speaking moments before. Deep in his soul, he knew that this new voice, although unfamiliar to him, was the voice of God. *"Son, I am going to heal you,"* He said, *"and you are to take my healing power to your generation."*[197] These unforgettable words would be emblazoned on Oral's heart and define his ministry for a lifetime.

At that moment, Oral understood not just that he would be healed, but also why God desired to heal him: he was to reveal the truth of God's healing power to a generation of people—and it would happen in ways he could never have imagined in that dark car on the way to a small-town Oklahoma tent meeting.

Releasing God's Power

The tent was filled to overflowing as the Roberts family walked in, with Oral leaning heavily on his parents' arms. Brother Moncey came over to Oral early in the meeting and encouraged him to look to God for the faith to be healed that night. Oral sat in a rocking chair with pillows propping him up. It was nearly eleven o'clock before it was Oral's turn in the healing line. Because he had sat in that chair while everyone else had been prayed for, Oral was the very last one to receive prayer. Brother Moncey walked over to him with a Holy Spirit anointing and prayed a short but faith-filled prayer.

Over seventy years later, Oral Roberts could recall those words: "Thou cursed disease, I command you in the name of Jesus Christ to come out of this boy's lungs; loose him and let him go!"[198] That was the first time Oral had ever heard a man command a disease to come out of someone. He never forgot the authority in the name of Jesus Christ to command disease. When his own healing ministry began years later, Oral would often refer to this as a "commanding faith prayer."

When Brother Moncey's hand touched Oral's head, he felt as though a pent-up force within his soul was released. The power of God came upon him and permeated his body from head to toe; his lungs cleared, and he could breathe. As the power of the Holy Spirit ran through his body, he shouted at the top of his voice, "I am healed! I am healed!"[199]

Immediately, Oral was able to take deep breaths from the bottom of his lungs without pain or coughing! The people around him shouted to God and raised their hands to Him in praise. They called out to hear

Oral testify of his healing and handed him a microphone. Oral stood up before them, trembling under the power of God. He was healed! As the words of testimony poured from his lips, Oral realized that his stuttering was completely gone, as well.

The Lord's presence clothed him as he spoke, and it was as though he had always been in the pulpit. Oral spoke for fifteen or twenty minutes—it was the first of thousands of sermons he would deliver on God's power to heal and deliver. A messenger of faith and Holy Spirit power was born that night in a vibrant tent meeting in a small town in Oklahoma, a messenger of God's healing power whose voice would be heard around the world!

For days after his healing experience, Oral still felt weak. It was Mama Roberts and her faith that again encouraged him to move forward in God. She explained that although he had been healed of tuberculosis, he had been in bed for more than five months, and so his body would need some time to regain its strength. Following her directions, Oral ate a little more and walked a little farther each day.

Within two months, Oral was able to preach a short message at a local revival meeting. When his parents took him for a follow-up lung fluoroscopy, his doctor found his lungs to be absolutely perfect. "Son, just forget you ever had tuberculosis. Your lungs are as sound as a dollar!"[200]

The Fire of the Holy Spirit

Oral began preaching in revival meetings at every opportunity he had. For nearly a year, he preached the Word of God and the power of the baptism in the Holy Spirit at Pentecostal Holiness meetings with his father. As his popularity as a preacher grew, he wrote an article in a Pentecostal Holiness newspaper crying out for the church's need for Spirit-filled young men and women. Yet, he still had not experienced the baptism of the Holy Spirit himself. How the yearning to have the anointing of the Holy Spirit burned within him!

In August 1936, the East Oklahoma Pentecostal camp meetings were being held in Sulphur, Oklahoma. Oral was to be licensed as a minister in the Pentecostal Holiness church at one of the last meetings. When he arrived, though, his mind was set on far more than that ordination. He was determined he would not leave those campgrounds without personally experiencing the fire of Pentecost. Oral began to seek God with all his heart for the baptism of the Holy Spirit.

Southern church camp meetings were full of excitement and expectancy. They were begun as early as the 1770s by Methodists, Presbyterians, and those of other denominations who wanted to dedicate time to God in prayer, praise, and teaching. The camp meetings were festive affairs celebrated annually by many church groups. There, friends and family could meet to fellowship and worship God. The Southern farmers, in particular, would take time in late summer to dedicate a week or so to the Lord.

In the earliest days, groups arrived in wagons and pitched tents in small groups around a central location. The largest tent would be the meeting place for all who attended. In later years, camp meeting sites were established with small, family cabins built around a meeting hall, where the congregation would meet during the days and evenings. Today, these gatherings are commonly referred to as conventions or conferences.

Whether in tents or cabins, there were praise, prayer, and teaching services all throughout the seven to ten days of each camp meeting, with the power of God falling upon the people in a great anointing. There was also a time of sweet fellowship as fathers, mothers, children, neighbors, and friends enjoyed eating, sleeping, playing, praying, and worshipping God together.

During one of the evening meetings at the Sulphur, Oklahoma, camp meeting, Oral Roberts cried out to God in prayer, feeling as though he could no longer wait for God's Spirit to fill him. As the time of evening worship and praise began, Oral opened his mouth to sing and was baptized in the Holy Spirit. He began to speak with other tongues, as the disciples had at Pentecost in the book of Acts. (See Acts 2:4.) He had received God's anointing to preach earlier in his ministry, but now he was empowered by the Holy Spirit as in the days of Pentecost!

> **As the time of evening worship and praise began, Oral opened his mouth to sing and was baptized in the Holy Spirit.**

A Busy Young Man

Oral was an intense young man, passionately searching for God and seeking to be used by Him in every way possible. Now that he had been baptized in the Holy Spirit, his intensity increased—all he wanted was more of God in his heart and in his life. At each evening camp service, he used his musical talent by playing the guitar in the young people's praise band.

One night, as he hurriedly mounted the steps to the stage, he sat down beside a young woman who was tuning her guitar. She was a pretty schoolteacher with brown hair, a warm smile, and a desire to serve the Lord as a missionary. With nothing but ministry on his mind, Oral didn't pay much attention to her that night. They spoke politely, and before the service began, he asked her if his hair was combed sufficiently. She answered yes, and he thought nothing more of it.

But the encounter meant a great deal more to the young lady, Evelyn Lutman Fahnestock. After meeting the handsome, dark-haired young man, Evelyn walked alone to her tent and wrote in her diary, "I sat by my future husband tonight!"[201] That was a young lady in tune with the Holy Spirit! She saw far more of God's will in that situation than Oral ever could have imagined. Wisely, Evelyn gave her thoughts and hopes to the Lord in prayer and returned to her teaching position in Texas that fall.

Early in his ministry, it was obvious to everyone who heard him that Oral possessed an unusual anointing to preach. Following the Sulphur, Oklahoma, camp meetings in 1936, he preached for two years, sometimes with his father but more often alone. He was excited to be preaching for the Lord, but he was also experiencing the lonely life of an itinerant preacher. At the end of those two years, Oral decided it was time to find a wife, but not just any wife. She had to willingly accept the rough roads of a Pentecostal preacher's life journey.

He Who Finds a Wife...

"Adam's wife came from his rib, while mine came from Texas!" Oral often joked.[202] As Oral began praying for a wife who would share his home and ministry, some friends told him about a wonderful girl named

Evelyn. After a few inquiries, he discovered that she was the same young woman he had met two years before at the Sulphur, Oklahoma, camp meetings. Oral could hardly remember what she looked like, but he was very impressed by the reports of her love for the Lord and her good reputation among other Christians.

Oral sent her a long letter about his ministry, along with a little booklet he had written. Evelyn wrote back eagerly, certain that this was confirmation of her initial feelings for Oral. They continued to correspond during the following months. From Evelyn's responses to his letter, Oral grew certain that she was the one for him. God was drawing their hearts together through their common love for Jesus.

The only thing left was for Oral and Evelyn to meet face-to-face and confirm that their relationship was truly from the Lord. One weekend in September 1938, Oral decided to drive the six hundred miles from Oklahoma to south Texas to meet Evelyn. Knowing how serious Oral was about this girl he hardly knew, Mama Roberts insisted on accompanying him!

She knew that the gifts bestowed on her son meant that he needed the prayerful support of a godly wife, and she wanted to make certain that his decision was the right one. Nevertheless, it had to have appeared strange for Oral to show up with his mother to meet a prospective fiancée. Evelyn and her grandparents accepted the visit from both of the Robertses graciously, however.

During that weekend, Oral and Evelyn talked a great deal and attended church together. They also spent a day alone fishing together on the Gulf of Mexico, but Oral quips, "All we caught was each other!"[203] By the end of the day, Oral knew that he had found the girl he wanted to spend the rest of his life with. Looking into Evelyn's eyes, he said joyously,

> My huge, happy, hilarious heart is throbbing tumultuously, tremendously, triumphantly with a lingering, lasting, long-lived love for you. As I gaze into your bewildering, beauteous, bounteous, beaming eyes, I am literally, lonesomely lost in a dazzling, daring, delightful dream in which your fair, felicitous, fanciful face is ever present like a colossal, comprehensive constellation. Will you be my sweet, smiling, soulful, satisfied spouse?[204]

★★★★★

What was Evelyn's answer to Oral's astonishing proposal? "Listen here, boy! If you are trying to propose to me, talk in the English language!"[205]

A Christmas Eve Wedding

Before the weekend was over, Oral and Evelyn were engaged to be married. Three months later, on Christmas Eve 1938, they celebrated a beautiful wedding at the church Papa Roberts pastored in Westville, Oklahoma. They were married by Oral's close friend, Reverend Oscar Moore.

Unfortunately, the newlyweds had to live apart for the next four months while Evelyn finished her teaching contract in Texas. In June, Evelyn left teaching for good to be the God-chosen helpmate of Oral Roberts.

For some men in the ministry, their wives are just side items in their service to God. But for Oral Roberts, his "darling Evelyn" was at the heart and soul of the years of ministry he offered to the Lord. From that time forward, next to the Lord, Evelyn was the dearest part of Oral's heart and life, truly a blessing from God. He often praised this beautiful, young woman who'd become his wife. She fit him "as a hand fit into a glove."[206]

What Happened to the Lord's Word?

Following his marriage to Evelyn, Oral received offers to pastor several small Pentecostal Holiness churches, first in North Carolina, then in Georgia, and then in Oklahoma. While pastoring during the next ten years, he also attended Oklahoma Baptist University and Phillips University, and taught one day a week at Southwestern Bible College. His days and nights were filled with church activities, and his latest church in Enid, Oklahoma, was growing. However, Oral Roberts was unsatisfied and miserable.

What had happened to the word the Lord had given him that he was to bring the message of God's healing power to his generation? Most of the people in the churches he served did not believe in or seem to care about the healing power of Christ. Oral recalls, "At this time, I had a feeling of destiny. A miraculous power was at my fingertips. I could feel it. I was frustrated and filled with inner conflicts, but I had the feeling that some-day God's power would come into my life and I would deliver humanity."[207] Even though Oral tried to drown out the voice of God with activities, he couldn't forget that clear call: "I have called you to proclaim My healing power...."

Oral as a young pastor

In 1947, Oral began to cry out to God for a new direction—a ministry according to the pro-phetic word given to him. Oral Roberts was near-ly thirty years old and feeling a dryness in his walk with Christ. In prayer day and night, crying out for God's power and anointing, Oral began a life-changing study of the four Gospels and the book of Acts, asking the Lord to reveal Himself. Oral spent nights on his knees reading the Bible, "sometimes laughing, sometimes crying; some-times shaken to the depths of my soul."[208]

Through reading the Word and praying, Oral discovered that the Jesus of the Bible was:

- a Man of heartfelt compassion and vibrant power.

- a responder to the desperate need of the people around Him, as Jesus spent two-thirds of His time healing the sick and performing miracles.

- a miracle worker whose works were to be surpassed by His dis-ciples through His name.

- a giver of the miraculous power by sending the Holy Spirit.

Jesus Is the Same Forever

Oral soon realized that nothing had changed; *"Jesus Christ is the same yesterday, and to day, and for ever"* (Hebrews 13:8). The plan was still for His disciples to accomplish "greater works" today than He had done. (See John 14:12.) Greater works through Oral Roberts! Jesus had transmitted His power to His disciples then, and Jesus wanted the same power to be with His disciples today—Oral was sure of it!

★★★★★

Oral's days of prayer and study also brought him to these Scriptures from John 14: *"I will not leave you comfortless: I will come to you"* (verse 18), and *"The Comforter, which is the Holy Ghost, whom the Father will send in my name...shall teach you all things"* (verse 26). Jesus comforted and healed the people when He was on the earth. Then, He sent the Comforter, the Holy Spirit, who would provide the *"greater works"* so that believers could heal people and set them free just as Jesus had done! The full significance of the baptism of the Holy Spirit came to Oral in a way he had never considered before. He realized that the power he had been waiting for had been with him all along. *"Ye shall receive power, after that the Holy Ghost is come upon you"* (Acts 1:8). Oral had had the Lord's healing, transforming power all along; he just hadn't known it.

> **Oral had had the Lord's healing, transforming power all along; he just hadn't known it.**

What about those of you reading these glorious testimonies of God's great generals? These men and women of God discovered His power that is available to believers today. The same power that raised Christ Jesus from the dead is the power that abides within each of us! The power that Jesus gave the seventy disciples to go and heal diseases and cast out demons dwells in you! You can make—you *must* make—a difference in the world around you as a disciple of Christ today. Look into His Word and embrace the truth of Jesus' statements to you. *"Ye shall receive power, after that the Holy Ghost is come upon you"* (emphasis added).

Oral's Greatest Discovery

During Oral's time of searching the Gospels and also the rest of the New Testament, a verse leapt off of the page and into his spirit. It was the second verse of 3 John: *"Beloved, I wish above all things that thou mayest prosper and be in health, even as thy soul prospereth."* Oral read the words again and was astounded. In the early Pentecostal church, poverty was often worn as an "honor badge" for the Lord. In all of his reading of the Bible, Oral had never grasped that Scripture verse before. He was certain that those words were for him—the answer to his questions about God's desires for His children.

He had questions such as, Does God bring poverty and sickness into our lives, as so many in the church believe? Does God want His children to be delivered in soul, mind, *and* body? As Oral joyously shared 3 John 2 with Evelyn, he declared, "Evelyn, we have it wrong. I haven't been preaching that God is a good God."[209]

Oral realized that true healing and prosperity begin in the soul of man but then move into his physical body, as well. As God desires a man to be well and strong in his inner man, He also desires his daily life to prosper. For Oral Roberts, this was a life-changing revelation.

A Fire Begins to Burn

Three other Scriptures began to revolutionize Oral's way of thinking. The first was Acts 10:38: *"God anointed Jesus of Nazareth with the Holy Ghost and with power: who went about doing good, and healing all that were oppressed of the devil; for God was with him."* Jesus went about doing good and not evil throughout His ministry, healing all of those who were oppressed by the devil. How well Oral now remembered Brother Moncey commanding the disease of tuberculosis to come out of him!

The next eye-opening Scripture was Luke 9:56: *"For the Son of man is not come to destroy men's lives, but to save them."* Jesus came to save men's lives from all that the devil wanted to afflict them with, including poverty and disease.

The final Scripture discovery Oral made was perhaps the greatest of all. It was the statement of Jesus in the gospel of John: *"The thief cometh not, but for to steal, and to kill, and to destroy: I am come that they might have life, and that they might have it more abundantly"* (John 10:10). At last, Oral had a real foundation for his faith. God was a *good* God who had come for the redemption of all of mankind. Oral could come to God and believe He was a good God who desired to see His people set free!

Oral Roberts's personal reaction to those scriptural truths was undeniable: "A thrill came in my soul that I still feel. A fire began to burn....I had an understanding of Jesus Christ that would thrill the world."[210]

Don't Cook Me Any Meals

Was it time to move out in faith? Was the Lord telling Oral that he should give up his church and move into a full-time evangelistic healing ministry? Oral believed that the time to bring the healing message of God had come, but he wanted to hear God speak a personal word to him affirming it. One morning, Oral walked into the kitchen, looked Evelyn in the eye, and said, "It is time for breakfast, but don't cook me any meals until I tell you."[211]

When someone turns to the Lord in fasting and prayer, what is he hoping to accomplish or receive? I believe the person has a passionate desire for God to move or to answer prayer—a desperate need of the heart. Fasting helps to communicate that need to the Lord on a level beyond everyday prayers. When we fast, we can speak to God more easily concerning the needs of our hearts, and we have the spiritual ears to hear Him. After twelve years of unfulfilling ministry in his life, Oral's fervent desire to hear from the Lord had reached a crisis point.

Over the next three months, Oral spent many hours fasting and praying. He lost nearly thirty-two pounds during that time and often found himself praying for the strength to continue.[212] Finally, feeling that he could no longer go on without an answer from the Lord, Oral went into his church study and locked the door. Slowly, he lay down on the small rug, prostrate before the Lord. He prayed, "God, I will not get up until You speak to me. You have to speak to me."[213] If he was to bring the Lord's healing message to his generation, then he had to hear from the Lord Himself!

Roberts remembers that life-changing day this way: I was one man striving with the Almighty. I felt my soul being poured out before Him like water. Time became eternity, and I lost sight of where I was and who I was."[214] In those hours, God finally spoke to Oral. He told him to leave the study and drive his car down the block. As Oral drove, he heard the Lord say, "From this hour you will heal the sick and cast out devils by My power."[215] Sensing the presence of God, Oral raced home, took Evelyn into his arms, and said, "Cook me a meal; the Lord has just spoken!"[216]

From that moment on, Oral Roberts was a man with a personal call from God that no man could deter!

☆☆☆☆☆

A Confirming Sign

Over the next few days, the plans for Oral's first healing meeting were put in place. The Robertses secured a downtown auditorium in Enid, Oklahoma, and the services were planned for the following Sunday at two o'clock in the afternoon. Oral continued to fast and pray as he nervously waited for that first meeting. He became so nervous about God's will that he decided to seek some type of confirming sign, as Gideon had done in the book of Judges in the Old Testament. (See Judges 6:36–40.) Before giving up his pastorate and launching a faith ministry, Oral needed one more solid confirmation from the Lord.

Although in hindsight this might seem like it was a foolish gesture on Oral's part, God knows that we are but dust, and that we often need to hear from Him in more than one way. There were three confirming signs that Oral asked the Lord to provide.

The first sign was that one thousand people would show up for the service, a good deal more than the two hundred people who were in his church service each Sunday morning. The second sign was that the offering would be as much as they needed to cover their expenses without their having to pull any money out of the people who were there. The third, and most important, sign was that Oral would have God's power to heal the sick in a manner that both he and the people there would recognize. If all three of these "fleeces" were answered, then Oral would know that his directions were from the Lord. If not, then he didn't think he knew or understood the Lord's call at all. It had to be all or nothing— all of God and nothing of Oral.

"In Jesus' Name, Be Healed!"

How faithful God is to His people, even when they question Him! When Oral arrived at the auditorium, some of his volunteers met him at the door with this exciting news: "There are over twelve hundred people already seated in the auditorium!" Oral's confidence was growing as an offering was received that totaled approximately three dollars over the amount needed to rent the building. Now, the time had come for this man of God to preach his first healing message.

★★★★★

I had not preached more than ten minutes until the anointing of God struck my mortal flesh. I began to tingle from the crown of my head to the sole of my feet with the presence of God.[217]

It was as though the Scriptures had exploded inside Oral's head. As he preached, and as God's anointing fell, two or three hundred people came forward to be healed, many of them weeping in anticipation.

As he walked toward the aisle, Oral stopped before an old German woman who showed him her stiff, crippled right hand. He touched her hand and spoke, "In Jesus' name, be healed!" The woman slowly opened and closed her right fist, realized it was loose, and cried out with joy, "I'm healed! I'm healed!"[218] The response of the people was immediate.

People crowded around Oral and began pulling at him, asking for prayer for their needs. He began to pray for all those around him. Six women from his local church stood there with their unsaved husbands, all of the men weeping because they wanted to be saved. God had answered Oral's prayers beyond his wildest expectations. The third sign had been received, and one of the mightiest healing ministries in the body of Christ began that day!

"I Can See! I Can See!"

Shortly after that first healing meeting, in early 1948, Oral and Evelyn decided to move to Tulsa, Oklahoma, where they could minister for the Lord in a larger city. Oral had an entire generation to reach with the healing message of God. Soon after arriving, Oral was invited to preach for a few days in the tent of Pentecostal Holiness pastor Steven Pringle, which seated one thousand people.

Since Oral was not well-known, the tent was not even half full the first two evenings. Then, when word of his on-fire ministry for Christ spread throughout the city's Pentecostal churches, the crowds grew, and miracles were recorded each evening.

One night, a blind man who had been brought to the meeting from Kansas City ran from the healing line shouting, "I can see! I can see!" The news traveled like an electric current through the crowd. From that night forward, the tent was filled, and Oral continued his healing messages in that tent for the next nine weeks.

As news of Oral's ministry traveled, invitations to preach began pouring in from many of the nation's major Pentecostal churches. For the first time, Oral saw that unity in the body of Christ could extend beyond his own Holiness denomination. He was delighted when he was invited to conduct healing meetings in an Assemblies of God church, and then was asked to conduct a crusade sponsored by three different Pentecostal denominations. Because healing was needed by all people and all denominations, Oral's ministry world began to expand.

Oral Roberts was brought to the entire nation's attention in an unusual way. During a Spirit-filled meeting in Brother Pringle's tent, an emotionally distraught man across the street pulled out a revolver and shot at Oral as he preached from the stage. The bullet sailed just eighteen inches above his head. While the identity of the assailant was never discovered, what Satan meant for evil, God used to great good. Newspapers throughout the country picked up the story, and evangelist Oral Roberts became nationally known overnight.

A Man Whose Quiver Is Full

Children are an heritage of the LORD: and the fruit of the womb is his reward....Happy is the man that hath his quiver full of them.

(Psalm 127:3, 5)

Children are a blessing of the Lord, and Oral and Evelyn were blessed with four children in their marriage. As children are for many parents, they were a source of unending joy to them, as well as a source of great sorrow later in life.

Just a year after their wedding, on December 16, 1939, Oral and Evelyn were blessed with their first child, a beautiful, dark-haired baby girl they named Rebecca Ann. During those earliest years, Oral was preaching at various church revivals. The little family of three traveled everywhere together, with Rebecca learning how to walk and talk while she and her parents were staying in the homes of pastors of the churches they visited.

When Rebecca was nearly four years old, Oral and Evelyn decided it was time to settle down, and the traveling stopped. Oral accepted his first pastorate, a church in Toccoa, Georgia, and in 1943, their second child, Ronald David, was born.

Evelyn and Oral both came from large families, but Evelyn thought that, with a busy ministry, two children would be just perfect. This was one time when Oral disagreed with her. He thought four children would be the perfect number. So, on November 12, 1948, Richard Lee Roberts was born. He would grow up to be very much like his daddy. Finally, two years later, the last Roberts baby came into the world. Lovely little Roberta was born with bright, blue eyes and a shocking wave of black hair.

By the time Roberta was born, Oral had left the pastorate and begun his tent and healing ministry in Tulsa. When the family outgrew the little house in Tulsa, Oral purchased a small farm outside the Tulsa city limits. Papa Roberts had encouraged Oral to buy a farm so that his children could experience farm life. For six years, the Robertses lived on that farm and spent many happy times together. Of course, for the family, those years were increasingly filled with the loneliness caused when a husband and father travels all over the world. The years ahead would show how this had affected the children's lives.

Oral and Evelyn felt great compassion for the people writing and a burden to pray for the author of every letter that was sent to them.

Filled to Overflowing

When Oral and Evelyn first moved to Tulsa in 1948, Oral's ministry was launched by the revival meetings in Brother Pringle's tents. Soon after those tent meetings concluded, letters began to pour in to the Robertses' small home from all over the country—letters of testimony, letters filled with prayer needs, and letters with offers to speak at churches. The letters started filling up every spare table and corner in their home.

Oral and Evelyn felt great compassion for the people writing and a burden to pray for the author of every letter that was sent to them. They would lay hands upon each letter and pray for the writer's needs, no matter how many requests arrived. All of these letters needed to be answered, as well. It quickly became an overwhelming task!

Three young women who had been blessed by Oral's preaching volunteered to help answer every one of those letters. So, Oral would prayerfully dictate his responses, and the girls would sit at the dining room table and write them down. Before long, the work could no longer be done on a voluntary basis, and those same young women became the first employees in Oral Roberts's ministry. As the letters continued to increase in volume, the Robertses turned their garage into a home office. Soon, the entire house became the office, and more workers were hired.

In order to answer so many questions about the healing power of God and the work of the Holy Spirit on the earth, Oral began his first monthly magazine, which he called *Healing Waters*. It was a wonderful way to stay in contact with the people who were writing, as well as to reach new people with the message of God's salvation and healing. Eventually, *Healing Waters* became the major link between Oral Roberts and his prayer supporters all over the world. That little house in Tulsa was bursting at the seams with the efforts of ministry outreach.

Within a few months, Oral was contemplating a new step of faith by purchasing land to build a ministry office. It was at this point that the Lord brought an amazing man of God and lifetime supporter into Oral's life.

Lee Braxton was a successful businessman from North Carolina who had read Oral's booklet entitled *You Need Healing, Do These Things*. He flew to an Oral Roberts healing meeting in Florida to see what this new minister was all about. Lee left Florida excited about what he had heard and seen during those meetings. A few weeks later, he traveled to Tulsa to check out the ministry firsthand.

When Lee saw the house overflowing with letters and understood the overwhelming amount of time and work involved, he spoke some practical wisdom into Oral's life. "This just can't all be handled by you, Oral," he exclaimed. "You need more help, and you need a ministry building."[219]

Lee Braxton helped Oral arrange for the bank financing needed; three months later, the building was complete, with a sign that read

"Turn Your Faith Loose" in neon letters shining out front. It would be the first of countless buildings Oral Roberts would build to promote the gospel of Jesus Christ. And Lee Braxton would remain a vibrant part of the Oral Roberts Evangelistic Association for the next thirty-three years. When Oral asked him how much he should be paid, Lee answered, "How about a dollar?" Though Lee was most likely kidding, Oral took him at his word and faithfully paid him one dollar each year. Lee enjoyed telling people, "I'm a dollar-a-year man!"

Soon after Lee became involved in the ministry, Oral began broadcasting the message of salvation and healing over the radio. Lee's experience as an organizer and business genius helped to promote Oral and increase his broadcasts from just a handful of stations to over one hundred stations across the country. God's message of healing reached the American airwaves as never before!

"God Spoke to Me Again"

In spite of all the attention Oral was suddenly receiving, he was adamant about keeping his focus on God. More than anything else, he wanted to know that the presence and power of God were with him when he preached and ministered to people. He continued to pray, longing to feel God's presence with him in a stronger way. That prayer was answered in spring 1948.

One Sunday night, Oral went to conduct a one-night crusade in an Assemblies of God church in the small town of Nowata, Oklahoma. During the healing time, Oral was praying for a young deaf boy when the Lord spoke to him again, saying, "Son, you have been faithful up to this hour, and now you will feel My presence in your right hand. Through My presence, you will be able to detect demons, and through My power they will be cast out."[220]

At that moment, Oral felt a burning sensation traveling down his right arm to his right hand. His hand was throbbing as though there was an electric current flowing through it. Was this really God, or was it his imagination? Oral knew that if it was God moving through his hand, the deaf boy standing before him would be healed. When Oral placed his hands on the boy's ear, he felt the Lord's power surge through his right hand, but he felt nothing at all in his left hand. Turning the boy away from his mother so that he could not see her mouth, Oral asked her to speak to her son. The young boy could hear every word his mother uttered! The people shouted praises to God for His miracle-working power!

His Right Hand on Fire

A few days later, Oral was invited to speak at a church in Tulsa. At the end of the service, a friend of the Robertses named Irma Morris came forward in the healing time. She had been diagnosed with tuberculosis, a disease Oral knew personally and despised. Oral could feel the fever on Irma's brow and smell the TB in her body, an odor he had known during his own sickness. Up to that moment, Oral had not told a soul about the power he felt in his right hand while praying for the sick, not even Evelyn.

Oral reached out to touch Irma's fevered forehead, feeling the power of God surge in his right hand. He commanded the TB to loose her body and set her free in the name of Jesus. "Oh, Oral, what did you do to me?" she cried. "Your right hand. It felt on fire when you touched me....Something in your right hand is causing a warmth to go through my lungs. My lungs are opening up. I believe I am being healed!"[221] God's presence charging through Oral's hand did not leave him at all as he moved along the entire healing line, laying his hand on each person standing there for prayer.

Late that night, Oral told Evelyn about the revelation from the Lord and the amazing thing that was happening with his right hand. He placed his right hand on her head as an experiment, but neither of them sensed anything different. However, a few minutes later, when Evelyn told Oral that she had been experiencing pain for a number of days, he laid his hands on her to pray. Immediately, they both were touched by the power of God surging through his right hand.

That night, they held each other and cried as they realized the special gift God had entrusted to Oral. Evelyn prayed that they would always recognize it as a gift from God alone and that it would remain precious to them.[222]

The Point of Contact

From this time, Oral began his earliest understanding of what he came to call "the point of contact." As Oral explained,

> A point of contact is something *you* do. And when you do it, you release your faith toward God, just as turning on the faucet makes the water come out, or turning on the switch makes the light turn on. It is not enough to have faith; you must release the faith you posses....You must *Turn Your Faith Loose.*[223]

This Holy Spirit-empowered idea became increasingly important as Oral's renown grew to the national stage.

Oral recognized that in the Bible, healings occurred after certain points of contact were made to release the faith of the individuals involved. In the Old Testament, for example, Naaman dipped himself in the Jordan River seven times as a point of contact to be healed of leprosy. (See 2 Kings 5:10–14.) In the New Testament, the woman with the "issue of blood" touched Jesus' garment and was healed. (See Matthew 9:30–22; Luke 8:43–48.) Jesus Himself told the lepers to go show themselves to the priest as a point of contact for healing. (See Luke 17:12–14.)

Oral Roberts lays hands on a young man.

In Oral's ministry, the power that he felt in his right hand became a point of contact for the people in the crowd. It was also a point of contact for Oral's own faith. He said that as he felt the warm presence of God moving through his hand, "my faith for healing seemed to leap out of my heart and up to God."[224] Later, with television audiences, Oral would encourage them to lay hands on the TV itself to initiate a point of contact to release their faith.

In later years, Oral would admit that there were things about God's healing power that he didn't understand. While he expected everyone whom he touched with his right hand to be healed, some were not. He simply learned to follow the Lord in obedience and pray in faith for everyone who came to him for prayer. He came to understand that the power was God's, the healing was God's, and the ministry was God's.

As Oral ministered in obedience to God's Word, many were either healed at the point of contact or greatly encouraged to believe God for a gradual physical healing and a closer walk with Him.

Tent Meeting Explosion

Oral Roberts was a pioneer in almost every area that he ventured into during his years of ministry. The first place this became evident was in the tent ministry. Tent meetings were a way of life in Pentecostal churches in the early twentieth century. Oral Roberts turned these small, relatively inconsequential tools into a viable ministry in the national limelight.

After concluding meetings in churches and auditoriums that could not hold the crowds that wanted to attend, Oral was ready to take a giant leap of faith. In the summer of 1948, he decided to order a tent of his own so that he could travel across the nation spreading the gospel of Jesus Christ. The first tent was large enough to seat 3,000 people; Oral named it the "Canvas Cathedral." This tent was larger than that of any other evangelist at the time.

Not willing to accept mediocre equipment to bring forth God's Word, Oral purchased a new Hammond organ, a Steinway piano, 3,000 folding chairs, two trailer trucks, and thousands of

Oral Roberts raises his hands during a tent meeting.

song books. The cost of the venture was nearly $60,000—an unheard of amount to spend at the time. But Oral knew that God had spoken. In order to speak to an entire generation about God's healing power, Oral would need the means to reach the people.

In Oral's earliest days of tent ministry, there were no frills or special music to draw the crowds in. There might have been a brief song or two, but his primary focus had been on preaching the Word of God. After one and a half hours of laying a foundation of the Word to undergird the faith of the people, he would offer them the opportunity to receive salvation in Christ. After that, the healing lines formed.

The first place Oral used his Canvas Cathedral was in Durham, North Carolina, a city that welcomed him with open arms. Although the tent could seat three thousand, on many nights, there were as many as nine thousand people in attendance. Oral could see overflow crowds that would encircle the outside of the tent to listen. He was overwhelmed by the response and kept his eyes on the Lord to give him the message for the people.

Each night while he was in Durham, a small number of deaf children from the local school for the deaf were brought to the meetings. And, each night, as Oral prayed for a different group of these children, their ears were opened to sounds and words; some could suddenly hear the music.

The crowd was electrified—and so was Oral! Many of those sweet, deaf children received a complete healing and were able to both hear and speak, moving the crowds to cry tears of joy. Those whose ears were not completely healed could hear sounds that were not possible for them to hear before.

Not without the Anointing

By the time 1950 arrived, Oral had been in the evangelistic healing ministry for three years. The number of people who came to hear him preach and receive a healing grew with each crusade. There were times when Oral felt completely overwhelmed by the needs of the people. To deal so closely in people's lives became tiring. As he faced the needs of thousands, knowing he was only human, just like they were, Oral took great comfort in feeling the presence of God in his hand.

He began to recognize the anointing of God more easily. He described it as "a divine power that had hold of my being....It was the power of anointing on me, and it began to change the impact of my preaching...the difference in results was easy to see."[225] Oral determined that he should preach or minister only when under God's anointing. To keep him humble, Oral's mother would often remind him, "No one wants to hear Oral Roberts; they want to hear God through Oral Roberts!"

Oral developed a special quiet time when he could wait on the Lord for His presence. At three o'clock each afternoon before an evening service, Oral would spend time resting and praying in preparation for the night's meeting. No one was to disturb him during this time alone with God.

As Oral waited upon the Lord, God's presence would come into his right hand and activate his faith to believe for the needs of the people. Oral made a vow to the Lord that he would not attempt to minister without sensing God's anointing power. He knew that without the Holy Spirit's presence at each meeting, he could accomplish nothing.

"Please Help Me!"

This vow was tested in the early 1950s at a crusade in the old Metropolitan Auditorium in Philadelphia, Pennsylvania. During his time of waiting on the Lord in prayer, Oral realized that he did not sense God's presence in his hand. How could he help the hurting without the confirmation of God's presence that night?

"Dear God," he prayed, "I have not been in this spot before. Please, will You help me?"[226] Oral had every intention of keeping his vow. In spite of the full auditorium waiting for him, if he did not get the okay from the Lord to proceed, he would not enter that place to minister.

When Oral's driver came to take him to the auditorium, Oral told him he was waiting on the Lord and would not be able to leave yet. In spite of the driver's repeated inquiries, Oral remained convinced that his decision was in obedience to the Lord. He would not move unless he knew God was going before him. Another ten minutes passed, then twenty minutes. Oral continued to pray, "Okay, God...I cannot go without absolutely knowing the anointing, Your presence, has come upon me."[227] Oral did the only thing he knew to do. He waited on the Lord rather than going out in his own strength.

> **As Oral waited, concerned about the crusade and yet trusting that God had a plan, he suddenly felt the surge of God's presence rush through his right hand.**

As Oral waited, concerned about the crusade and yet trusting that God had a plan, he suddenly felt the surge of God's presence rush through his right hand. He jumped up, ran to the door, and told the driver it was time to go.

Oral walked into the evening service in the Metropolitan Auditorium energized by the Holy Spirit. The people were already on their feet waiting in anticipation for what the Lord was going to do. Many people were healed that night, more than at any previous Oral Roberts service. Lives were changed throughout Philadelphia, the City of Brotherly Love, because of Oral's obedience to the vow he had made before God. He recognized that it was God who was in charge and that everything that happened depended upon His power and His timetable.

Oral has his own definition for the anointing of God:

It is a time when God separates you from yourself and fills you with His glory so that when you speak, it is like God speaking, and when you act, it is like God acting...the glory of the Lord that comes upon you at the time of the anointing removes all fear, fills you with a holy boldness, and gives you revelation knowledge of how and what to do.[228]

From beginning to end, it is all up to God!

Turning Disasters into Miracles

The 1950s was a decade of many different kinds of miracles in Oral Roberts's tent ministry. After just one year of using the Canvas

Cathedral, Oral purchased a new tent that was large enough to seat 7,000 people, and he traveled back and forth across the country ministering the saving, healing power of God. An astounding miracle of divine protection occurred in 1950 in Amarillo, Texas. On a very windy September night during the Amarillo crusade, a storm suddenly struck the tent. High winds came sweeping in, and the lights went out.

As lightning flashed across the sky, "the huge tent was tossed straight up into the sky,"[229] then floated slowly to the ground a few yards away. As the winds struck the tent area again, the heavy, steel poles, weighing a thousand pounds each, seemed to fall to the ground, landing between the chairs and the aisles, but not on a single individual. Later, it was confirmed that a tornado had hit the tent.

In the darkness, the people hardly realized the tent was gone. Instead of running in panic, they remained calmly in the tent area. Roberts gratefully recalled, "It was as if a thousand hands took control of the situation."[230] As Oral lay on the stage after being knocked down by the wind, and as the lightning continued to blaze overhead, several hundred people spontaneously began to sing God's praises.

Getting up on the platform in the pouring rain, Oral announced to the people that they should just calmly walk to their cars and leave the area. Then, he attempted to find Evelyn and their two-year-old son, Richard, who were somewhere in the crowd. The ministry staff quickly reassured Oral that Evelyn, who was six months pregnant with Roberta, and little Richard Lee were safely hidden under the preaching platform.

Whether it was because of angels or God Himself, the protection of all 7,000 people that night was astounding. The tent and everything around it were destroyed, but, other than a few minor injuries, every person had been spared. Everyone saw the love and power of God that night in a way that exceeded anything Oral Roberts could have ever imagined. Newspapers the next morning announced that God's miraculous protection had been over the crowd.

The day following the physical devastation, Oral received telegrams of encouragement from across the country, as well as some funds needed to purchase another, larger tent. With great concern, Lee Braxton flew in from North Carolina to encourage Oral to continue boldly in the ministry.

As they walked around the devastated tent the next day, Oral could feel his spirits sinking. Lee sensed the discouragement and said, "Oral, the miracle here means that this ministry can't go under for going over! God is not through with you yet. I'll begin a search of tent making companies, and we'll have a tent made that seats ten thousand and is built to withstand storms like this."[231] This time, by God's grace, Oral Roberts was able to purchase a tent to seat ten thousand people. Believers and nonbelievers alike flocked to that tent wherever it was set up to hear the Word of God from Oral Roberts's growing ministry.

Two Giants in God's Kingdom

Another blessing of the Amarillo, Texas, disaster came in an unexpected way. After the Canvas Cathedral had been demolished, friends of Oral and Evelyn invited them to spend a few days in Tacoma, Washington, to get some much-needed rest. The friends paid for their airfare and secluded Oral and Evelyn, determined that they should rest and relax. Within a few days, the couple felt the Holy Spirit's renewing strength, and the concerns of the ministry seemed less overwhelming.

Before they returned to Tulsa, they were invited to take a short trip to Portland, Oregon, to visit some other friends and attend a Billy Graham crusade. Billy had become well-known after a powerful crusade in Los Angeles, and Oral was very excited about the effect of this man's ministry on the nation.

As Oral and Evelyn were leaving their hotel room to head to the crusade, they met Billy Graham, who was leaving the hotel at the same time. Billy recognized Oral and invited him and Evelyn to share a cab with him and his wife, Ruth. Oral was honored by the invitation but was shocked by Billy's next request a few moments later: "Oral, I want you to lead in prayer tonight."[232]

Oral responded with concern. "Billy, you can't be serious. I don't want to be a problem for you by being on the platform...you know my ministry is very controversial."[233] Both men were dynamic soulwinners who spoke to thousands about the gospel of Jesus Christ, but they both knew that the baptism of the Holy Spirit and the preaching on modern-day healing were points of controversy in Oral's ministry.

At Billy's insistence, Oral did sit on the platform that night, and he prayed before the crusade for the Lord to anoint the services that evening. He was blessed by the opportunity and experienced firsthand the graciousness and the God-honoring ministry of Billy Graham, the man Oral often referred to as "the number one evangelist in our generation."[234]

Later that evening, the Robertses and the Grahams met again unexpectedly in the hotel coffee shop. The Grahams insisted that the Robertses join them for a late-night snack. Engaged in warm conversation, Billy told Oral that he and Cliff Barrows had visited one of Oral's crusades two years earlier in Florida. He recounted that they had been moved by the souls won to Christ and the people healed through Oral's ministry. Billy Graham freely admitted that he believed God healed people in the present, and that Ruth's own sister had been healed at a Pentecostal meeting.[235] Finally, Billy shared with Oral, "God has not called me to pray for the sick, but He has given you the gift."[236]

The unexpected trip to Portland laid the groundwork for a relationship of friendship and mutual respect between these two giant men of faith for decades to come. Years later, Billy Graham had a significant role in the dedication of Oral Roberts University. Between the two of them, they would reach millions of men and women with the message of Jesus Christ in the second half of the twentieth century.

At Oral's Side

There were countless men by Oral's side in the years of his ministry but few whom he held more dearly than Bob DeWeese. Bob had been gifted by God as a pastor, a teacher, an evangelist, and an administrator. He had a very effective ministry in his own right. But Bob believed that God had called him to use his gifts to support Oral Roberts and his ministry.

When he came on board in the early 1950s with his warm enthusiasm and joyful love of Christ, he and Oral developed an instant relationship that would last. For thirty years, Bob and Oral were a team "welded together like long-lost brothers."[237] Oral appreciated all of Bob's gifts, but especially his unshakable faith in the power of God to move in the present to save and heal broken lives.

As Oral's associate evangelist, Bob would speak to the afternoon crowds at the crusades. With his effervescent love for God, he would walk confidently onto the stage and preach a dynamic message of salvation in Jesus Christ. His daily testimony of God's faithfulness and the miracle-working power of the Holy Spirit always built up the people's faith to believe for healing during the evening services.

During the healing crusades, prayer cards became an important part of the process of praying to heal the sick. During the afternoon services, Bob would explain the use of the prayer cards and how the sick could expect to be prayed for during the services. Bob would explain that because the people with prayer needs often numbered in the thousands, some individuals might have to wait for a service or two before they would be called to come into the healing line.

In addition to preaching the word of faith, Bob was instrumental in working with the sponsoring pastors of each crusade and making sure everything flowed smoothly in spite of the thousands of people present. He visited the sponsoring pastors in each city months before the healing campaign arrived to make certain that everything was organized and ready for Oral Roberts's team.

> **Oral believed that the healing line gave each hurting individual the opportunity to come forward for prayer as an acknowledgment of his or her need for God and as an act of faith in His healing power.**

God's Healing Line

From the first night of Oral Roberts's healing ministry in the auditorium in Enid, Oklahoma, the healing line was the manner in which people received prayer for healing. Oral had received prayer in a healing line years earlier when he had been suffering from tuberculosis. More important, Oral believed that the healing line gave each hurting individual the opportunity to come forward for prayer as an acknowledgment of his or her need for God and as an act of faith in His healing power. It also gave Oral the opportunity to touch each one of them with his right hand, even if it was very briefly.

✻✻✻✻✻

This personal touch for each individual was important to Oral. Not only was it a "point of contact," but he also believed with all of his heart that it was the reason God had anointed his right hand—so that each person in need could feel Jesus' personal touch. The healing line was always preceded by an altar call, since the salvation of the soul was the first order of business in God's kingdom. After that, Oral would call for people who had physical needs to come forward. Masses of people would respond to the word of faith to be healed.

As the numbers of those who wanted to enter the healing line climbed into the thousands, Oral and his ministry team realized that they had to come up with a way to reach everyone. Those who wanted prayer for healing still filled out prayer cards explaining their physical needs. Then, local pastors who sponsored the crusade would interview each person and validate his or her prayer needs. After that, the people who desired healing prayer would be told that their prayer cards would be called when possible, but that they might have to wait throughout the entire crusade before it was their turn.

Personal attention from Oral Roberts, aside from a brief touch, was not possible. The time available and the strength he had would not permit it. Oral always took the time to pray for those too sick to enter the healing lines before he prayed for the others, though.

After that prayer time was complete, Oral would stand in front of the platform and lay his right hand on each individual as he or she walked by, praying for Christ's healing power to touch him or her. Because the touch was so personal, it was much more exhausting for Oral than just praying for general ailments in the congregation would have been.

Even though there were restrictions and waiting lines, thousands of people traveled from near and far to hear the Word and to be prayed for by this anointed man of God. At times, the healing lines extended for nearly a mile. After praying for and personally touching each person in line, Oral would be so exhausted that he would need to be carried out of the tent by Bob DeWeese and other men on the ministry team.

During the 1950s, as Oral traveled across the nation and conducted approximately one crusade a month, he became known as the nation's "faith healer." Stories of his ministry were published in both *Look* and

Life magazines, which, at the time, were the most popular news outlets in the United States.

In this decade, Oral spoke to more than eight million people, preaching in tent meetings and on radio and television programs, and witnessing God's miraculous power in the lives of Pentecostal and non-Pentecostal people alike. Tens of thousands of people flocked to see the power of the Holy Spirit moving in Oral's meetings. He possessed an unusual anointing to preach, and the fruit of that anointing was thousands of salvations and countless healings by the power of God.

Healing Miracles

There was one thing Oral was certain of in the success of the healing ministry: All miracles come *from God alone*. One of the greatest early miracles that occurred was in Goldsboro, North Carolina, during a sixteen-day-crusade. Oral rented a B-29 hangar because it was the largest facility in the area. It would seat ten thousand people with room for a few thousand more to stand.

Oral Roberts loved it when his meetings were full. He often remarked that empty seats were a waste, for he "never saw an empty seat converted or healed!"[238] The first meeting in Goldsboro was filled to overflowing, and there was a sense of excitement in the place. However, as Oral walked onto the stage to greet the people, he knew immediately that the excitement was really a hostile curiosity. The people sat in their seats with their arms crossed, and their facial expressions showed disbelief. The buzz of excitement had nothing to do with faith in God's miracle-working power.

So many people in that hangar were doubting God's Word on healing that it was like a "force field of doubt" between Oral and the people. It would take a miracle of the Holy Spirit to break through and reach anyone for Christ. The Holy Spirit reminded Oral that the Word of God alone could break down that force of doubt and fear. Instinctively, Oral knew that the Word would have to be presented in a way that would cause the doubters to realize how real God still was. The faith of the people in that cavernous room could be set on fire by the Word of God!

Oral faced a crucial decision. Would he stand on the Word and the anointing of God to believe for saved souls and healed bodies? Or, would the hostile attitude of the people make Goldsboro a city lost to God's touch? Oral *knew* that the Word of God was true and wouldn't return to Him without accomplishing its purposes. (See Isaiah 55:11.) So, he boldly preached the full Word of God and believed that there would be a breakthrough with miraculous signs and wonders following.

"I Want to Run!"

It wasn't until the fifth night of the crusade that Oral saw the Holy Spirit break through the people's hostility. A mother and her twelve-year-old son, who wore an extended leg brace on his right leg and used crutches, came through the healing line. As they approached, the Holy Spirit stirred inside of Oral. The excitement of God grew, and, in his heart, he knew "a mighty healing was about to happen!"[239]

The young boy's name was Douglass Sutton. He and his mother approached Oral with a faith that shone on their faces. They had not been intimidated by the lack of belief in that room. They had heard the Word of God, and they believed that He could do what His Word said.

As Oral touched the boy with his right hand, he spoke two words: "Jesus, heal!" Immediately, the presence of God moved down Oral's arm and through his right hand into that boy's hip bone. God was at work

Oral Roberts and a boy with the crutches he once used

to heal that night! Oral asked the mother and then the son, "Do you be-lieve God has healed this hip?" They both responded with a resounding, "Yes!"

Oral would always ask questions so that those being healed could proclaim their faith in God's miraculous power at work. He asked that young mother what she wanted her son to do, and she responded by tak-ing off his leg brace. When Oral asked Douglass what *he* wanted to do, Douglass replied, "I want to run!"[240] His mother nodded with a smile, and that young boy began running down the long hangar aisle!

In an instant, the current in the room changed completely. Men and women began singing the praises of God while tears ran down their fac-es. Oral himself cried as the power of God moved among the people of Goldsboro. When Douglass ran back to hug his mother, she touched his hip and could feel the complete restoration God had done to that bone. That set off another round of glory shouting at the goodness and mercy of God to heal.

For over fifteen minutes, the people cried out in thanks to the Lord, and there was no stopping them! How everything in that place had changed! God had been faithful to His Word.

Night after night, until the crusade ended, people came forward to receive salvation for their souls and healing for their physical bodies. Local newspapers and radio stations covered the remaining days of the crusade with reports of God's power moving in eastern North Carolina. During the final service, over twenty-five thousand people gathered in-side and outside of that hangar waiting on the glory of God. With the strength of the Holy Spirit, Oral personally laid hands on ten thousand sick people that afternoon, praying with the faith to believe God for the miraculous.

"I'm Moving to My Mother's!"

Discovering the biblical secret of sowing and reaping, which Oral called "the miracle of seed-faith," will be a lasting legacy of his ministry. His discovery came in a very natural way, born out of his own need, as well as the need of one of his church members in his early ministry in Enid, Oklahoma.

When Oral and his family had first arrived at the church in Enid, they had discovered that there was no parsonage. Oral, Evelyn, and their children were to stay with a family from the church in a rather small home. As the weeks wore on, and they still had no place of their own, the usually easygoing Evelyn threatened to take the children and move in with her mother until something was done about their living conditions. "I'm serious, Oral, I'm moving to my mother's!"[241]

That Wednesday night, Oral went alone to the evening church service. After the message, he explained to the congregation the desperate need for a church parsonage. Oral felt the Holy Spirit impress him to donate his entire week's salary—$55—in faith for a down payment on that parsonage. He plunked his paycheck down on the altar and then turned to face the congregation. "Who else would like to help?" he asked. To his amazement, nearly every person in the congregation walked forward enthusiastically and laid money on the altar. When the money was counted, the amount was enough for the entire down payment.

Evelyn wasn't very happy with Oral's donating his entire week's salary, since it was supposed to have been used to pay for their groceries and other needs. Had he done the right thing? Oral slept restlessly that night before he was awakened by a loud knock at the door at 4:30 a.m. Groggily, he opened the door to find a farmer who was a member of his congregation standing there with a concerned look on his face.[242]

What the man didn't know was that he was about to share an amazing biblical principle of sowing and reaping that would stay with Oral Roberts and his ministry for the next seventy years!

The Miracle of Seed-Faith

After apologizing for the early hour, the farmer, whose name was Art Newfield, explained the reason for the intrusion. Art was in trouble because he had been playing the stock market and was about to lose everything he had, including his farm. That night at church, Oral had given his last $55, and everyone else had come forward to give, but Art hadn't given anything out of fear because of his losses. Then, when he'd gone home, he hadn't been able to sleep. God had been speaking to him and hadn't let him go. Art had gone into his backyard and dug up the last of his money, $400 in all. That said, he thrust four one-hundred-dollar bills into Oral's hand.

> **Intrigued by the principle from God's Word, they stayed up the rest of the night reading the Scriptures on sowing and reaping, giving and receiving. Oral experienced a burst of joy with this fresh word from the Lord.**

It was then that the farmer spoke the words that Oral would never forget: "This is not just money I'm giving you, Pastor. *It is seed.* I'm a wheat farmer, and I know how to plant seed in order to have a wheat harvest. I'm sowing this seed to you as a man of God for the Lord to get me out of this trouble I'm in, so I can get back to farming, something I know how to do."[243]

After Art Newfield left, Oral showed Evelyn the money, and they rejoiced at the Lord's provision, which went far beyond their expectations. They were also humbled by the great need in Art's life and the magnitude of his faith. Intrigued by the principle from God's Word, they stayed up the rest of the night reading the Scriptures on sowing and reaping, giving and receiving. Oral experienced a burst of joy with this fresh word from the Lord—a principle of God's faithfulness.

God was encouraging Oral and Evelyn to give out of their need and then to expect the Lord of the harvest to multiply the seed sown, as well as to meet their needs in return. Their expectation was rooted in the place in the Bible where Jesus said, *"Give, and it shall be given unto you; good measure, pressed down, and shaken together, and running over, shall men give into your bosom"* (Luke 6:38). But it was the revelation of 3 John 2 that really opened Oral's eyes to the truth of seed-faith: *"Beloved, I wish above all things that thou mayest prosper and be in health, even as thy soul prospereth."* He claimed that Scripture was "the greatest discovery Evelyn and I ever made about health, prosperity, and spiritual blessings."[244]

From that experience and those Scriptures, Oral developed his teaching that would become known as "the miracle of seed-faith." With this

✶✶✶✶✶

life-changing revelation, Oral began to sow a seed of faith in every area of his life and then expect a miracle harvest from the Lord in return.

In Matthew 17:20, Jesus compared faith to a mustard seed, saying that such a small amount could move mountains. Oral believed that faith should be like a seed that is sown in order to reap a harvest in God. Growth and harvest are the purposes of sowing seed, as determined by the Creator. God doesn't expect us to sow a seed that will just die in the ground and never produce a harvest. His desire is that we plant seeds in faith in good soil, with the water of the Word and the sunshine of God's Holy Spirit. Those seeds will grow to produce the harvest of the Lord.

God Moves Mountains

God promises to move the mountains of our lives as we plant seeds of faith. Oral shared the teachings on seed-faith in the early years of his ministry during a crusade in Spokane, Washington. As he explained God's laws of planting and harvesting, an older gentleman named William Skrinde walked up to the altar with a donation and a pledge to support the ministry on a monthly basis. He didn't know how he would do it on Social Security, but he wanted to plant his seed in faith.

William prayed, "Lord, You promised to multiply it, so I'm going to do it, and I'm going to depend on You as my source to multiply it back."[245]

At the conclusion of that evening's service, Oral encouraged the people to go home and seek the Lord for the blessings that He might have already provided—things they might have missed. Oral said, "Look to God to give you ideas. Think about some idea that never came to fulfillment. Be expectant. Open your eyes. See what you've put away that you could turn into something."[246] That last statement surprised even Oral, but he was certain God had prompted him to say it.

William Skrinde went home, meditating on all that the Lord had said through Brother Oral. He had been an inventor for much of his life and remembered a project he had put away in his attic. Several years earlier, William had invented an instrument that he'd believed would help Jeeps with a wheel problem they were having. However, each time he had submitted his blueprints to Jeep for consideration, they had been rejected.

✯✯✯✯✯

William retrieved the blueprints from the attic, prayed over them, and made several adjustments to his designs. Trusting the Lord as his only true Source, William submitted the blueprints to Jeep once again. This time, they were accepted! In William's case, his answer from the Lord was not a small one. The company paid William Skrinde millions of dollars for his ideas.

Brother Skrinde would become one of the largest donors to the building of Oral Roberts University in future years. There are plaques on several buildings on the ORU campus with William Skrinde's name on them. He donated thousands of dollars to see the Word of the Lord go forth in the lives of young people. Seed-faith, my friends, works when we plant in faith and look to the God of the universe as the Source of our harvest.

There Is No Retirement in God

No one watched the successful crusades and miracles of Oral Roberts's evangelistic ministry more closely than Ellis and Claudius Roberts. They were delighted to see God's Spirit moving through their son's life. Ellis had worked hard during Oral's childhood to establish twelve different local congregations for the Pentecostal Holiness church. Unfortunately, by the end of the 1940s, there was little work left for Ellis to do, and he found himself without a place to minister.

Oral's oldest brother, Elmer, built a small house for his parents behind his own home, where they lived a rather bare existence. The fire of the Holy Spirit had never died out in their hearts, though, and they still ministered for the lord whenever the opportunity arose.

Oral longed to have his parents near him and his ministry in Tulsa. After a few years of successful crusades, Oral and Evelyn were able to build his parents a small home near them so that the elder Roberts could experience the excitement of the ministry and be near their grandchildren.

As Oral's ministry grew and his testimony became better known, churches began inquiring about his parents and their work for the Lord. Invitations addressed to Rev. Ellis Roberts and Sister Roberts came in from many churches in the Southwest asking them to conduct revivals. What a glorious way to spend their "retirement" years. Papa Roberts preached the Word of God, and Mama Roberts prayed for the healing of the sick with the same fiery faith that she had implanted in Oral's heart and soul as a boy.

For ten years, Papa and Mama Roberts preached in Pentecostal church revivals, often seeing two or three hundred people come to the Lord during a single crusade. They were loved and accepted wherever they were called, and their success brought immeasurable joy to Oral and Evelyn.

"Oral Roberts, Get Out of Australia!"

For reasons known only to God, trials are one of His greatest tools for maturing us in our faith.

My brethren, count it all joy when ye fall into divers temptations; knowing this, that the trying of your faith worketh patience. But let patience have her perfect work, that ye may be perfect and entire, wanting nothing.

(James 1:2–4)

After seeing God move miraculously in the lives of thousands of people, Oral faced one of his severest disappointments overseas. Many of the Pentecostal churches in Australia had been asking Oral to come to them for nearly two years. They wanted him to bring his tent so that they could experience the move of God the same way as it had been experienced in America. The large tent was shipped over to Australia for two crusades—one in Sidney, another in Melbourne. Oral reached out to his supporters for help with a new World Outreach campaign centered on the trip to Australia.

In spite of all the planning, excitement, and spiritual anticipation, from the moment that Oral Roberts and his staff stepped off of the ship in Sydney, they were greeted by a hostile Australian press. Each newspaper printed something more condemning than the one before. The Roberts ministry team was certain that it was a conspiracy by Satan to discredit Oral before the Lord could move.

Even though the bad press didn't diminish, the Sydney crusade was still a tremendous success. Oral's tent, which had been expanded to seat eighteen thousand people, was filled to capacity each night. Oral moved in the power of the Holy Spirit as he preached about God's goodness and power to save, deliver, and heal. During the eight-day crusade, thousands of people came forward for salvation, and many received healings as a result of their increased faith in God. However, when Oral and the team traveled to Melbourne for the second crusade, it was a startlingly different experience.

> **From the moment Oral walked into the tent on the first night, he could sense the people's hunger for God. He sensed a special love for the Lord among the people of Melbourne.**

The Melbourne crusade began on a Sunday and was scheduled to last eight days. From the moment Oral walked into the tent on the first night, he could sense the people's hunger for God. He sensed a special love for the Lord among the people of Melbourne. The first night, there was an overflowing crowd, and several hundred people came forward during the altar call. However, the next morning, the Melbourne press published articles that Oral called "anti-God, anti-Bible, and anti-America."[247] Surprised, Oral, Bob DeWeese, the sponsoring pastors, and the staff gathered to pray for God's anointing to continue for redeemed lives. They prayed and bound the enemy's forces over Melbourne.

The second night opened with another large and expectant crowd of worshippers. Suddenly, the service was disrupted by several hundred burly men from the local longshoremen's strike. They began spewing all the hateful words about Oral Roberts's ministry that they had read in the newspapers. With their own anger at the unresolved strike, the longshoremen were used as tools of destruction in Satan's hands. The riotous men ran down the aisles of the tent, cursing and yelling, then jumped onto the stage and slapped Oral Roberts.

Unbelievably, the Melbourne police officers who were stationed at various entrances in the tent stood there with their arms folded, not responding to the violence in any way. Later, Oral learned that there is no law in Australia protecting church services from outside disruptions.

The police hadn't been obligated to protect them! The service limped along to a conclusion that night.

After a day of intense prayer and agonizing discussions with the sponsoring pastors, Oral opened the meeting on the third night. Only one half of the seats were filled, and, once again, the longshoremen rushed into the tent, spewing the same ugly curses, ridiculing the people, and spitting on Oral. And still, the meeting proceeded through the time of healing.

The next day's press talked about the healing lines, ridiculing the concept of healing, and denying the testimonies of people who had been healed. The reporters would not even follow up with those who had testified of healings to judge if the accounts were true. Oral was certain that it was healing in the name of Jesus that had so inflamed the local press. The devil was working overtime to sow discouragement, fear, and dissension among the crusade-goers.

Protection in Jesus

With renewed determination, Oral Roberts opened the fourth night of the Melbourne crusade. The sponsoring pastors had invited a high-ranking leader in Melbourne to come to the crusade and persuade the rowdy men to stop their harassment. Not only did the longshoremen refuse to heed this leader, but they actually rushed the stage and spit on him. He was shocked and humiliated by their behavior. This time, the longshoremen broke up the service, refusing to allow it to continue to the end.

In anguish, Oral was rushed to a car to escape, while Evelyn was taken by some members to a different vehicle. Oral watched in horror as a group of men rocked the car that Evelyn was in, trying to overturn it. Thankfully, when they realized that Oral Roberts was not inside, they left the car alone. Oral's car sped down a side street and escaped harm's way.

The U.S. Embassy sent word to Bob DeWeese that it was no longer safe for Oral to stay in Melbourne; they could offer no protection to him and his family. While Oral slept at a pastor's house that night, his staff had the tent and all of the equipment packed up and loaded on the first ship leaving Melbourne's harbors. The next morning, they put Oral and Evelyn on a plane bound for the safety of home.

What Satan means for evil, God can always turn to good. In spite of the great anguish Oral experienced over the "failure" of the Australian crusades, the Lord did turn them into great good for Australia. The Christian churches there discovered that they had no protection under the law, and they lobbied for changes soon after the incident. A well-known Australian pastor spoke daily on his broadcasts about the event, exposing the unscrupulous behavior of the press.

One year later, when Billy Graham arrived in Australia for a crusade, he reported to Oral that great things had happened there since Oral's trip the year before. He knew Oral was still hurting from his Australian experience, so Billy sent him a telegram to say, "Dear Oral, I know that you had a difficult time here, yet for your encouragement I have met many people who were blessed through your God-anointed ministry."[248]

January 1956 had begun in a painful way in Australia, but God turned Oral's mourning into joy. During that year in America, nearly two million people attended Oral Roberts's crusades. The tent was filled to overflowing in every city where they ministered, and tens of thousands came to know Christ as Savior! God uses all things to bring glory to His name when we are faithful to His direction.

"Hollywood Preacher"

As the crusades of the 1950s grew in intensity, Oral's desire to see more people experience those crusades grew, as well. The mounting popularity and astounding potential of television fascinated him. Just like a "pioneer" in the wilds of early America, Oral was always looking for new lands to discover in his quest to spread God's healing Word.

In spite of the television professionals, who insisted that Oral could not televise his crusades successfully, he was determined to find a way. His friend, Pastor Rex Humbard, of Akron, Ohio, encouraged Oral that with God, this, too, was possible! Pastor Humbard had been the first pastor in the country to televise his church services.

Venturing into the unknown with confidence that God was with him, Oral launched his television ministry in 1954. He actually went into the movie studios—considered by most Christians at the time to be tools of Satan—and he applied what he learned to filming his tent meetings. During a crusade in Akron, Ohio, Oral paid over $42,000 to have three crusade services filmed. Wanting the full impact of the crusades to reach the people, Oral wasn't interested in broadcasting the sermons alone. He arranged to have the bustling of the huge audiences as they entered the tent, the altar call for salvation, the healing lines, the laying on of hands for the healing of the sick, and the actual miracles filmed for the entire nation to experience! Oral longed for the programs to communicate the excitement and power of God that was present in healing crusade meetings.

As an added benefit, television audiences experienced what most people in the crusades could not. Because the cameras captured close-ups of Oral, the television "congregation" could see his fervent expression and the sincerity with which he prayed for those in need around him. They also had the privilege of seeing thousands of people respond in faith to both the salvation message and the healing prayers. In this way, Oral Roberts extended his faith for God's healing power into the homes of millions of Americans.

> **Oral Roberts extended his faith for God's healing power into the homes of millions of Americans.**

Confirming God's word to Oral, healing testimonies began to pour in from the television audiences to his Tulsa headquarters. One of the most glorious was a testimony of the healing of the young, paralyzed wife of an army sergeant living in Wichita Falls, Texas.

Anna Williams was the young woman's name. Three tragic things had happened to result in her paralysis. First, in 1951, she broke her leg in an automobile accident; then, twenty months later, she was diagnosed with the dread disease polio. Finally, in 1953, she had a second serious diagnosis of what was termed "spinalitis," a crippling disease that paralyzed her from the waist down and confined her to a wheelchair.

On Sunday, May 1, 1955, Anna was sitting in her wheelchair beside her husband watching the Oral Roberts telecast of a crusade. Before the healing prayers began, Anna's faith for her own healing had been growing within her heart. When the time for prayer came, she could not place her hand on the television set as her point of contact to release her faith. So, she placed her hand over her heart instead, and she cried out to God to visit her in the room and heal her paralyzed legs.

Immediately after she prayed, Anna turned to her husband and asked him to help her stand up. Slowly, Anna began walking away from the brown leather wheelchair seat. She took tentative steps at first and then began taking more confident ones. As a smile spread across her face, tears streamed from her husband's eyes. Rejoicing, Anna called a friend to come to her house to see what the Lord had done. When the friend arrived, Anna borrowed her high heels and began to dance around her living room! She was healed that day!

Monday morning, May 2, the Wichita Falls, Texas, newspaper headlines read "Paralyzed, She Walks after Prayer!" The news quickly spread throughout the nation, being picked up by the national newswires and announced by Paul Harvey on his national broadcast. Faith for the miracle of healing grew in the nation; miracles were now occurring through the fledgling medium of television.

"I'm Supposed to Be Healed Today!"

"Suffer little children, and forbid them not, to come unto me," Jesus said in Matthew 19:14. Even young children had their faith for healing enlarged through Oral Roberts's television broadcasts. Willie Phelps was a young boy who had been afflicted at six years of age with Perthes disease, a flattening of the hip bone due to a lack of blood flow to the hip. From the time of his diagnosis until he was ten years old, Willie had worn a shoe with an extra two-and-a-half-inch heel and had used crutches. He often experienced pain because of the inflammation in his hip.

One evening, Willie and his mother were watching a televised Oral Roberts crusade. At the end of the program, Oral announced an upcoming crusade in Roanoke, Virginia. Willie turned to his mother with a certainty that comes only with childlike faith, and said, "Mom, if you take me to that meeting, I know I will be healed."[249]

After Willie's mother agreed to go, he simply responded, "Mom, when that meeting is over and I get healed, will you take me to get new shoes?" "Of course," replied his mother, with tears of hope streaming down her face.

Willie's father was a farmer who worked late into the afternoon. By the time they left for the crusade and drove forty miles to Roanoke, the family was too late to get inside the crusade and thus couldn't sign up for the healing time. The same thing happened to them each of the remaining evenings of the crusade—they stood outside to hear the message but couldn't get inside to receive the healing power.

On the final night of the crusade, Willie and his parents traveled the forty miles from their home, praying fervently that the Lord would open a way for them to get inside the prayer service. As they stood outside of the large building, unable to get in once again, an unusual thing occurred. An usher had noticed the little boy with crutches who had stood outside each evening, and he opened a side door, motioned the family in, and led them to a small room where they could watch the service.

Oral prayed for two or three thousand people to be healed that evening, touching each of them with his right hand. He left the service totally exhausted. As he walked down a back corridor to return to his hotel, Oral noticed a young boy sitting in a room with his head bowed and a pair of crutches on the floor beside him. Oral asked him what he was doing, and he replied that he was waiting for Oral Roberts.

"I'm Oral Roberts," Oral answered. "What do you want with Oral Roberts?"

"I'm supposed to be healed today!" the boy replied confidently.[250]

Oral was so exhausted that he hardly knew what to say. He explained that he had just prayed for thousands of people and that he didn't have the faith to pray for anyone else.

"I don't know about that, Mr. Roberts," the boy said. "I just know I'm supposed to be healed today."[251]

Seeing what great faith the boy had, Oral agreed to pray for him. But he told Willie that his faith would have to be strong because his own was so weak at that moment. Oral reached out and touched Willie Phelps, prayed a prayer for his healing, and then went back to his hotel. In his exhaustion, Oral was just hoping that the Lord would answer the prayer.

✦✦✦✦✦

It wasn't until one year later, when Oral and Evelyn went back to Roanoke for another crusade, that someone reintroduced Oral to little Willie Phelps. After hearing Willie's testimony of healing, Oral invited him onto the stage, where Willie shared about his miracle.

Following Oral's prayer that previous year, Willie had requested that his mother take his shoes off of his feet. He had put down his crutches and placed his bad foot on the floor. As Willie took a step, he realized that his bad leg, which had been shorter, was just as long as the other one. He walked across the room to his mother, then asked her, "When am I going to get those new shoes you promised me?"[252]

Willie went to school the Monday following the crusade and walked in without his crutches. When his astounded classmates and teacher asked him what had happened, Willie shared the power of a God who heals: "A preacher prayed for me, and God healed me!" he proclaimed.[253] The whole school rejoiced at the wonder of a God who still heals people today.

Oral and Evelyn kept in touch with Willie Phelps for many years. The last time they spoke with him, he was fifty years of age and was still well and whole.

Abundant Life in Christ

Although Oral's television ministry was popular from the beginning, there were two major challenges he faced in going on the air in the big-city markets. One was persuading television stations to carry a program with a theme as controversial as supernatural healing. The second challenge was convincing his financial partners to send in sufficient funds to pay for it. With Oral's astute business sense and arresting personality, though, both of these challenges were overcome. The ministry began with thirty-one stations in 1955, and, by 1957, the programs were airing on over 135 of the nation's five hundred television stations.

The gospel of Jesus Christ was moving through the television airwaves across the nation! Without leaving their living rooms, people were being touched by the message of Jesus Christ, and lives were being changed. Thousands of additional letters began to pour into the Oral

Roberts Evangelistic Association headquarters each day—letters filled with the testimonies of the saved, healed, and delivered.

As Oral's ministry outreach of the 1950s continued to expand, so did his main contact with his supporters. The monthly magazine *Healing Waters*, which Oral had begun in 1948 to explain the importance of God's healing power today, continued to attract more readers. As Oral's television ministry began to expand beyond the subject of healing alone, he changed the name of the magazine to *Abundant Life*. From 1950 to 1956, the number of subscribers jumped from ten thousand to one million. *Abundant Life* provided the strongest lifeline between Oral Roberts and the contributors on whom he depended for both prayers and financial support. These same supporters would be greatly needed for Oral's next mandate.

"Build Me a University"

"You are to build Me a university. Build it on My authority and on the Holy Spirit." Build God a university. Of all the things that Oral Roberts had pioneered or presented as God's direction for him, none seemed more overwhelming than this one. Oral Roberts, the Oklahoma farm boy without a college or seminary degree, was to build God a university?

Oral believed he first heard this word from the Lord in the backseat of the car the night he was healed of tuberculosis as a seventeen-year-old. The first part of the word—bringing healing to his generation—made sense to Oral. The second part—building a university—he had hidden in his heart, unsure of what God meant by such a statement. Now, in the 1960s, as the tent ministry and healing evangelism movement appeared to be waning, Oral turned his attention to God's next move in his life.

By the time 1960 had arrived, the crowds at the healing crusades were becoming smaller. Oral felt the stirring in his heart to move into another area to reach the world with Christ's message of healing.

How did God want him to extend his worldwide passion for the Word and the power of the Holy Spirit even further than his ten ministries could reach? How would he pass the power of God's Word to the next generation even after he was gone? Oral began to reflect on God's word to him from years before: "Build Me a university."

✴✴✴✴✴

Dinner with Pat Robertson

One night in 1952, Oral Roberts was driving around Tulsa, Oklahoma, and pulled his car up to a piece of property on the corner of 81st Street and South Lewis Avenue. Helping his children out of the car one at a time, Oral stood with them and Evelyn. In wonder, the children looked up at their father. What were they doing standing in front of this empty lot?

Oral said, "Children, we are going to pray. I believe someday the Lord wants a school on this property that will be dedicated to Him."[254] The family prayed and then drove away, leaving the outcome in the Lord's hands. It wouldn't be the last time that the Roberts family would lift this piece of property to the Lord in prayer.

Eight years later, Oral was eating dinner with Pat Robertson of *The 700 Club* in a restaurant in Norfolk, Virginia. As they discussed the move of the Holy Spirit on the earth, Oral began to write down words on a napkin as they came to him. The theme concerned educating the young people of the future, training them to bring forth the good news of Jesus Christ.

What Oral scratched down on that napkin in the restaurant later became a resounding theme to all the students who entered Oral Roberts University in years to come:

Raise up My students to hear My voice, to go where My light is dim, where My voice is small and My healing power is not known. To go even to the uttermost bounds of the earth. Their work will exceed yours. In this, I am well-pleased.[255]

Oral didn't believe that these words came from him. They were a message from the Lord, and the time had come to consider building a school. Oral realized that a school would be the key to "perpetuate my ministry and multiply it thousands of times, a ministry that otherwise would die."[256] It would be a school where ministers of the gospel would be trained to go out to the whole earth in the name of Jesus Christ.

"This Is Not Your Calling"

When Oral first announced his plans to build a university under God's direction, his associates were shocked and worried. Given his

✶✶✶✶✶

full-time ministry of traveling, preaching, and bringing healing to others, there weren't many people who could understand why he would ever pursue such a radically different vision. Even his closest aides were filled with concern. At first, they dismissed it as one of Oral's many brainstorms. Later, they called him into a meeting where they expressed their great concern that he was leaving his "true calling."

Manford Engel, executive vice president of Oral Roberts Evangelistic Association, was the group's spokesman. He said, "Oral, each of us has left our profession to serve with you in taking God's healing power to your generation. We feel that building this university will stop the flow of healing. Also, there will be no place for us....If you persist in building the university, all of us have decided to leave."[257] Oral was hurt that these men who had served so closely with him did not understand his new vision. He explained one more time that his desire regarding the university was to expand the healing concept to include the "whole man"—his mind and his emotions, as well as his physical body.

Then, he spoke words that were as painful for him to say as they were for his fellow workers to hear:

God Himself called me to build Him a university on His authority and the Holy Spirit. I am not leaving the healing ministry; it is my life. But God does not operate in a vacuum. He is constantly moving forward, and I have learned that we must move with God. I have to obey God and start building Him a university, permeating every part of it with the divine principle that God is a healing God. I may fall on my face. I may fail. It may never fly, but I have to do it. If you leave me, it will break my heart. However, if I obey God, as I intend to do, He will raise up another team to serve with me.[258]

With great sadness, Oral left the room to pray. The team he'd left behind got on their faces to pray for God's direction, as well. After several hours, they met again in Manford's office. The men told Oral that they understood it was God's call for him to build the university—a newer, broader facet of the Oral Roberts evangelistic ministry. They announced to Oral, "We're not leaving. You lead, and we'll follow."[259] With the misunderstandings behind them, this team of "God's men" moved forward with an exciting new plan to build "God's university."

"This Is the Day"

It was the fall of 1961. For nine years, Oral and his family had prayed for the land on the corner of 81st Street and South Lewis Avenue. Oral believed in his spirit that it was the spot God had chosen for the university to stand. Five hundred dollars of seed money was all that Oral had at the time. Often, he would drive out and walk the land, praying in tongues and asking the Lord what to do and who to work with. He could picture tall, graceful buildings filled with students who wanted to bring honor to the Lord and spread His Word.

However, when Oral's lawyer, Saul Yager, approached the property owners, they insisted that it was not for sale. They were a rich, oil family who had owned the corner acreage for years, and they wanted to keep it in their holdings. The attempts to purchase the property dragged on for weeks.

Oral continued to pray and wait. One day, while in California, Oral sensed the Lord's voice say, *This is the day.* He could see the land in Tulsa in his mind—the buildings that would soon make up the campus, the students eagerly searching for the Lord's answers to their life quests, the young people sharing the gospel of Jesus Christ.

He called Saul. "Go today and buy that land." Impatiently, Saul insisted that Oral was wasting his time. But Oral replied, "I'm telling you, Saul, I know today is the day. Buy it today."[260] Saul got off the phone and called the owner's attorney, who, like Saul, was of the Jewish faith. Saul explained Oral's insistence that today the owner would want to sell the land.

The second attorney contacted the owner, and his response marveled them all. "I woke up this morning and decided that if Mr. Roberts's lawyer approached me today, I would sell."[261] The attorneys were amazed at the way God had worked in the situation. Oral was thankful to the Lord, but not surprised by His unfailing faithfulness.

Oral's Vision Becomes Personal

Oral's original vision for the school was to build a university of evangelism primarily to bring young, foreign nationals to the United States and train them to go back to their own nations and preach the gospel. In February 1962, construction began on three buildings that would house the evangelistic school. However, by the summer, Oral's vision had expanded to building a fully accredited university with a wide range of academic programs.

Whenever Oral suddenly changed direction, there was always some tension among his team members. After he and his team had ironed out their differences, they came up with a unified plan. They would build a full university by 1965, dedicated to excellence in academics under the guidance and presence of the Holy Spirit.

One personal reason why the university became such a growing vision in Oral's heart was the great need he saw for Christ-centered education in his own home. Oral's oldest son, Ronnie, had enrolled at Stanford University in California in the fall of 1962. Ronnie was academically gifted, and Oral and Evelyn were proud of his accomplishments. His desire was to be fluent in several languages, and his acceptance to Stanford was a source of family pride.

However, it wasn't long after arriving at Stanford that Ronnie began to question his Christian belief system and the personal relationship that he had with Jesus Christ. Oral made a trip to Stanford and was invited to speak to the student body. He was well-received, and that helped Ronnie for a little while, but the questions and doubts slowly cropped up again.

Oral explained to his evangelistic team, "I get this fighting instinct to get this school going sooner than we intend because it has come home; it's in my family. This is affecting my family."[262] Oral saw many young Pentecostals leaving the faith as he had once done because they were going to universities

> **Oral saw many young Pentecostals leaving the faith as he had once done because they were going to universities where God was not lifted up or even believed in. His answer was to build a major "class A" university where God was supreme.**

where God was not lifted up or even believed in. His answer was to build a major "class A" university where God was supreme, Jesus was Lord, and the Holy Spirit's work and power in the world were given their rightful places.

A Band of Brothers

What did Oral Roberts know about actually building a university? He knew he needed a man with an academic vision who shared his own fervor about the Holy Spirit's role in the Christian life. He found that person in a boyhood friend, Raymond Corvin. Raymond was a member of the Pentecostal Holiness church and had served as president of the Southwestern Bible College for the previous sixteen years. His credentials were sound for the job, as he held a doctorate in religious education and had also earned a second doctorate in general education. In Raymond Corvin, Oral had found a kindred soul to work with him on his vision of excellence in education.

The university could not be formally established until a board of regents was appointed. Oral and his group of advisers began to formulate a forty-one-member board of dedicated and Spirit-filled leaders from around the country. Lee Braxton became the obvious choice as head of the board, with Oral as president of the university and Raymond Corvin as chancellor.

Lee felt it was essential that the university be named after Oral Roberts. His name had become a "symbol" to the Pentecostal and charismatic supporters whose children would probably be the first university students. Of even greater importance, Oral's name would help to insure the continued financial support of the thousands of believers who had been touched by his ministry for so many years. On November 27, 1962, Oral Roberts University was formally established, with the goal of opening its doors to students in just three short years, the fall of 1965.

Lee Braxton was invaluable in helping to establish Oral's vision. Braxton brought another vital university leader to the school, Dr. John D. Messick, the former president of East Carolina College in North Carolina. With his Ph.D. from New York University, his years of experience in education, his ability to think innovatively, and his firm belief in the baptism of the Holy Spirit, John Messick became the perfect man to design the rigorous academic program for Oral Roberts University.

A School for the Whole Man

The longer Oral Roberts prayed and meditated on his vision for the school, the more his focus expanded to include the "whole man." Oral's first priority was to train evangelists to spread the good news of Jesus Christ throughout the earth. His desire was for students to be filled with the Holy Spirit and to understand the power that God gives to accomplish great things through the Holy Spirit in Jesus' name.

Oral and his team developed eight major goals for the university in the months before the school opened. Those goals were: "education excellence, a climate of positive faith in God, an atmosphere of the Holy Spirit, spiritual and moral purity, a search for truth, a permanent projection of the healing ministry, in-residence exposure, and no worthy student denied for lack of finances."[263]

Oral Roberts University

In the university's early years, Oral looked for ways to involve the whole man in the students' education. The students had their academic classes, mandatory chapel, and a required physical fitness program that emphasized the importance of taking care of their bodies, "God's temples of the Holy Spirit."

★★★★★
213

Oral was tremendously proud that the emphasis on strong academics would raise the level of education at ORU beyond anything attempted by the Pentecostal schools of the past. In all of these important areas, nothing was as important to Oral as the spiritual purpose of the university. He fought continually to protect the vision that was ORU's purpose for existence. "ORU was never intended to be purely an educational institution, but a tool, an instrument, for the higher purposes of our calling."[264]

In later years, Oral explained the success in building the university when they had no real understanding of how an institution of learning should be developed with these words: "By the Holy Spirit, I was given an understanding beyond myself that the central core of all we offered at ORU was to be wrapped around the fact that all truth was in Jesus Christ. He was to be the center of the university....We did not have to look outside Him for the truth."[265] When the first university catalog was printed, it stated firmly, "ORU is a Christian institution with the distinctive charismatic dimension of the baptism with the Holy Spirit and the gifts of the Spirit."[266]

Buildings beyond Belief

Most people probably would have envisioned a small group of efficient but inconsequential buildings on this new Tulsa campus. But Oral Roberts was the same man who, even when he had nothing, believed that only the best piano, best organ, and best sound system were suited for the Lord's work in the tent ministry days. Oral used that same standard of excellence in planning the buildings that would house God's work at Oral Roberts University.

Of all the adjectives one could use to describe Oral Roberts, *innovative* would be near the top of the list. In everything he did through his years of ministry, being creative and thinking outside the box were essential parts of the story. Thinking along this creative vein, Oral hired architect Frank Wallace to design and erect a spectacular series of buildings on the ORU campus. The central structure in the first stage of construction was the Learning Resources Center, a six-story building with nearly four acres of floor space. The ORU library was located in this building, as were the first classrooms and administrative offices.

Oral had an amazing ability to look toward the future when designing anything for his ministry. Just as Oral had visited Hollywood to learn about the best methods before designing his television programs, he visited several major universities with Wallace and other team members, looking for cutting-edge building innovations. As a result, the interior of the Learning Resource Center was designed with curriculum innovation in mind and was wired to facilitate the latest electronic media of the time. In 1965, the design of the Learning Resources Center brought ORU national and international attention, with the Ford Foundation naming the center "the most innovative facility of its kind."[267]

> **Oral had an amazing ability to look toward the future when designing anything for his ministry.**

Prayer Is at the Heart

Nothing that Oral has ever attempted in his life has been without controversy. The newest ORU controversy was focused on the Prayer Tower built at the center of the Oral Roberts University campus. The two-hundred-foot building was designed to be the school's focal point, located in a sunken garden at the center of the campus. Made out of glass and steel, the building resembled a giant cross. When lit, the gas flame on the top of the tower could be seen for miles around the Tulsa landscape.

There were academic administrators who objected to the building, saying that a place of prayer should not be so obviously displayed on campus. For Oral, the Prayer Tower was the heart of the ministry, as well as the heart of the campus. There was a circular observation deck on top where the prayer team could look out over the campus and pray for the work of the Holy Spirit in the lives of the students, the faculty and their families. Prayer to a God who hears and answers His people was at the center of the university's purpose for existence, and Oral intended for it to remain at the center of ORU forever.

In the building years, from 1965–1975, the Oral Roberts University campus expanded to include the Mabee Center, a state-of-the-art sports arena for the ORU basketball team. The Mabee Center was also opened to the Tulsa community to hold special events, and it provided a stage for the performing arts. Oral was deeply committed to giving something of value back to the city of Tulsa for the kindness extended to him and his ministry over the years. In the early 1970s, several high-rise dormitories were added to the campus, as well as additional classrooms to accommodate the more than two thousand students who were enrolled by 1972.

One of the most beautiful buildings on campus, Christ's Chapel, was built with a sanctuary large enough for the entire faculty and staff of over two thousand to be seated together at a chapel service or a special event. Later, it was expanded to seat over four thousand people. Many celebrated and dedicated men and women of God have shared their hearts and ministries in that chapel, including Kenneth Hagin, Kathryn Kuhlman, Corrie ten Boom, and Billy Graham.

In the course of nine years, the campus became awe-inspiring. At the time, the *Chronicle of Higher Education* wrote, "The campus itself is an impressive, $60-million collection of futuristic buildings in one of Tulsa's classiest suburbs. It ranks as one of the city's most popular tourist attractions."[268] Oral believed that the accomplishment was because of the Holy Spirit's gift of "the working of miracles." He was convinced that the beautiful campus was a result of the Holy Spirit's miracle-working power. They had started ORU *with* nothing and *from* nothing, yet, there it stood before them. For many years, the ORU campus would be the top tourist attraction in the state of Oklahoma, outpacing even the Oklahoma Rodeo for the reservation of rental cars and hotel rooms.

Dedicated to the Lord Forever

Oral Roberts woke up on the morning on April 2, 1967, knowing that the God of the Bible was truly the God of the impossible. On that beautiful, spring afternoon in Tulsa, Oklahoma, Oral Roberts University was to be formally dedicated. It had been built by the power of God's Word and the unswerving belief of Oral, his team, and his tens of thousands of supporters that *"with God all things are possible"* (Matthew 19:26). It was a university built with Holy Spirit inspiration that recognized the Spirit as the miracle-working power of God, dwelling on the earth.

As Oral walked across the university campus that day, he was overwhelmed by the beautiful buildings of glass and steel that rose all around him, a testimony of God's faithfulness to His promises. He was grateful for the supporters who had captured the vision and worked with him to see this day come to pass. And he was humbled by the men and women who would be with him later that day to dedicate the university to the Lord. He was particularly humbled by Billy Graham's enthusiastic agreement to speak at the dedication ceremony.

When Oral and Billy had attended the World Congress on Evangelism in Berlin in the fall of 1966, Oral had asked Billy if he would assist him in dedicating the new Christian university the following spring. Despite the negative counsel of his closest advisers, Billy welcomed the opportunity to stand with Oral on the platform and dedicate the school and its students to God's purposes for them. Billy was not afraid of public opinion; his desire was to see the Word of God prosper in this new educational institution.

Billy Graham spoke that historic day on "Why I Believe in Christian Education." He recalled the early Christian founders of America's greatest universities—ones that had long since deserted their biblical roots. He commended Oral Roberts and his staff for building a school that would honor the Lord Jesus Christ without apology. Billy thanked God that "here at Oral Roberts University, these young people are being taught not only how to make a living, but how to live."[269] Then, Billy challenged Oral "to remember the university's founding, to savor it, and to protect it."[270]

The generous support of Billy Graham benefited the image of the young university. In an interview later that day, Billy Graham affirmed that Oral was on "the right track in making the university deeply spiritual and biblical, but at the same time the very highest in academics."[271] No longer was the school considered necessary or valuable only by Pentecostal believers. Oral Roberts and Billy Graham had stood side by side on a platform once again and announced to the world that this was an institution where all who believed in Christ's saving power were invited to learn and grow.

Decade of Change

What a tumultuous time the 1960s were in America with the Vietnam War, political unrest, and student protests. The decade brought times of great change to the country—and to the church, as well. During this time, as the Pentecostal influence through healing crusades began to fade, a new movement of the Holy Spirit, called the "charismatic movement" by many, began to pervade mainstream Protestant and Catholic churches. At the same time that the baptism of the Holy Spirit and speaking in tongues were being embraced by some Christians in almost every denomination, attendance at the Pentecostal crusades where these beliefs were preached was receding.

Oral Roberts's heart was still in preaching and praying for healing. Still, as the number of people in attendance diminished, the crusades were shortened to six days and then eventually to three days. Many times, his tent was left in Tulsa, and the crusades were held in large auditoriums to save both time and money. For the Oral Roberts Evangelistic Association, even though the attendance numbers were smaller, the Word was still going forth; Bob DeWeese was still preaching during the daytime sessions, and people were coming forth for healing prayer in the evening services.

To continue to preach to capacity crowds, many Pentecostal evangelists, including Oral, began to travel overseas to find new audiences for their messages. Oral committed to one overseas crusade a year, telling his partners that there was still much to be done to bring the healing message to the millions of people outside the United States. During the 1960s, Oral and his team traveled to cities in Europe, Russia, India, Indonesia, Australia, New Zealand, Vietnam, Chile, and Brazil. In most of those nations, he was welcomed warmly, and the gospel was received with open ears and hearts.

As late as 1968, Oral was still declaring that he longed to continue to lay hands on the sick and see them recover. At the same time, his spirit was stirring within him that God had something different for him to do, and he sensed it from the center of his being. The university was moving forward strongly, but what else was brooding in Oral's spirit?

The Year of Upheaval

Nineteen sixty-eight has been branded the year of greatest upheaval and change in the decade of the 1960s. The same could be said for the ministry of Oral Roberts. It was a "midlife crisis" year of great proportions. During those twelve months, Oral finally came to the realization that it was time to end the crusades. The Lord had made it painfully obvious to him that his years of tent ministry were finished. It was heartbreaking news for most of his evangelistic team. After thirty-eight years of close ministry, Bob DeWeese cried at the news and left the Oral Roberts Evangelistic Association to pastor a Pentecostal church in Ohio for several years. He returned to the ORU ministry some time later and remained one of Oral's closest friends.

Changes were afoot at the university in 1968, as well. John Messick, as executive vice president of ORU, had been instrumental in setting up the school's academic programs, but he continually fought with Oral. In Messick's personal crusade to keep the academics strenuous, he tried repeatedly to deemphasize the spiritual emphasis of the university's mission. Finally, the men came to a mutual decision that it was time for Messick to leave. He was succeeded by Carl Hamilton, a young man who shared Oral's belief that the spiritual undergirding of the school should be just as strong as the academic one.

At the same time, there was a different kind of dissension between Oral and his longtime friend Raymond Corvin, the university's chancellor. Corvin had been a key figure in the School of Theology and all of the spiritual aspects of ORU. As a dogmatic Pentecostal, Raymond had little use for the more inclusive spiritual direction in which the school was moving. As the student population grew, more professors were hired who did not have the same Pentecostal backgrounds as the earlier instructors. The new professors were often part of the up-and-coming charismatic movement or were members of mainline evangelical Protestant churches. Corvin fought the changes vehemently. By the end of 1968, he had also offered his resignation as a way to end the internal conflict of the university's administrative team.

Oral Goes Methodist

A final, shocking change of 1968 set the Pentecostal world abuzz. Oral Roberts, after a time of great prayer, as he assured his supporters, resigned his ministerial position in the Pentecostal Holiness denomination and joined the Methodist church, receiving ordination as a ministry within the mainstream denomination. What a stir reverberated through the Pentecostal community! What had this favorite son of the Pentecostal church done?

As a young boy, Oral Roberts had joined the Methodist church. When his family's passion for Christ had grown, they had joined the Pentecostal Holiness church, where Oral's father had become an ordained minister. The Pentecostal Holiness church actually had strong historic ties to the Methodist church when the move of the Holy Spirit had been accepted in the denomination. Oral could claim simply to be returning to the church of his youth. But so much more was at stake in his shocking and controversial decision.

For some time, Oral had felt restrained by certain theological positions of the Pentecostal church. The list of don'ts made it difficult for him to present the gospel in more acceptable cultural terms, such as through his new television specials. The Pentecostal Holiness ties also made it increasingly difficult to accept professors and students at ORU who had backgrounds in denominations other than Pentecostalism.

A few years earlier, Evelyn had begun to attend the Boston Avenue Methodist Church in Tulsa, participating in the women's ministry whenever she had the opportunity. Oral had attended at times and had become friends with Dr. Finis Crutchfield, the church's influential pastor. The men had discussed the possibility of Oral's changing his ordination to the Methodist church.

In the meantime, Oral and Evelyn, understanding the powerful impact this decision would have on the Pentecostal church, prayed for the Lord to direct them to the right decision. At the World Evangelism Conference two years earlier, Oral had seen the mainstream denominations opening up to the message of the Holy Spirit's power.

Possibly the most striking influence in his decision was the charismatic movement, which was in full swing across the denominations of America. Christians across the nation were embracing the baptism of the Holy Spirit, including speaking in tongues and the gifts of the Holy Spirit. Oral saw the Methodist church as one of the most open denominations to this move of God.

Oral had a meeting with Bishop W. Angie Smith, who presided over the Oklahoma Conference of the Methodist church. With an open heart to how God was moving through the Holy Spirit, the bishop said to Oral, "We need you, but we need the Holy Spirit more than we need you, and we've got to have the Holy Spirit in the Methodist church."[272] Oral saw that statement as an acceptance of him and his ministry by the Methodist clergy. On March 17, 1968, Oral and Evelyn joined the Boston Avenue Methodist Church in Tulsa. Two months later, Oral was ordained as an elder of the Methodist church.

The Robertses' decision sent shock waves through the Pentecostal church, even among some of their closest friends. When Mama Roberts heard about it, she thought Oral had lost his mind and demanded to speak to him on the phone immediately. After he reassured her that his decision had been made after much prayer, and that it had come to him directly from the Lord, Mama Roberts relaxed and set her faith in her son's ability to hear God's will for his life.

Many of Oral's Pentecostal supporters were not nearly as generous in their reactions. Feeling rejected by the man who had been their champion, they wrote hurt-filled letters, withdrawing their prayers *and* financial support. They had helped him to build the university of his dreams and to take the message of Holy Spirit power around the world, and he had "deserted" them. For a time, the ministry lost as much as one half of its Pentecostal financial supporters.

Oral wanted to be kind and not to strike back at the protesters and the reporters who questioned him. He wrote many letters explaining his love for the Lord and his certainty that this was God's direction for his life. In the end, Oral's response was, "I have become a Methodist because it was the will of God."[273]

The Electronic Church Is Born

Ever a trailblazer, Oral began to contemplate new ways to reach the millions of unchurched people who had never heard the full

> By 1968, millions more American homes had TVs, and Oral was certain it was time to use that avenue to reach them.

gospel of Jesus Christ. He had cancelled his televised tent meetings in 1965, but, by 1968, millions more American homes had TVs, and Oral was certain it was time to use that avenue to reach them again.

As the crowds at the crusades dwindled, Oral talked more about reaching out to the television audiences. He was excited about the new awareness of the Holy Spirit's power that accompanied the charismatic movement and sensed that the country would be open to a Christian television program that promoted Jesus Christ in a more contemporary fashion.

When complaints came from team members or ministry support-ers about the "Hollywood" use of television to spread the gospel, Oral reminded each critic, "We have to go where the people are, because they are not coming where we are."[274] It was much like the apostle Paul de-scribing how he preached to different audiences:

> *And unto the Jews I became as a Jew, that I might gain the Jews; to them that are under the law, as under the law, that I might gain them that are under the law; to them that are without law, as without law, (being not without law to God, but under the law to Christ,) that I might gain them that are without law. To the weak became I as weak, that I might gain the weak: I am made all things to all men, that I might by all means save some.* (1 Corinthians 9:20–22)

In Athens, when a group of philosophers brought Paul to the Ar-eopagus and invited him to speak, instead of referencing the unknown Old Testament, he referenced all the idols they had built to various gods. Specifically, he said, *"For as I passed by, and beheld your devotions, I found an altar with this inscription, TO THE UNKNOWN GOD. Whom therefore ye ignorantly worship, him declare I unto you"* (Acts 17:23). Paul was not afraid to use the contemporary culture around him in order to share the gospel.

Oral Roberts wrote to his supporters in *Abundant Life* about his un-changing principles of walking with Jesus Christ—principles of truth that would never change in his heart or ministry. However, he reminded them that the methods to reach people for Christ are different from the principles. Over and over, he proclaimed, "I am married to the *principles*; I am not married to the *methods*."[275] Oral moved forward with his new television plans, continually looking for the best ways to reach people for Jesus.

Ralph Carmichael was the foremost expert on prime-time specials in the late 1960s, and Oral contacted him with a plan to produce several prime-time specials on the major networks that would reach a younger audience for Jesus. Oral would present the gospel with a short "sermon," but the main messengers would be the World Action Singers, gifted music students from ORU. Oral's youngest son, Richard, and his wife, Patti, would be featured singers on the program, as well. Carmichael was delighted to have the opportunity to present the gospel and bring clean entertainment to the audiences.

In the first two years of the specials, featured celebrities included Pat Boone, Anita Bryant, Dale Evans, the Lennon Sisters, Jerry Lewis, and Johnny Cash. After the initial protest of some Pentecostal supporters, who accused Oral of selling out to Hollywood, the programs were met with great success and increased his support base to nearly one million people.

Soon, Richard and Patti became celebrity singers known around the country as a result of the successful shows. They sang and performed around the nation and were lauded as the perfect, young Christian couple by many people in the audiences.

A National Celebrity

For Oral Roberts and the evangelistic association, the first half of the 1970s was full of miracles and abundant living. The prime-time television programs made Oral Roberts a national celebrity, accepted by Americans as a Christian minister to whom they could easily relate. The clean-cut image of the World Action Singers was much more pleasant for audiences to watch than the constant barrage of rebellious youth seen on so many national news programs.

At NBC, where the prime-time specials were produced, Oral became a star. His successful shows led to his appearance on shows hosted by Dick Cavett, Dinah Shore, Mike Douglas, and Johnny Carson. Oral also appeared on a Jerry Lewis telethon and was interviewed by Barbara Walters on *Today*. Oral was open and charming during his interviews

Oral Roberts hosted several network television specials.

by all of these celebrities. While he admitted the mistakes of some of his early methods, he stuck firmly by his belief that God still heals today, and that He heals as an answer to our prayers.

Oral found himself in a whirlwind of activity. He was traveling and preaching, producing a series of successful television shows, administrating a growing university, and editing *Abundant Life* magazine. Oral Roberts had gone from being a tent evangelist full of controversy on the fringe of Pentecostalism to becoming a university president and a television personality. The religion editor of the *New York Times* wrote a complimentary article describing Oral's change in ministry, saying, "Oral has, as it were, gone straight—and made it to the big time. The tent was folded in 1968 and replaced by a television studio."[276]

Through all of this activity, Oral continued to seek God's will for Oral Roberts University. In addition to his other ministry activities, Oral could be seen on ORU's campus, interacting with students in the activities center, inviting groups of students into his home to meet with him and Evelyn, and speaking an inspiring word at the weekly chapels.

The World Turns Upside Down

From the day that Oral and Evelyn's first child, Rebecca, was born, she was a source of joy to them and their family. She grew up in the limelight and, while a little irritated with all the attention at times, accepted her father's role in international ministry. Rebecca went to college for two years at her parents' insistence but really just wanted to work in the offices at Oral Roberts Evangelistic Association.

Rebecca entered Oral's world of ministry with eagerness. She brought her enthusiastic love of the Lord and her knowledge of her father's passionate heart to every job assigned to her in the front office. Her zest for the Lord did not escape the notice of a handsome young man who was handling the printing work in Oral's office.

Marshall Nash was the son of a Pentecostal Holiness superintendent from Georgia who had known the Roberts family for years. When Marshall came to Tulsa to work for Oral, it was with the understanding that he would help with the business side of the ministry. Marshall loved the Lord and was blessed with a quiet, steady personality and keen business insight.

Rebecca and Marshall fell in love from the first days of their working in the office together. They were married on the Robertses' front lawn in Tulsa and began their life together. With a real passion for business, Marshall left the ministry to work in real-estate development. He built a wonderful relationship with the Tulsa realty community, and his intuitive business sense paved the way for a prosperous career in real estate. By the time they celebrated their tenth anniversary, the couple had become millionaires. Rebecca rejoiced in the birth of their three children and remained deeply in love with her husband.

Coping with Grief

The morning of February 12, 1977, began like any other. Oral and Evelyn were home getting a little rest from their busy television schedule. Early in the morning, Collins Steele, Oral's administrative assistant, arrived at the door of their home in tears. "I have some bad news. Marshall and Rebecca died last night in a plane crash over the Kansas wheat fields on their way to Tulsa. I'm so sorry."[277] The Nashes had spent a few days in Aspen, Colorado, and had been flying home in a private airplane with friends.

God is a God of goodness and mercy, but in this world, we can experience great tribulation, as well. And, sometimes, it seems as if the world is crumbling around us. Only a steadfast faith in the God of the universe will keep us going. As Oral and Evelyn clung to each other, Oral prayed

✭✭✭✭✭

in the Spirit. Quietly, he whispered to Evelyn the words of assurance that God gave him: "God knows something about this we don't know."[278] As Oral and Evelyn rode over to Marshall and Rebecca's home to give the heartbreaking news to their children, they repeated God's word over and over and held on to His mercy.

How do you tell three children between the ages of five and thirteen that their dear parents are gone? Oral and Evelyn held the children and cried, praying and believing God that this painful nightmare would somehow pass.

Two days later, a memorial service was held at Mabee Hall to honor Rebecca and Marshall. It seemed as though half of Tulsa was present to bid farewell to this vibrant young couple. With tears in his eyes, Oral spoke of God's faithfulness, and he raised his hands in praise during Handel's Hallelujah Chorus. God had Oral's beloved daughter secure in His arms. Even in their heartrending grief, Oral and Evelyn wanted the world to know that they were confident that Rebecca was in Jesus' care.

Within the first few days after the tragedy, Billy Graham sent a telegram of condolences:

> Beloved Oral, sometimes we have to look at heaven through tears. Those tears sometimes become telescopes that bring heaven so much nearer. Ruth and I will be praying for you and Evelyn and for the family that God's grace will be more than sufficient. We love you in the Lord.[279]

Thousands of others reached out to help the Robertses in their grief. Finally, Oral made the decision to go on television and share the pain of their loss, as well as the faithfulness of God. This was a hard choice for Evelyn, who was much more private and reserved than Oral. But they went together to the ORU television studio and recorded the broadcast, believing fervently that God would minister to their own grief and help thousands of others who had experienced similar loss. Red-eyed and weeping before the cameras, the Robertses reaffirmed their faith in God and urged those watching to be sustained in the faithfulness of the Almighty.

Months later, in her booklet *Coping with Grief*, Evelyn reminded those questioning God's love, "God didn't *take* my daughter away. He *accepted* her. He *received* her when the accident took her life."[280] In spite of the depth of the pain they felt, for Oral and Evelyn Roberts, God remained the One who is faithful and true.

"My Son, My Son!"

"O Absalom, my son, my son," was the cry of David's heart in 2 Samuel 19:4 when his son defied him and his kingdom and chose a life of rebellion. When it came to the Robertses' oldest son, Ronald David Roberts, how often similar words must have come from Evelyn's lips. From the time that Ronnie—as he was known in the family—enrolled at Stanford University, his life was never as his parents had hoped it would be.

Ronnie was extremely gifted by the Lord, and Oral and Evelyn had always believed that God had great plans for him. When he was a child, he could preach and explain the Word of God and would pray forth healing for those in need. Oral saw him as a "successor" to his own ministry.

Yet Ronnie never saw things the same way. From his first questions at Stanford, Ronnie's independence and his desire to be removed from his father's presence and ministry grew. Stanford had initially been Oral's idea because Ronnie was so intellectually gifted, and Evelyn had supported the plan because they'd been proud of their firstborn and his gifts.

Later, though, Evelyn questioned the motives of their hearts. Had their pride in their son's abilities prompted them to send him to such a godless environment? How much of Ronnie's struggle of faith was their fault? Within months of Ronnie's entrance into Stanford, the university put him under a psychiatrist's care to help him end the "confusion" in his mind. Eventually, Ronnie left Stanford, but not to return to his parents or their way of life. He immediately joined the army, hoping to get into foreign affairs. Ronnie was gifted in learning foreign languages and wanted to serve his country. He became fluent in several languages and was stationed with the Security Division of the U.S. Army, but he was still unhappy with his life.

Just before he was discharged from the army, Ronnie married Carol Croskery, a beautiful flutist with the Virginia Philharmonic Orchestra. By then, Ronnie was fluent in six languages besides English and was studying to become a foreign diplomat. A short time later, the couple

⋆⋆⋆⋆⋆

moved to Los Angeles so that Ronnie could obtain his Ph.D. from the University of Southern California. Then, before he actually finished his doctorate, Ronnie and Carol moved back to Tulsa so that he could teach several foreign languages at a magnet school there. Obviously, life was unsettled for Ronnie, and he was never certain of the path he wanted to follow.

Something Is Very Wrong

Soon after Ronnie returned to Tulsa to teach, Oral and Evelyn began to suspect that something was very wrong. Ronnie often slept for long spells during the day, and when he was awake, he "just wasn't himself." When they spoke with him, their brilliant son seemed to be distracted and unsure of what was going on around him. One day, his wife, Carol, came to Oral's home quite distraught. She had found a large bill from a drugstore where Ronnie had been obtaining prescription drugs, apparently illegally.

The Robertses were shocked; they knew so little of the world of drug addiction. Ronnie confessed to his parents and wept over his addiction because he wanted to be free. He went into drug rehabilitation for a month, but nothing seemed to help. His parents prayed and cried with him. Ronnie confessed his sin and repented before the Lord, yet, somehow, his mind seemed to become increasingly distorted and depressed.

Finally, Carol decided that she needed to leave Ronnie for the sake of their two children. Oral and Evelyn's hearts were broken, but they still believed that God would bring Ronnie to his right mind. Oral often scolded himself for not understanding the horrible pitfalls of drug addiction better than he did. Perhaps there was something to be done to save Ronnie before his mind became too damaged by drugs.

After his divorce with Carol became final, Ronnie returned to his parents' home one more time to receive prayer. Oral didn't fully understand at the time how badly Ronnie's mind had been altered by the drugs. He and Evelyn prayed for Ronnie, the son who had been so sensitive to the Lord and His Word. Oral laid hands on him and prayed for his deliverance. Saddened, Ronnie looked up at his father and asked the question, "Dad, have you ever known a real drug addict to be delivered?"[281] Oral assured Ronnie that he had known of many addicts delivered in his years of ministry.

Ronnie left the Robertses' home still unconvinced of his deliverance. Three weeks later, on June 9, 1982, Ronnie was found dead. Oral's son, Richard, brought the news to his father. "The police have just informed us that Ronnie is dead," Richard said, choking out the words.[282] When Oral asked what had happened, Richard explained that the police had found Ronnie slumped over the steering wheel in his car, dead from a bullet wound. The police believed it had been suicide.

Stricken, Oral cried, "But Ronnie, in spite of being on drugs, loved the Lord. He wouldn't have taken his own life." When Oral reached Evelyn, they wept and clung, shaking, to each other as though there was no tomorrow. Suicide—how could Ronnie have taken his own life? They were ministers of faith—how could this be happening to them? Suicide was the cruelest possible end to their son's life of promise.

Once again, the body of Christ around the world offered their condolences, their support, and their love. But, this time, it was much more difficult. Oral and Evelyn wrestled with many conflicting emotions. Evelyn questioned, "Oh, is there something we could have done that we didn't do?"[283] Spiritual questions arose as they searched the past, wondering what they could have changed.

It is never easy to battle one's demons when you are also part of a family that lives within the glare of the national, religious spotlight. Oral and Evelyn knew that Ronnie's mind had been destroyed by the years of prescription drug addiction—that he had lost control of his mind. In fact, Ronnie's hell had been a lethal combination of drug and alcohol addiction, depression, and a struggle over sexual orientation. In most prominent families, such problems are usually swept under the rug and dealt with in private. The Robertses were facing their family crisis in the headlines of the local and national newspapers.

The Lord's comfort finally came in a visit from Kenneth Hagin Sr. and his wife, Oretha. They visited the Robertses' home with a message they believed was directly from the Lord. The word was from 1 Corinthians 5:5, which says, *"To deliver such an one unto Satan for the destruction of the flesh, that the spirit may be saved in the day of the Lord Jesus Christ."*

✯✯✯✯✯

Kenneth Hagin's encouragement was confident. He believed that the Lord wanted the Robertses to know that Ronnie had not gone to hell. His flesh may have been stolen by Satan, but his spirit was with the Lord. Brother Hagin assured them that in the cases he had known of suicide among believers, the individuals who had taken their own lives had not been right in their minds. The Word of God in 1 Corinthians, as well as Brother Hagin's encouragement, brought Oral and Evelyn the peace of mind that they had been seeking. After that evening, the healing process over the horrific tragedy of Ronnie's death began in their hearts.

A Marriage Dissolves

The 1960s and 1970s had seen the ministry of Granville Oral Roberts flourish. The university had risen from a small idea to an educational institution of national prominence within and without the Christian community. In addition, the successful television programs and prime-time specials had given Oral a place of acceptance and prominence that was rarely seen among preachers who believed in and practiced the gifts of the Holy Spirit. Oral Roberts's ministry outreach had moved beyond his wildest dreams. Who could have foreseen the painful trials of the 1980s?

It actually began at the end of the successful 1970s, just two years before Ronnie's suicide, with the announcement of another kind of death—the death of Richard and Patti Roberts's marriage.

The young couple had met at Oral Roberts University in the mid-1960s and married in 1968. Patti had been on fire for Christ. She was a talented vocalist who had, along with other ORU singers, accompanied Oral on several of his overseas mission trips. At the time, Patti had been excited about what the Lord was doing in the Oral Roberts ministry.

Richard, on the other hand, had not been quite as sure about his faith. He had just rededicated his life to the Lord after several years of rebellion. During that time, he had used his singing gift to entertain in nightclubs and bars. When Richard had finally returned to the Lord and to his father, he'd dedicated his singing talents and gifts to be used for God's glory. Patti had been thrilled that Richard had wanted to take his rightful place within his father's ministry.

For eight years, from 1968 to 1976, the couple had sang and ministered together, growing into a more viable part of the Oral Roberts sphere of public influence. The years on the prime-time specials had brought fame and fortune to the young couple, and they'd performed to Christian audiences around the nation.

They also experienced a lifestyle quite different from the average Oral Roberts University graduate's. They'd been regarded as celebrities by many Christians and had been invited to sing at churches and concerts all over the country. With the success of the prime-time specials, the producers at NBC had also regarded them with some respect. Their celebrity status had gained them the opportunity to spend time with famous people and to enjoy the luxuries of a nice home, a country club membership, expensive cars, and a second house in Palm Springs, California. Oral and Evelyn had already purchased a home in Palm Springs. The desert gave Oral some relief from his allergies and provided them with a "retreat" from the demands of the growing ministry.

Unfortunately, behind the smiling faces, singing, and hand-holding of this young couple were days of tension and nights of fighting. There were pressures on both of them to maintain a picture-perfect marriage in the eyes of the public. At the center of the tension was Richard's increasing devotion to his father's ministry and Patti's increasing desire to escape from Oral's overshadowing presence in their lives.

A Ministry for Herself

By the end of 1976, Patti had resigned her role in the Oral Roberts television specials and had formed her own ministry, Patti Roberts International Outreach. She performed solo concerts for churches and civic programs with the ultimate goal of ministering internationally. Richard had encouraged his wife to find her place in ministry, and Patti had spoken increasingly of her search for "personal fulfillment" and of "finding a dream of my own."[284] At one point, Kathryn Kuhlman asked Richard and Patti to her house where she counseled them, and things seemed to normalize for a while.

In 1977, Patti took her ministry team to Tehran to perform and preach the gospel for the first time. Much of the trip was funded by Richard. Two years later, on Patty's third trip to Tehran, Richard accompanied her on the journey, hoping to obtain a better understanding of her ministry.

In the end, unable to hold the marriage together any longer, Patti Roberts sued Richard for divorce on the grounds that they were incompatible. Their marriage ended in March 1979. Many close family friends believed that Patti had grown weary of living under Oral's shadow. Although Patti had been the one to persuade Richard to join his father's ministry more than ten years earlier, she was now the one who wanted him to break away. Richard believed that serving in his father's ministry was his call from God, and he was convinced it was where he should remain.

No one who loved the couple wanted to take sides or blame either one of them. The entire Roberts family was heartbroken about the divorce, knowing that it was not in God's plan for His children. It was particularly hard for Oral to understand because God had given him such a stable, loving relationship with Evelyn. They were truly lovers of each other in every sense of the word and remained devoutly committed to their marriage covenant, no matter what circumstances they faced.

In spite of the number of marriages Oral and Evelyn Roberts had been instrumental in saving through their ministry and through their solid example of a godly marriage, they could not do the same for Richard and Patti. After the marriage ended, Patti wrote a book entitled *From Ashes to God*, in which she claimed that her discomfort with the lavish lifestyle of the Robertses contributed to the marriage's downfall. Since Patti had also enjoyed that lifestyle, it is hard to say what part this really played. In the end, no one but the Lord and the couple involved know exactly what kept that marriage from remaining intact.

The God of Second Chances

After the divorce, Richard stayed faithful to the ministry and remained in the Word of God. He looked to the Lord to heal him from the pain of a failed marriage. Together, he and Oral prayed for the role he was to have in the ministry from that point on. How would Oral deal with a divorced son in leadership in his ministry?

Oral prayed long and hard to the Lord concerning Richard's continued role in the ministry. Some of Oral's friends thought that he should send Richard away for a few years before allowing him to return to public ministry. All of Oral's counselors and friends pledged that they would be in prayer with him for God's perfect will in the situation.

As Oral prayed about the devastating divorce involving his own son, he began to study God's Word concerning grace and mercy. Wasn't God the God who took the deceiver, Jacob, and transformed him into Israel, the father of a great nation? Wasn't God the God of Peter, who, after he had denied Christ three times, was still called by Jesus to be a leader and feed His sheep? (See John 21:16–17.) God was the God of mercy and grace.

In many Pentecostal circles and at the university itself, there were many people who judged Richard initially as being unfit for ministry because he was a divorced man. He went through a baptism of fire as he was hounded by reporters and saw details of his marriage and divorce spread in the national papers. Patti went on a number of talk shows to defend her position, which was very difficult for the Roberts family to understand. Ultimately, Richard turned to the Lord and sought His comfort and direction in this difficult time.

In the first few months after his divorce, Richard spent his time ministering on the ORU campus when he had the opportunity. Gradually, he began to receive more and more invitations to preach and sing at churches in the Southwest. People who had predicted that Richard would be out of the ministry completely were surprised to see the Lord begin to move through him in evangelism. Preaching on God's healing power became a signature part of Richard's message, and many churches received him as they would have received his father! God was changing Richard Roberts and forming him into His man to do His work.

Lindsay Roberts

If Richard's divorce was difficult for some people to understand or accept, a whirlwind romance followed by a remarriage ten months later was an even greater strain. Lindsay was attending ORU to become a lawyer, but she realized that she wanted to marry Richard from the day they first met.

✮✮✮✮✮
233

In a time when Christian leadership was reserved for men only, their marriage became a second chance to give Oral a grandson—a leader to take the mantle for the third generation. Richard already had two daughters, Christine and Julie, with Patti, but there was an expectation for there to be a male heir to Oral's legacy.

All seemed to be going according to plan when Lindsay became pregnant and gave birth to a boy—Richard Oral Roberts. Those hopes were soon dashed, however, when their baby died within thirty-six hours. According to Lindsay, a nurse in the hospital asked if she was going to remain a Christian. Lindsay said, "More than ever."

Another Kind of Medical Miracle

> That a healing evangelist would have any interest in the field of medicine was shocking to some. However, Oral saw it as God's plan to bring healing to the whole man: spirit, soul, body, mind, and emotions.

In the mid 1970s, as Oral Roberts University was growing by leaps and bounds, Oral believed it was time to expand the graduate studies program to include a School of Law and a School of Medicine. That a healing evangelist would have any interest in the field of medicine was shocking to some. However, Oral saw it as God's plan to bring healing to the whole man: spirit, soul, body, mind, and emotions. He believed that God could use both prayer and the hand of medicine together.

While Oral was praying over the details of the School of Medicine, God moved a physician into the Tulsa area who would become Oral's partner in this new venture.

Dr. James Winslow was an orthopedic surgeon who knew very little about the power of God to heal. Soon after moving to Tulsa, James's wife, Sue, was diagnosed with advanced cervical cancer. Wanting an answer beyond medicine, Sue began attending a prayer meeting at a Methodist church, where she received salvation and the baptism in the

Holy Spirit. She began to pray for the Lord's healing power to do "the impossible" in her life.

Each time she lay on the hospital table to receive her chemotherapy treatments, she prayed earnestly, "Lord, let *Your healing power* go into every cell of my body."[285] By the time those treatments were complete, Sue was completely healed from cervical cancer, and it never returned to her body again!

In the following months, James was asked by the ORU athletic department to provide medical care for the basketball team. As a result of his agreement, Oral was referred to him for a sore knee. Thus began a friendship—and a miracle in the making.

After getting to know Jim on the golf course and through long talks on medicine and healing, Oral shared with him his desire to open a School of Medicine at ORU. Although Jim was surprised at the idea, he believed that God had had him in mind as the leader of the new medical school all along.

Healing a Surgeon's Hand

When Jim Winslow met Oral Roberts, more would happen in his life than a new avenue for his medical career. Jim had always attended church and believed that God existed. But a personal relationship with Jesus wasn't something he'd ever thought much about. After some months of knowing Oral Roberts, he naturally grew more and more curious.

On a Saturday morning in the mid-1970s, Jim Winslow had an accident with his lawn mower, cutting his hand with the blower blades. Orthopedic surgery by his fellow physicians didn't seem to have done much to help the injury, which had left him with little feeling in his right fingers. His future as a surgeon was in great jeopardy.

Jim called Oral on the phone, then drove to the Robertses' home battling the fear that his surgical career was over. Jim recognized his great need for the Lord. For five hours, Oral shared the plan of salvation with Jim and explained the personal relationship that Jesus desires to have with His followers. During that time, Jim received an assurance of his faith in Christ and the experience of the baptism of the Holy Spirit with speaking in tongues.

As Oral prayed for Jim's hand, he felt the power of God surging through his right hand once again. After the prayer time, Jim went home to tell his wife, Sue, what had happened. They continued to pray together using their prayer language and believing for Jim's healing. Within weeks, his hand was healed sufficiently for him to continue his practice in surgery. Jim Winslow was ready to hear God's next miraculous step for his life.

The Great Medical Challenge

Oral Roberts was passionate about his vision for a medical school. He announced to his ministry team that he wanted the School of Medicine to open by 1978, and he appointed Jim Winslow as the dean. One major hurdle that Oral hadn't foreseen was that the medical community has a great deal of control over what happens within medicine. A school of medicine could give young doctors three years of medical training; however, without a three-to-seven-year residency program for the students to attend after school, their credentials would not be accepted anywhere in the United States.

Any school of medicine would have to have its credentials accepted by a hospital so that the doctors could receive the residency training they needed. The question was, would any hospital accept the students of Oral Roberts University, with its highly controversial doctrine on supernatural healing?

After months of negotiations with the three hospitals in the Tulsa area, Jim Winslow had not reached an agreement with any of them for an affiliation with the ORU medical school. Oral, always determined to follow what he believed to be the Lord's command, declared that the medical school would open in December 1977, even if the hospital affiliations had not been secured. One month later, ORU welcomed its first twenty medical students, who had come to the school in faith that the problems would be solved with time.

The City of Faith

On February 11, 1977, a tragic airplane crash claimed the lives of Rebecca and Marshall Nash. Grieving, the Robertses went to their home in Palm Springs to have a time of privacy and prayer with Richard. Trying to deal with the pain of Rebecca and Marshall's deaths, Oral spent a great deal of time with the Lord. After a few days of prayer, he told Evelyn that the Lord was speaking to him once again.

Oral wrote these words from the Lord in his journal: "You must build a new and different medical center for Me. The healing streams of prayer and medicine must merge through what I will have you build...."[286] Oral received a vision for the buildings of a new medical and research center. The Lord told him to call it the City of Faith. When Oral returned to Tulsa, he didn't share the word about the new direction with Jim Winslow or anyone else for six months. He was waiting on God's perfect timing and allowing the idea to take root in his own mind.

Oral's vision from the Lord in the deserts of Palm Springs was not a small one. He envisioned three medical towers—one sixty stories tall, another thirty stories tall, and the other twenty stories tall. These towers would house the doctors, clinics, diagnostic center, hospital, research center, and rooms of prayer partners. Oral saw it all in great detail and wrote about each phase in his journal.

More than that, he continued to write the Lord's subsequent words to him. The medical center was to use "medicine, but more than medicine; prayer, but more than prayer...the atmosphere was to be charged with faith and hope, where My healing love permeates the whole place."[287]

On September 9, 1977, Oral Roberts shocked Tulsa and much of the Christian community with the announcement that he was building again; this time, it was a medical center called the City of Faith!

"He'll Get the Money from God"

When someone asked Saul Yager, Oral's Jewish attorney and longtime friend, where Oral would get the money to build something as large as the City of Faith, Saul answered emphatically, "He's going to get the money from God."[288]

Some of Oral's other team members weren't as positive. Oral's top advisers repeatedly questioned the details of the expansive vision. As Evelyn recounted, "The men at the office came to [Oral] one day and said, 'Now, Oral, you've got so much done. Can't you go back to the Lord and see if we can't stop right there?'"[289] A few years later, one had to question whether their words of caution weren't from the Lord. But there was no stopping Oral and his determination to fulfill what he believed to be God's directive.

Oral explained the full plan, as the Lord had revealed it to him, to his partners and financial supporters. Then, he asked them to consider making a seed-faith planting into the work. When the money came in, they worked on building the towers; in the months when money was tight and few funds came in, they stopped building for a time. Oral's partners gave as they had in the past, and many of them gave above anything they had given before.

One man with little involvement in the ministry sent a check for one million dollars at a time when it was desperately needed. When Oral asked him why, he simply replied that God had told him to do it.

A Battle All the Way

The City of Faith was a battleground from its inception. All new hospital construction had to be approved by the Oklahoma Health Planning Commission and issued a certificate of need for the construction to move forward. Seventy-eight percent of the physicians in Tulsa voted to oppose the new hospital on the grounds that it would provide duplicate services of what was already available in the city.

In the end, Oral convinced the medical agency that just as his university had been misunderstood in the beginning but had proven beneficial to Tulsa, the Medical Center would prove the same. The certificate of need was issued, and the building began. Still, the fights in court continued. The next conflict was over a separation of church and state issue because of the spiritual affiliation of the hospital. Even as the hospital was being built, both sides fought determinedly to win.

By April 1981, the final decision had been made, and the City of Faith received its final, official certificate of need. If only the troubles had ended with that decision! The financial burden of building the complex debt-free, as the money was provided, put a huge strain on everyone and everything connected with Oral Roberts.

In order to keep the building going, Oral consistently had to make special appeals to his financial partners. They responded in amazing ways, providing $38 million in one year alone. One month, as Oral spoke of his desire to see the work of God continue on the building, his supporters sent in $18 million in a thirty-day period! It was an astronomical amount of money from a believing public. But the strain on the rest of the Oral Roberts Evangelistic Association was enormous, just the same.

A 900-Foot Jesus

Public criticism of Oral Roberts was not an unusual thing in his ministry. But many struggles in building the City of Faith led to more than the usual number of strange predictions from Oral and corresponding public outcries.

In May 1980, when funding for the City of Faith was at a low point, Oral stood looking at the unfinished towers before him. He reported that at that time, he saw a vision of Jesus—900 feet tall. His words were, "I felt an overwhelming holy presence around me. When I opened my eyes, there He stood...some nine hundred feet tall, looking at me....He stood a full three hundred feet taller than the six-hundred foot tall City of Faith. There I was, face-to-face with Jesus Christ, the Son of the living God."[290]

Oral described Jesus lifting the City of Faith in the vision, then telling him that He would encourage Oral's partners to continue supporting the work financially, and that the City of Faith would be completed. Oral was convinced that he should share his vision with his partners.

The outrage from critics in Tulsa and around the country was immediate. Some called the vision "blasphemous" or claimed that Oral had gone "berserk"; others simply ridiculed him. Oral answered the critics by saying that he had seen Jesus with his spiritual eyes, not his physical eyes. Over half a million of Oral's partners believed that the Lord had appeared to him, and they contributed nearly five million dollars to complete the next phase of the construction. Still, the difficulties with the City of Faith continued.

Too Many Empty Beds

On November 1, 1981, the City of Faith was dedicated to the Lord. Religious and political leaders from around the country attended the event, and President Ronald Reagan sent a congratulatory letter to Oral. All looked well on that glorious day.

However, things quickly fell behind in the medical complex. The hospital was not attracting the patients from out of state, as was originally projected. By 1983, the hospital was one year behind in the planned estimate for filled hospital beds. By 1984, only 130 beds were occupied. That year, layoffs claimed 334 employees of the ministry, including one fourth of the hospital's 907 employees.

The City of Faith placed a financial burden of one million dollars a month on the Oral Roberts Evangelistic Association. And the hospital wasn't the only part falling behind in expectations. There was not enough money to fund the completion of the research center. Only three floors had been completed, and the research equipment wasn't there for the cancer research that Oral had promised his followers.

It was in the midst of these many intense months of building and waiting on God that Oral's son, Ronnie, took his life. Feeling as though life was falling apart, Oral pressed harder into the Lord and looked for some positive message concerning the medical research that could come out of Ronnie's death. In addition, it was during this time of grief that Oral announced his prediction concerning cancer.

Oral believed that God had told him, "There will be some kind of major breakthrough in cancer prevention by the end of this century. I'm predicting a major healing coming in the world."[291] Oral's hope was that, with the Spirit's leading, a cure for cancer could be found within the walls of the City of Faith. But it wasn't to be.

"God Is Going to Take Me Home!"

In 1986, the City of Faith had been open for five years, but the debt and struggles had never ended. Oral, along with both the medical and university administrators, had cut expenses as much as possible. Much to the dismay of the ORU administrative team, this had included cutting back on improvements to Oral Roberts University to allow whatever money was available to flow toward the medical buildings. In spite of every effort, by 1986, the City of Faith was $8 million in debt, with no relief in sight.

Once again, Oral went before the Lord with the need and believed that God told him to present the critical need to the partners. Once again, Oral's message was controversial enough to send the national media into an uproar. Appearing on his Sunday night television program, which had the largest audience of all his shows, Oral conveyed the word he had received from the Lord during his prayer time:

"I told you to raise $8 million to carry on My medical work. You have from January 1 to March 31 to get it done. If you don't then your work is finished, and I am going to call you home."[292]

By this time, Oral Roberts was just turning sixty-nine years old. Perhaps he was weary of the fight to maintain all that he believed God had called him to do. He admitted that he briefly welcomed the idea of going home to be with the Lord, of finding a place of rest. However, Oral was certain that the Lord spoke this word of direction and exhortation to him.

Naturally, Oral made the announcement on his weekly Sunday evening show because he wanted the millions of viewers to understand the seriousness of the financial need. By the next day, news services across the country and in others parts of the world reported that Oral Roberts had said, "God was going to kill him if he did not raise $8 million right away."[293]

To a passionate man like Oral, this announcement made perfect sense. God wanted Oral and everyone else involved with the ministry to know how serious He was about His work. Some listeners embraced the message as from the Lord Himself. Pentecostals, in particular, understood it differently from the mainstream press. Most understood this to mean that if the fund-raising effort failed, Oral's work for the Lord on earth would be complete and he would eventually be called home. However, others, Christians and non-Christians alike, saw it as another fund-raising ploy designed so that Oral could get the money he needed to complete his pet project.

Oral committed to spending the next couple of months in the Prayer Tower praying for God's will to be done. He vowed to

> **Oral committed to spending the next couple of months in the Prayer Tower praying for God's will to be done.**

the Lord that he would not leave the Prayer Tower until the money had been raised. News helicopters flew around the tower to show their audiences where Oral Roberts was in retreat, turning it into a sensationalized story. On the other side, charismatic ministers and encouraging friends arrived at the Prayer Tower to join with him in prayer.

Oral was determined to ignore the media's scoffing, to believe God, and to stand in faith, as he had done so many times before. As the donations came in, the March 31 deadline came closer and closer. Oral and Evelyn continued to telecast their Sunday evening shows from the television studio in the Prayer Tower.

One Sunday night in March, Oral went on the air and announced that he had only $1.6 million left to raise in order to reach their goal. Evelyn, who was sitting in the front row of the audience, interrupted him from off camera and reminded him that the actual figure was only $1.3 million. In God's provision, a man in Florida who had not yet made a commitment to Christ was watching the show that evening. He decided that if such a high profile man would allow his wife to correct him on national television, then he must not be all bad. He decided that he should be the one to give the remainder of the money, and he called in to the television show. On his first attempt, the person who took the call thought he was joking and hung up on him! Fortunately for Oral Roberts, the man was persistent and called back a second time. This time, the call was put through.

When the gentleman arrived in Tulsa with a check for $1.3 million, he revealed that he owned several successful dog racing tracks. Not put off by how he had earned his money, Oral asked him if he knew the Lord. Admitting that he did not, this seeking man held Oral's hand and repeated the sinner's prayer after him. The Lord's word had come to pass, and a new soul had entered the kingdom of God!

Scandal Hits the Church

Although the City of Faith had a short rejuvenation in capital, the expenses were still prohibitive. Then, a scandal rocked the body of Christ and changed the finances of all the ministries with programs on the air.

In 1986, Jim Bakker of the PTL ministry was accused of having an adulterous affair and, subsequently, was indicted for fraud as a result of the methods he used in raising funds to build a Christian vacation/ retreat center. Later that same year, Jimmy Swaggart, a popular Assemblies of God televangelist, was accused of repeated visits with a prostitute. Shortly after the accusations came forth, he confessed the validity of the statements.

The infidelities of two men of God with prominent television ministries, and the national media exposure they attracted, shook the body of Christ and created distrust in the hearts of thousands of supporters of their ministries and other ministries. Contributions to the Oral Roberts Evangelistic Association fell off dramatically as a result. Many churches in America were affected in the same way.

Unfortunately, the cost of running the School of Medicine, the School of Dentistry, and the City of Faith had not fallen off a bit—and so the debt load and strain continued.

"You Can Add No More to It"

With a great deal of emotional distress, Oral Roberts closed the School of Dentistry in 1987 while still struggling to keep the rest of the medical dream alive. Over the next year, the American Medical Association resumed its intense evaluation of the School of Medicine, requiring additional and costly changes for continued accreditation. And the expenses in the other medical areas continued to rise. Finally, in 1989, with a broken heart, Oral Roberts came to the realization that the School of Medicine and the City of Faith would have to close, or his entire ministry would be at risk.

The dream of merging prayer and medicine appeared to have been destroyed. Oral, a man who fought like a lion when he believed he was right, felt as though he had entered his own Gethsemane. He cried tears of anguish at the loss, while his medical foes denounced the entire work: "You hate to say it, but almost everything that has happened was totally predictable."[294] Those words were spoken by C. T. Thompson, an executive at St. Francis Hospital in Tulsa and an outspoken opponent of the City of Faith from its inception.

Although Oral's ultimate dream was not realized as he had hoped, he received encouragement from unexpected sources. Dr. Harry Jonas

✶✶✶✶✶
243

of the American Medical Association assured Oral that he had "forever changed medicine and the way the medical world looks at it...this idea of combining medicine with prayer, with a view toward wholeness, is an idea whose time has come...the fact is, the idea is bigger than you are."[295]

A year earlier, David Wilkerson of World Challenge in New York City had given Oral a word that the City of Faith was to close, but that God was pleased with Oral. Wilkerson stated, "You have made the point He wanted made. The world knows it, the church knows it, and you are to close these institutions." Wilkerson went on to say, "Oral, you've done what God wanted you to do. It's over, as far as this place is concerned, but the concept is released, and you can add no more to it."[296]

Problems in the Palace

In hindsight, I believe it would have been better for Oral to follow the biblical pattern of King David and King Solomon in building the temple. It was David who gathered all the material, but it was Solomon who finally built the temple. Likewise, Oral probably should have let his son, Richard, build the hospital. If he had, I believe that Richard would still be there today. But Oral was adamant that no debt would be left behind when he stepped down from the ministry.

Oral and Evelyn Roberts in 1997

In the end, one criticism of Oral's leadership would be that he didn't utilize his children effectively. Richard was second in line and had the burden of taking over all that his father had built. Oral's daughter, Roberta, became a brilliant lawyer with a successful legal career. It would be interesting to imagine what would have happened had Roberta taken over ORU, allowing Richard to continue the ministry. This would have been nearly impossible, however, because of Oral's inability to allow women a place in leadership—a problem that continues to plague other Christian leaders.

By default, Richard took over as ORU president in 1993. Oral and Evelyn moved to California soon after Richard took over. Oral believed

⋆⋆⋆⋆⋆

that as long as he lived in Tulsa, Richard would never be able to lead properly. People would always be turning to Oral to know what to do. Walking in Oral's shoes turned out to be a difficult fit for Richard from the beginning. Unlike Oral's humble beginnings, Richard had been "raised in the palace" of public fame and celebrity. He didn't relate to the general public effectively. Problems soon developed in his relationships with both the faculty and students.

In November 2007, Richard resigned from the presidency of ORU after being named in a lawsuit alleging the improper use of university funds and resources for both political and personal purposes. Despite residing in California, Oral continued in his role of chancellor while Tulsa-area pastor Billy Joe Daugherty was named the executive regent to assume the administrative duties of president. In 2009, Oral handed over the leadership of the university to its incoming president, Mark Rutland.

California

Unlike Tulsa, living in Newport, California, allowed Oral and Evelyn to lead unassuming lives. Health problems also led to a decline in Oral's activities. He underwent a couple of angioplasty procedures; the last one almost killed him on the table. Doctors were ready to let him pass away, but Oral rebounded.

While Oral lived in California, I was able to meet with him on several occasions. Once, when he was appearing at a church in Irvine, California, I asked him if he had a favorite Oral Roberts joke. After years of ministry, fund-raising, and even some controversy, there certainly was no shortage of Oral Roberts jokes. He asked me what mine was. I told him of the story in which Oral Roberts and Billy Graham died. Unfortunately, heaven was not yet prepared for them, so they had to wait in hell. It wasn't long before the devil pleaded with heaven for them to leave. It turned out that Billy Graham was saving everyone, and Oral Roberts was raising money for air-conditioning.

Oral smiled and said his favorite was the story that claimed that he couldn't golf. Every time he tried the holes would heal up.

In 2005, Oral's beloved wife, Evelyn, died after complications from suffering a fall at the age of eighty-eight. Today, far too many pastor marriages end in scandal or divorce. Other ministry couples are content to lead completely separate ministries. Evelyn was a strong woman but also a perfect fit for Oral's type-A personality. Often, she would sit in the front row of his appearances and correct him out loud if he recalled details incorrectly in his stories, just as she had done with the fund-raising amount for the Medical Center. Oral and Evelyn ministered together and loved each other to the end.

The Passing of a Legend

On December 15, 2009, Oral Roberts died at the age of ninety-one. On his passing, Pat Robertson said,

> I am grieved at the passing of my dear friend, Oral Roberts. He was a pioneer in healing evangelism and in Christian education. He inspired a generation of young people to follow his lead in the charismatic ministry. We were friends for over fifty years and I will miss him. My sympathies to those children who survive him.[297]

Oklahoma Governor Brad Henry stated,

"He taught me how to love, and he taught me how to forgive. He prayed for the very ones who opposed him."

> Oklahoma and the nation have lost a truly remarkable man of God. The influence and impact of Oral Roberts and his ministry are beyond measure. His faith, compassion and charity have left a legacy that will be felt for generations to come. Our thoughts and prayers are with Reverend Roberts' family and loved ones during this difficult time.[298]

Five days later, nearly four thousand mourners filled the Mabee Center on the ORU campus for a memorial service. Pat Robertson opened the service with a prayer to the Lord: "You sent us a man who [sic] we know and loved, and who walked with God and never gave up the common touch. I know you broke the mold with Oral."[299]

Oral's daughter Roberta spoke of remembrances of her father: "When he was praying for someone, he had his mind on one thing and one thing only, and that was the need of the person with whom he was dealing." Richard also eulogized his father, saying, "He taught me how to love, and he taught me how to forgive. He prayed for the very ones who opposed him."[300]

Several other leading figures in Christianity also paid their last respects:

I will always treasure the last conversation I had with your father. I'm sure he heard the words: "Well done, good and faithful servant."[301]
—Billy Graham

Today we celebrate the homegoing of a true man of God.[302]
—Benny Hinn

He was a spiritual father to millions around the world. He opened the door for all of us who are now in Christian television.[303]
—Paul Crouch

His legacy will continue to bear fruit. He was a true man of God.[304]
—David Yonggi Cho

A video tribute featured comments from former Presidents George H. W. Bush and Jimmy Carter, as well as Jerry Lewis, Roy Clark, collegiate basketball coaching legend Eddie Sutton, and others.

Finally, Denver, Colorado-based Bible teacher Marilyn Hickey spoke, reminding the audience that Oral Roberts was one of the first to "blast the world" with God's message of healing, and for that, Roberts had paid a great price. "Now," she said, "you can go all over the world and find the healing message." Later, Hickey said, "I love this about Oral, who said, 'The game is not over until I win.' But he won. Oral went to heaven with many victories. One of them is ORU. That's one of the major things I learned from Oral Roberts. He didn't believe in losing."[305]

After her remarks, Hickey encouraged all in attendance to place their hands on any part of their bodies that was sick as she prayed for healing. Then, the service closed with a call to salvation—a fitting and honoring tribute to a man who spent his life delivering God's message of healing and salvation to a sick and dying world.

✴✴✴✴✴

CHAPTER FOUR

ENDNOTES

178 David Edwin Harrell Jr., *Oral Roberts: An American Life* (Bloomington, IN: Indiana University Press, 1985), 25.
179 Ibid., 26.
180 Oral Roberts, *Expect a Miracle: My Life and Ministry* (Nashville, TN: Thomas Nelson Publishers, 1998), 37.
181 Harrell, *An American Life*, 28.
182 Oral Roberts, *Expect a Miracle*, 34.
183 Harrell, *An American Life*, 30.
184 Oral Roberts, *Expect a Miracle*, 13.
185 Ibid., 43.
186 Ibid., 15.
187 Ibid.
188 Ibid., 18.
189 Ibid., 19.
190 Ibid., 28.
191 Ibid.
192 Ibid., 29.
193 Ibid., 45.
194 Ibid., 46.
195 Harrell, *An American Life*, 5.
196 Ibid.
197 Ibid., 49.
198 Ibid., 50.
199 Oral Roberts, *My Story* (Tulsa and New York: Summit Book Company, 1961), 35.
200 Oral Roberts, *Expect a Miracle*, 51.
201 Oral Roberts, *My Story*, 43.
202 Ibid.
203 Oral Roberts, *When You See the Invisible, You Can Do the Impossible* (Shippensburg, PA: Destiny Image, 2005), 91.
204 Harrell, *An American Life*, 46.
205 Ibid.
206 Oral Roberts, *Expect a Miracle*, 50.

207 Oral Roberts, *Expect a Miracle*, 53.

208 Harrell, *An American Life*, 65.

209 Ibid., 66.

210 Oral Roberts, *Expect a Miracle*, 74–75.

211 Ibid., 77.

212 Ibid., 78.

213 Ibid.

214 Ibid., 89.

215 Ibid., 90.

216 Ibid.

217 Ibid., 93.

218 Ibid., 84–85.

219 Ibid., 106.

220 Ibid., 91.

221 Ibid., 94.

222 Ibid.

223 Oral Roberts, *My Story*, 153.

224 Oral Roberts, *Expect a Miracle*, 98.

225 Oral Roberts, *Still Doing the Impossible: When You See the Invisible, You Can Do the Impossible* (Shippensburg, PA: Destiny Image, 2002), 72.

226 Oral Roberts, *Expect a Miracle*, 103.

227 Ibid.

228 Ibid., 108.

229 Oral Roberts, *My Story*, 133.

230 Ibid.

231 Oral Roberts, *Expect a Miracle*, 125.

232 Ibid., 128.

233 Ibid.

234 Ibid.

235 Harrell, *An American Life*, 179.

236 Oral Roberts, *Expect a Miracle*, 130.

237 Ibid., 149.

238 Ibid., 113.

239 Ibid., 114.

240 Ibid., 117.

241 Ibid., 124.

242 Oral Roberts, *Still Doing the Impossible*, 167.

243 Ibid., 167–168.

244 Oral Roberts, *A Daily Guide to Miracles* (Grand Rapids, MI: Fleming H. Revell Company, 1978), 35.

245 Evelyn Roberts, *Evelyn Roberts' Miracle Life Stories* (Tulsa, OK: Roberts Ministries, 1998), 70.

✮✮✮✮✮

246 Evelyn Roberts, *Miracle Life Stories*, 70.

247 Harrell, *An American Life*, 75.

248 Oral Roberts, *Still Doing the Impossible*, 192.

249 Oral Roberts, *Miracle Life Stories*, 40.

250 Ibid., 41.

251 Ibid.

252 Ibid., 42.

253 Ibid.

254 Harrell, *An American Life*, 206.

255 Ibid., 207.

256 Ibid.

257 Oral Roberts, *Expect a Miracle*, 165.

258 Ibid., 166.

259 Ibid.

260 Ibid., 170.

261 Ibid., 171.

262 Harrell, *An American Life*, 121.

263 Ibid., 219.

264 Ibid., 220.

265 Oral Roberts, *Expect a Miracle*, 165.

266 Harrell, *An American Life*, 221.

267 Ibid., 223.

268 Ibid., 225.

269 Ibid., 229.

270 Ibid.

271 Ibid., 230.

272 Ibid., 294.

273 Ibid., 299.

274 Ibid., 262.

275 Ibid., 272.

276 Ibid., 303.

277 Oral Roberts, *Expect a Miracle*, 197.

278 Ibid., 198.

279 Harrell, *An American Life*, 331.

280 Ibid., 332.

281 Oral Roberts, *Expect a Miracle*, 208.

282 Ibid.

283 Harrell, *An American Life*, 340.

284 Ibid., 341.

285 Oral Roberts, *Expect a Miracle*, 256.

286 Harrell, *An American Life*, 334.

287 Oral Roberts, *Expect a Miracle*, 273.

[288] Oral Roberts, *Expect a Miracle*, 281.

[289] Harrell, *An American Life*, 381.

[290] Ibid., 405.

[291] Ibid., 392.

[292] Oral Roberts, *Expect a Miracle*, 289.

[293] Ibid., 290.

[294] Harrell, *An American Life*, 391.

[295] Oral Roberts, *Expect a Miracle*, 301.

[296] Ibid., 299.

[297] http://www.cbn.com/cbnnews/us/2009/December/Oral-Roberts-Hospitalized-After-Fall/.

[298] http://www.tulsaworld.com/ourlives/article.aspx?subjectid=58&article id=20091215_58_0_TheRev592630.

[299] http://www.tulsaworld.com/news/article.aspx?subjectid=19&article id=20091221_11_0_tablet688063.

[300] Ibid.

[301] Ibid.

[302] Ibid.

[303] Ibid.

[304] Ibid.

[305] Ibid.

CHAPTER FIVE

CHARLES & FRANCES HUNTER

"If We Can Do It, You Can Do It!"

"IF WE CAN DO IT, YOU CAN DO IT!"

When God speaks a new word, the hearer is often caught unaware. Yet, doing new things is God's specialty. In February 1973 in El Paso, Texas, God did a new thing in Charles and Frances Hunter's lives and ministry. They were conducting revival meetings at a local church and were sitting up front along with the pastor.

"Did God just speak to you?" Frances and Charles asked each other, wide-eyed with surprise.

"Yes, He did!" they answered simultaneously.

"What did He say?" one asked the other.

"He said to announce a miracle service for Tuesday night!"

"Yes, that's what He just said to me!"

Stepping to the podium, Charles looked out over the expectant faces at the crowded Sunday night service. "God just spoke to both of us that there will be a miracle service on Tuesday night! Okay, Pastor?" Charles asked.

Pastor Bob Lewis nodded his head in the affirmative.

"Jesus will pass by this church on Tuesday night to heal the sick. Go out and tell your friends to bring the sick, the lame and the crippled, and He will heal them!"[306]

This was not a casual statement for the Hunters to make. They had never conducted a miracle service before or felt led to announce one. In many churches around the country, they had preached on the miracle of salvation through Jesus Christ. Those who thirsted for more of God were then led into the glorious baptism of the Holy Spirit. But this night, in this Southern Baptist church in El Paso, Charles and Frances heard God speak to their hearts and learned that He wanted to do more. They moved out in faith that He would bring healings and miracles.

And the miracles began that very night. Pastor Lewis and his family were thirsting for more of God. After the Sunday night service, Charles and Frances asked Bob, his wife, and their youngest daughter if they would like to receive the baptism in the Holy Spirit. The Lewis family walked into the Hunters' motel room and prayed eagerly together, and the Holy Spirit descended on them as on the day of Pentecost. Together, they began praising God in a new language.

The next morning, the Lewises' twenty-year-old daughter saw the excitement on her parents' faces and declared, "I want to be baptized in the Holy Spirit, too."

They explained God's gift to her and prayed, and she was immersed in the Holy Spirit, as well. However, their son, Bob Jr., wasn't quite as excited. He even called his family "holy rollers." But God wasn't finished with him yet!

A Miraculous Day

The Tuesday morning church service was full of people eagerly anticipating what God would do there that night. But God wasn't going to wait for the evening. He was ready to move right then. A young woman, Mary, had walked into the service early, full of tears, anger, and deep needs. Bob Jr. and his sister took her into another room to pray while the service began. Before long, Bob Jr. walked to the front of the assembly with good news: Mary had accepted Jesus as her Savior.

✯✯✯✯✯

He stuttered his way through that statement, just as he had stuttered all of his life. Charles walked up to the microphone and said, "Bob, Jesus would like to heal your stuttering. Is that okay?"

Eagerly, Bob responded, "Okay!"

Charles prayed for him, saying, "Father, sweep through Bob's entire life and erase from his memory anything negative which caused the stuttering and, in Jesus' name, heal him."

"Now, Bob," Frances said, "step to the microphone and read from the Word of God."

Opening to the center of the Bible, he read four verses *with no stuttering*! The morning service exploded with applause for the Lord!

That evening, Bob Jr. shared his testimony before the overflowing crowd without a single slip or stutter. A round of joyful applause arose from the congregation because Bob had been healed by the power of God when Jesus passed by.

The congregation was electrified. They had already seen the healing of a boy whom they had known for years. Then, an eleven-year-old girl walked to the altar in tears. When Frances asked her what was wrong, she said that she had been deaf, and now she could hear! She said she was crying because the music sounded so beautiful and so loud. Her mother, who was working in the children's nursery, ran into the sanctuary, praising the Lord for this miracle. Her daughter had been deaf in one ear, with little hearing in the other, since birth. Later that week, a doctor administrated an audio test that confirmed that both ears were perfectly normal!

As the congregation praised the Lord for His faithfulness, things began moving faster and faster. The most astounding miracle of all was when the formerly deaf young girl brought a friend forward who insisted that she had just been healed, as well. Questioning the child, the Hunters discovered that she had been born with cerebral palsy!

Frances looked down at the little girl with the faith-filled eyes and asked, "Honey, how do you know that you were healed?"

The child answered in faith, "Jesus touched me...I felt Him."

Charles reached down and lifted the little one up onto the platform. "Can you walk?" he asked her.

✰✰✰✰✰

Gingerly, she took a step.

"Can you run and leap like the man in the Bible story who was healed?"

Within minutes, she was walking and leaping across the front of the church![307]

Two days later, Pastor Lewis called the Hunters to tell them that the little girl's legs had straightened, and she was playing happily on the playground at school with her friends. The Hunters discovered that this little one had told her mother before the miracle service, "Take off my braces. I'm going to leave my crutches at home, too, because I'll never need them again."[308] Praise the Lord for the faith of a little child!

Marked for His Purpose

Frances Hunter often referred to herself as a "marked woman." She—and Charles—had been marked by God for His amazing purposes! She was truly a woman who had an indelible brand burned into her by the fire of God. She said, "I am a marked woman because wherever I go that brand goes with me and whatever I do that mark shows on me....When God puts a seal on you, it's done with indelible ink and you cannot get it out."[309]

Frances and Charles Hunter

Frances and Charles Hunter had been marked by God to lead multitudes into a saving knowledge of Jesus Christ and the powerful gift of His Holy Spirit. They had been marked for healing—to be healed themselves, as well as to bring healing in the name of Jesus to untold people around the globe. The "Happy Hunters," as they were known because of their joyful ministry, had been marked for marriage to each other, as well. They brought glory to God through their loving devotion to one another wherever they traveled.

As two of God's generals, the Hunters served a powerful purpose in bringing God's message of healing to the nations. Before the Hunters, people who desired healing went to see the "gifted ones," including Kathryn Kuhlman, Oral Roberts, William Branham, and A. A. Allen. These godly servants had truly received gifts of healing from the Holy Spirit.

But in His eternal plan, God was ready for a shift of focus. He used the Hunters to transform the course of the healing ministry, making people realize that ordinary believers can be used to heal the sick. If the Hunters could heal, so could Grandma; so could young Johnny.

This transformation had astounding significance. It was a major move of God, a shift of doctrine throughout the culture of Full Gospel Christianity. Do you understand how significant it is that these two people who were sold out to God could change the mind-set of an entire religious group that includes 660 million Pentecostals in the world today?

> **God was ready for a shift of focus. He used the Hunters to transform the course of the healing ministry, making people realize that ordinary believers can be used to heal the sick.**

I have ministered in over one hundred countries. When I fellowship with other brothers and sisters in Christ throughout the world, we often talk about healing ministries. Oral Roberts's name comes up, A. A. Allen's name comes up, but then the people always say, "But Frances and Charles taught our whole church how we can do it ourselves through the power of the Holy Spirit within us!" Just how did these two ordinary people of the twentieth century become two of God's generals and have such a tremendous impact on the Christian church worldwide?

A Cry from the Shoe Box

A tiny cry came from the worn, brown shoe box sitting atop the old bedroom dresser. A startled midwife turned from her patient and looked down at the scrunched face of the two-pound baby girl flailing her arms. This little one should have died. Yet, the feeble cry grew stronger by the minute. This was Frances Eileen Fuller's entrance into the world on May 8, 1916.

Her mother had gone into labor two months early. It was painfully difficult, and the midwife worked hard to save Dessie Fuller's life. Certainly, there was no hope for the tiny baby girl, so the midwife had laid her little body in the shoe box to be buried later. But from that first breath of life, Frances was destined to do far beyond the possible! She met each situation and every obstacle with determination and joy, blessed by God with the will to overcome.

It would be some years before Frances realized that her success came from a God who loved her and had called her for Himself.

Frances had a difficult childhood in Chicago, Illinois. Her mother was stricken with tuberculosis and lived in a sanatorium off and on for nearly ten years before she died. The Fullers were often destitute, but the love of Fred Fuller for his daughters, Frances and her older sister, Kathleen, kept life exciting. Fred was a wonderful storyteller and a hard worker, and his outlook on life kept the girls hopeful and secure. They attended church regularly, even though no one ever shared the personal message of Jesus Christ with them. The Fullers moved around for work and eventually settled in St. Louis, Missouri. Still, Frances grew up happy and determined to make something special of her life. Somewhere within herself, she came to disdain the word *can't*.

Overcoming Odds

During high school, Frances determined to be the fastest typist in the city of St. Louis. With lots of practice, she reached her goal of one hundred and twenty-five words per minute. At the height of the Great Depression, when little work could be found, she landed an excellent job with the Southwestern Bell Telephone Company and quickly advanced in her assignments year after year. In her mid-twenties, Frances and several girlfriends decided to treat themselves to a vacation out West. They traveled to a Colorado dude ranch, where Frances met a handsome young ac-

Frances and her first child, Tom, in 1945

countant named Larry Steder from her original hometown of Chicago.

After several months of taking turns visiting one another in Chicago and St. Louis, Frances and Larry were engaged. Their wedding plans were interrupted by Pearl Harbor and World War II because Larry rushed off to enlist in the navy. When they discovered that he would be stationed in the U.S. for quite a while, the young couple decided to go ahead with their marriage plans. They lived on a naval base in New York and then San Francisco until late in the war, when Larry had to ship out to Okinawa. Frances moved back to Chicago to be close to her mother-in-law while Larry was gone. Frances was pregnant, and a handsome, brown-eyed baby boy that they named Tom was born in September 1945. Soon after this, Larry was discharged from the navy and returned to his young wife and newborn son. The Steders excitedly set up their first home in a suburb of Chicago. Frances's heart was full to overflowing with happiness.

Painful Years

Cancer is an ugly word today, and it was a death sentence in the late 1940s when Larry Steder was diagnosed with brain cancer. It was just two years after the end of the war, and the young couple was devastated by the news. Larry battled the disease for two more years while Frances kept the family going with her work as a self-employed cosmetic consultant. Successful as always, she was able to provide for them while Larry fought the disease in a veterans hospital. But Larry lost the battle, and when he died, Frances became a widow at the age of thirty-three.

And widowhood became another challenge for her to overcome.

Fighting overwhelming grief herself, Larry's mother moved from Chicago to Florida to be closer to her other son. Just as in the Old Testament account, in which Ruth followed her mother-in-law, Naomi, to remain close to her, Frances moved, along with little Tom, to Florida to give them a sense of family and to keep Tom close to his grandmother. It was also a way to help ease the pain of losing her husband.

Always the life of the party, Frances found herself filling the empty months after Larry's death with social occasions—opportunities to share a few drinks and laughs with friends in her Florida neighborhood. Before long, she met a successful builder named Walter Gardner. He soon proclaimed his love for Frances and her precious son, Tom. Swept off her feet by his sweet talk, Frances did the one impulsive thing in her life that turned disastrous.

Shortly after Frances and Walter were married, she discovered that he was an angry and sometimes abusive alcoholic. He had deceived her with his disingenuously pleasant personality in order to convince her to marry him, and he never showed her or Tom any of the love he had professed to have. After five years of suffering abuse, some of it life threatening, Frances divorced Walter and obtained a court order for her protection.

One great gift from the marriage was the birth of her daughter, Joan, who became the apple of her mother's eye and a source of blessing to Frances throughout her life.

Life Starts at Forty-nine

With two children to support, Frances turned back to her typing skills. What started out as a secretarial service quickly developed into a full-service printing business with scores of satisfied customers. Everything that Frances Gardner touched turned to gold. Life became easy, with the exception of the little voice inside her that said something was still missing.

These were the years when Frances became a "wild sinner." For ten years, she smoked five packs of cigarettes a day, drank martinis every night, and was the life of every party with her off-color stories and crude language. She thought she had life by the horns!

Yet each week, a young pastor named Peter Slagle would come into her printing shop and speak to her about the amazing things that were happening in his church. He never pressed Frances too hard but patiently showed her the love of Christ and the excitement in his own life. She was intrigued, yet she was also afraid to follow her heart, so she listened to him for four years without ever making a move.

As Frances was driving home from her son's new apartment late one night, her car was struck from behind by another vehicle. Everything seemed to be fine until three months later, when she discovered she had lost sight in her left eye. The fear of eye surgery overwhelmed her, and, like many panicked people, she cried out to God for His help. She asked Him to protect her from the pain of the surgery.

Lying in a hospital bed the night before the surgery, Frances experienced a miracle. She had been reading a verse from Psalm 23 to the nurses a few minutes earlier, trying to appear spiritual. After they left, she turned back to the psalm to finish reading and discovered that the two pages were completely blank—wiped clean! *Where did the ink go?* she wondered. Suddenly, she saw a hand write the words "Frances Gardner, I love you" in red across the blank pages. "God had dipped His finger in the brilliant red blood of Jesus and had written a very special message just for me," Frances wrote of the event.[310]

Overwhelmed by God's love for her, Frances cried out, "God, I take back that prayer, and I don't care how much it hurts tomorrow. I promise You this: when I get out of this hospital, I will spend the rest of my life seeing what I can do for You, and not what You can do for me."[311] Frances was in shock, but she knew that God had made it clear that He loved her personally, and with that message, He had captured her full attention.

As soon as Frances was well enough, she made a beeline for Pastor Slagle's church. It was a Church of God, non-Pentecostal congregation. (This is different from the Pentecostal denomination that is also called Church of God.) It was a holiness congregation, and the people loved and served the Lord. Frances heard a message about being born again, a concept she did not really understand, but she still attended the church every Sunday for nearly nine months. Every week, she wept through the closing hymn of "Just as I Am" yet still refused to surrender herself completely to the Lord.

God sent another young Christian man into Frances's printing shop, this time to have copies of *The Four Spiritual Laws*, a publication of Campus Crusade for Christ, printed for distribution. After Frances's curious questioning, Ed Waxer led her through the four biblical steps to salvation and established her need for a personal Savior. The following Sunday, February 8, 1966, Frances Gardner walked down to the altar of Pastor Slagle's church as a "wild sinner" and committed her life to Christ. That morning, at the age of forty-nine, Frances was born again. She uttered the life-changing words, "God, I'll make a deal with You. I'll give You all of me...in exchange for all of You."[312] And she never rescinded that commitment for the rest of her long, God-honoring life.

A Notorious Soulwinner

The Sunday after Frances had gone to the altar, attendance at Pastor Slagle's church nearly doubled. Frances brought twenty new people to church that morning to hear about the saving grace of Jesus. She later remarked, "I have been a soulwinner since the day I got saved, even though I didn't know what I was doing!"[313] Devoted friends and curious strangers accompanied her to church that morning to hear what Frances's powerful God had to say.

As the months passed, Frances looked for new ways to serve the Lord in the church. Her enthusiastic love for Christ was a beacon of light to many teenagers, so she started a youth group called Alpha/Omega, where many young people were led to the Lord, including her own daughter, Joan.

Frances exuberantly shared, "When Jesus came into my life, He opened my mouth, and I haven't shut it since!"[314] She witnessed with confidence to friends at parties, where she no longer drank, and they listened in astonishment while their drinks sat untouched.

Two years and many witnessing opportunities later, she wrote her first book, entitled *God Is Fabulous*, to introduce the world to a God who is personal, exciting, and desirous of giving His children incredible lives today. Frances knew that her call was to be an encourager—"someone to remind people that Jesus Christ is the most exciting Man who ever lived!"[315] In this book, Frances shared her passion for leading others to Christ. She proclaimed loud and clear, "There is no thrill in the world which compares to leading someone to Jesus!"[316] The little book became a quick seller, and Frances received an invitation to be the first woman to speak at the 1968 national camp meeting of the Church of God (COG), non-Pentecostal.

The afternoon of the convention, Frances prayed silently, "God, let Your Holy Spirit move in this auditorium like He has never moved before!"[317] Then, she stood before an audience of five thousand people and spoke from her heart about a God who had delivered her from smoking one hundred cigarettes a day, drinking strings of martinis, and living a life of sin. He was a God who loved her and lived daily in her heart, who gave her the opportunity to lead others to Him, and who would be her Savior and Redeemer for the rest of her life.

Frances ended her message with closed eyes and a simple prayer: "God, may I have been the woman You called me to be. May I have said what You told me to say."[318] When she opened her eyes, she was astounded to see over half of the congregation nearly running to the altar for prayer, some to meet Jesus for the first time, others to repent of their hardened hearts over the years. The church leaders shouted at them to stop coming forward, as there was no more room up front. Overwhelmed by the reaction and unsure of the next step, Frances walked off the platform and quietly left the building by a back door. Meanwhile, a leader in the denomination who was usually stoic ran from the meeting with uncharacteristic enthusiasm, shouting that the Holy Spirit had fallen inside the auditorium.

> **She stood before an audience of five thousand people and spoke from her heart about a God who had delivered her from smoking one hundred cigarettes a day, drinking strings of martinis, and living a life of sin.**

Where was this new and exciting life taking Frances Gardner? Ultimately, she was on a God-ordained collision course with a man by the name of Charles Hunter.

Across the Country

On the morning of July 23, 1920, Charles Edward Hunter was born as the fifth of six children to James and Minnie Hunter in Palo Pinto, Texas. Like Frances, he was born into a poor family, but there the similarities ended. Instead of growing up in a city environment, surrounded by lack and sickness, Charles was raised on ranches in the Southwest surrounded by the beauty of God's creation, and there was always enough growing on the land to provide for the family's basic needs.

✦✦✦✦✦

When Charles was still a child, an itinerant Baptist pastor came to the small town where his family lived and shared the powerful message of God's salvation through Jesus Christ. Charles's parents surrendered their lives to God's call that day and sensed His supernatural peace and presence in their lives.

The Hunters diligently worked in rural Texas as peach farmers, while their children grew up and then moved on. Charles knew from his early teens that he wanted to be an accountant—and a successful one!

He even stated that the mayor of Houston would be one of his clients someday. As a young teenager, Charles went forward to the altar at church to accept Jesus Christ into his life while his parents watched with great joy. By the time he was eighteen, he was leading youth groups and Bible studies. God was a part of his life, but a comparatively small part. The center of his life was still himself.[319]

Charles Hunter in the U.S. Air Force, 1944

When World War II broke out, Charles enlisted in the Army Air Corps, which later became the U.S. Air Force. He enlisted as a private and had to serve only twenty-one months before he was discharged. During that time, he was promoted to captain, and he could have had a career in the Air Force. But his dream was to return home and establish his own certified public accounting firm.[320]

Life in the Slow Lane

One by one, Charles's life dreams were fulfilled. He and his best friend, Leonard Helvering, started a CPA firm, and their first client was actually the mayor of Houston! Charles was a frugal, hardworking man who intended to be successful in every area of his life. He met and married his first wife, Jeanne, and they had a solid, love-filled marriage for twenty-seven years, although they had no children.

Through their married years, Charles and Jeanne Hunter attended church each week without fail. Their faithfulness became a source of pride for Charles, who sometimes found himself judging those who did not attend church as faithfully. He served the church in many ways—as a deacon, an usher, the church treasurer, a board member, and even a member of the church choir. He and Jeanne always supported church projects and tithed consistently. To everyone who knew them, they were pillars of the church second to none.

However, when Charles reflected on those years, he said that, spiritually speaking, he was a "dried-up prune."[321] Realizing how dry their life in Christ was, Charles and Jeanne decided to attend another church in the area. They sensed God's presence in the church and in the hearts of the believers there.

In the spring of 1968, around Easter, Charles joined a group of men in the congregation who met for prayer on a weekly basis. One morning, Charles experienced a strong longing for more of Christ. Without a special invitation from the pastor or an altar call, Charles went to the church altar, bowed humbly before the Lord, and said to Him, "Take *all* of my life and make me spiritually what *You* want me to be. Take all of Jeanne's life spiritually and make her the person You want her to be."[322]

"Hydrogen Energy"

For Charles and Jeanne, everything changed. Charles compared his new life in Jesus to "hydrogen energy" available to us when we turn God loose to use our lives for His glory. He and Jeanne were able to minister to others in a powerful way, pray together in the presence of the Lord, and impact others for Jesus. It was the most fulfilling time they spent together.

Devastating news came just a few months later. After a number of tests and a disquieting visit to the doctor, they discovered that Jeanne had ovarian cancer. The mass in her lower abdomen was growing, and her condition was terminal. This was not the direction their lives were supposed to take! Jeanne wrestled with the Lord for several days.

Seeking the Lord for His strength and comfort, Jeanne felt her fear pass away. Their pastor came to pray with her, and she let her fears slide away for good. During those final six months of Jeanne's life, with Charles always by her side, her faith and testimony remained strong and blessed those around her. Later, Charles wrote about this precious time with his wife in a book entitled *A Tribute to God*, "She attained a faith in God—a far greater faith than I have ever seen—and approached eternity with such an eager positive assurance that there was absolutely no room for doubt that she was personally, literally, a child of God going to her eternal home joyfully."[323]

On May 29, 1969, Jeanne went home to be with Jesus. Charles always remembered his first wife as a precious child of God who shared years of happiness with him, and his time of grieving was also filled with rejoicing that she was now with Jesus. In the months following Jeanne's death, Charles threw himself more vigorously into sharing the gospel of Jesus along with others from his Church of God congregation.

A Date with God's Destiny

Ever since the powerful Church of God camp meeting where Frances had delivered a memorable message with an apparent move of God, word had been spreading about her throughout the denomination, and she was inundated with invitations to speak at many different churches and Bible schools. One particular pastor who had attended the 1968 camp meeting returned to Houston and shared with his brother Charles about the remarkable events that had occurred. He also handed Charles the famous speaker's new book, *God Is Fabulous*.

> **Charles Hunter read the book from cover to cover and was determined to meet this spitfire for Jesus.**

Over the next few days, Charles Hunter read the book from cover to cover and was determined to meet this spitfire for Jesus. When he learned that Frances would soon visit Houston to speak at a Christian college and several churches, he called her office in Florida and invited her to stay in his home while she was ministering in Houston. He explained that he would, of course, stay elsewhere, but Frances misinterpreted the offer and hung up on the "dirty old man."

When Frances arrived in Houston, she was shocked to see Charles listed as the leader of one of the sessions on her itinerary. She determined to greet him coldly, but when she finally met him, a cold façade was impossible. When they shook hands, she felt the electricity of the Holy Spirit flowing between them! Getting to know him over the next two days convinced her that she had been wrong about his intentions.

Charles had also been assigned to drive Frances to the youth meeting at his church. After she spoke there, he volunteered to drive her to her next appointment—visiting her friends from Campus Crusade for Christ at their home. He ended up joining her, and the two of them stayed up late into the evening, sharing with these friends stories of God moving among His people. When Charles finally drove Frances back to her hotel, they were both reluctant to end the evening. So, they sat in the car and continued to share, then spent another hour praying for the needs of others. During that time, Charles gave Frances nearly twenty-seven of his business cards in case she ever needed to contact him.[324]

Love Letters through Jesus

As soon as Frances got back to Florida, she sent Charles a thank-you letter for his helpfulness during the trip and for the donation he had given to her ministry. The next day, she felt compelled to write him another letter, inviting him to a "Party for the Lord" service at her church on New Year's Eve. Thus began a dynamic, ongoing correspondence between Charles Hunter and Frances Gardner. They wrote excitedly about their love for Jesus Christ and all the things He was doing in and through their lives. Within weeks, the letters shifted focus to a growing admiration and love for one another.

Their notes were filled with professions of faith that God was the one in control of their destinies because they had surrendered their entire lives to Him. Charles began to speak in faith about God's plans for them from the beginning, writing, "I know God has a very definite purpose in your entering my life and I'm very glad and will stand by, ready to run with Him when He says go!"[325] When they were discussing their common mission of leading others to Jesus, Charles wrote, "You 'enthuse' people and cause masses to accept Christ. I 'enthuse' people and constantly press for nothing short of TOTAL commitment of their lives. Maybe He wants me to follow along after you and talk further to those seeds which fall on good, rich ground and [see] their lives flourish."[326]

★★★★★

His statement proved to be prophetic, for in the decades that followed, what he had hypothesized was exactly what would happen. The two of them would minister together, Frances leading the way by sharing the plan of salvation and speaking about the power of the Holy Spirit, and Charles following her, helping believers to receive the baptism of the Holy Spirit. It was a ministry match made in heaven!

One Minute after Midnight

After six weeks of correspondence, it was obvious to Frances and Charles that they were in love and wanted to be married. But their first desire was to glorify the Lord, so they continued to pray for His guidance. With Frances's ministry calendar full, there were no free weekends available for a wedding for two years, and since she and Charles were dedicated to keeping God first in everything, neither one of them wanted her to cancel a commitment. What to do?

One night in mid-December, just ten days before Charles was scheduled to arrive in Florida for the Christmas visit, Frances cried out to the Lord, "God, I just don't know when Charles and I can get married, but *You* do, so I am going to ask You to reveal it to me, and confirm to Charles exactly when we should be married!"[327]

In just a couple of days, God spoke to Frances's heart: "1969 was Jeanne's, 1970 is yours—start it off right the first minute, at the Party for the Lord."[328] Frances was stunned because she received this message on December 19—just eleven days before their wedding date, according to the Lord—and Charles hadn't been told yet!

Frances wrote to him right away, explaining that God had given her the date, and so now he needed to ask for a confirmation. Just a few days prior, she had penned these words: "Common sense tells me things like this just don't happen. They don't work. It's impossible, and yet I was never more certain of anything in my life than I am of God's hand in our relationship."[329]

Soon, Charles called Frances and read to her from a letter he had written, saying, "I feel utterly confident that your answer is also the same exact date and exact time and my heart is about to jump out of my chest!!…At the New Year's Eve Party for the Lord at midnight—to start the Fabulous 1970 year."[330] They marveled at God's faithfulness and planned their wedding in excitement.

Despite some difficulty in obtaining a marriage license on such short notice, the wedding went as planned. Frances changed into a wedding dress just after the Party for the Lord, and the dynamic ministry team of Charles and Frances Hunter was born! Just a few weeks before the wedding, before the confirmation from God, Charles had written to Frances, "We can never look selfishly at our blessings when [God's] main purpose in teaming us as partners is for reaping

Charles and Frances cut their wedding cake on January 1, 1970.

a harvest of souls for Him and glorifying Him by our totally dedicated service to Him for the rest of our lives. WOW FOR GOD!"[331] "Wow for God" is probably what Frances and Charles were saying once the Lord really teamed them as partners in ministry as well as in marriage.

Life Begins with Jesus

God had brought Frances and Charles together because they both loved Him and they both loved each other. But in the first months of their marriage, love and ministry did not mesh together well. Frances traveled extensively to minister without Charles, which was much harder on him than he'd imagined it would be, even though he had the company of Frances's daughter, Joan, with whom they made their home in Houston.

Eventually, Charles withdrew more and more from his accounting practice until he was traveling with Frances nearly full-time. When it was possible, Joan, who had just turned sixteen, would join them. Charles had a father's love for Joan from the beginning and legally adopted her as his own child soon after he and Frances were married.

In their early days of traveling together, Charles saw his job as a silent, loving supporter of Frances's ministry. At each event, he would escort her onto the platform and stand behind her to pray while she preached. They continued to write books, sometimes together and sometimes on their own. As the Lord was touching thousands of lives for Jesus, they heard growing reports about a tremendous move of the Holy Spirit sweeping across the nation. Initially frightened by a movement they had been warned against, they avoided the new "charismatic" meetings.

Well-meaning Christians gave the Hunters books like John and Elizabeth Sherrill's *They Speak with Other Tongues* and Pat Boone's *A New Song*. Some days, they were intrigued by the message; other days, they were annoyed; but through it all, they prayed that God would grant them discernment.

In early 1971, the Hunters flew to Pittsburgh to preach for several days. On a rare night when their schedule was empty, they attended a meeting of the Charismatic Conference at the First Presbyterian Church in downtown Pittsburgh, where Kathryn Kuhlman ministered on occasion. They were curious about the charismatic service going on that evening, but they sat in the back of the church "just in case" they needed to make a quick escape.

From the beginning, Frances noted how the singing was different from anything she had ever heard. As the congregation sang "Amazing Grace," Frances thought, *They do not sound like we sound in our church.* All of a sudden, the congregation began to sing a beautiful harmony of sounds in tongues. Startled, Frances turned to Charles and asked, "What is that? Whatever it is, it sure is pretty, isn't it?"[332] As the Presbyterian pastor spoke, Frances was certain that she had never heard so much power in a message. But when there was an altar call for those who wanted to receive the baptism of the Holy Spirit, Charles and Frances hightailed it out of there and ran a block down the street before they stopped to talk about what they had just witnessed.[333]

The Anointing of Kathryn Kuhlman

The morning after their visit to the charismatic meeting, the Hunters went back to the First Presbyterian Church, this time to attend a Kathryn Kuhlman healing service. Their curiosity concerning the power of God's Holy Spirit was growing. As they approached the church, they came upon crowds of people lined up outside, waiting for a seat—and every seat inside was already filled. Right beside them stood a man cradling his daughter in his arms. Her entire body was covered with lumps.

Shortly after their arrival, an usher began calling the Hunters' names. Miss Kuhlman had learned that they were outside and knew that Frances was a well-known author, and she had sent someone to escort them to reserved seats near the front. Charles and Frances were eager to see God move in that church and grateful that the Lord had provided seats with a good view of everything that was happening.

The praise and worship at the opening of the service was glorious. Miss Kuhlman walked out onto the platform to sing "How Great Thou Art" with the choir and the congregation. The presence of the Holy Spirit was strong in the sanctuary. And then, the healing reports began. Miss Kuhlman did not lay hands on the sick during these meetings. She just waited as the Spirit of God moved through the auditorium and healed a number of people. She would invite them to come forward to the platform to testify of how and when God had healed them.[334]

Kathryn Kuhlman flowed with the gift of the Holy Spirit called a "word of knowledge," and she would often point to an area of the auditorium where she believed a healing was taking place. It might be a woman whose hearing was restored or a man who could now walk without his brace. That morning, Miss Kuhlman announced that there was a little girl with cancer and lumps all over her body who was being healed by the power of God at that moment. Much to the Hunters' amazement and joy, the little girl they had seen outside the church came running down the aisle, looking perfectly healthy without a single lump on her body! The assembly, including the Hunters, erupted with a spontaneous offering of praise to God.

> **Kathryn Kuhlman flowed with the gift of the Holy Spirit called a "word of knowledge," and she would often point to an area of the auditorium where she believed a healing was taking place.**

This was also the first time that Charles and Frances saw someone "go down under the power," an experience that is also called being "slain in the Spirit." Often, when a person was touched by God's Holy Spirit, he would fall back at the power of His presence. Many believers compared it to the incident with Jesus and the guards who came to arrest Him at the garden of Gethsemane. When the guards asked for Jesus by name and He responded, "I am He," the guards fell backward on the ground in His presence. (See John 18:4–6.)

The spiritual atmosphere in Kathryn Kuhlman's meetings was always quiet and reverent. She maintained that this was out of respect for the Holy Spirit. She would walk around the room, and the people would stand to their feet as she passed. To some, she would reach out her hand and simply say, "Bless her, Jesus," or "Bless him, Lord," and those individuals would fall gently to the floor under the power of God's Holy Spirit. While they lay there in His presence, many would be healed of physical, emotional, and mental diseases. Many people were slain in the Spirit as they approached the platform or even right where they stood.

This was still such a new thing to the Hunters at the time, and Frances remained skeptical. *Well, she's such a tiny woman; she's not going to knock me down!* she thought. But when Miss Kuhlman approached and asked Frances to step into the aisle, she simply spoke the words, "Jesus, bless my sister," and Frances floated to the ground, surrounded by the presence of the Holy Spirit. Frances shared years later, "I don't know if she even touched me. I was down on the floor and felt the power of the Holy Spirit flooding over me. I never questioned the power of the Holy Spirit again. That really changed my life forever; it does something to you."[335]

Frances and Charles became friends of Kathryn Kuhlman and were involved with her ministry for the next five years, until Kathryn passed away in 1976. Frances insisted, "We saw more power in her services than we have ever seen since then. That was God's choice. It was His power, and He gave it as He willed."[336]

"God Was Still After Us!"

After their first visit with Miss Kuhlman, the Hunters still didn't understand much about the baptism in the Holy Spirit, but, as Frances said with a laugh, "God was still after us."[337] In the summer of 1971, the Hunters attended the Christian Booksellers Association International Convention in Denver. Their booth was set up directly across from that of George Otis, author of *High Adventure*, his personal testimony, and *You Shall Receive*, a book on the baptism in the Holy Spirit. George was filled with enthusiasm and a vibrant joy in the Lord. He and Charles hit it off immediately because they had similar backgrounds. George had been a successful businessman and the general manager for Learjet when he came to Christ and left everything behind to spread the gospel all over the world. At this point in the 1970s, he was very instrumental in leading many people into the baptism in the Holy Spirit, including Pat and Shirley Boone.[338]

A few weeks later, when George traveled to Houston to preach, he stayed in the Hunters' home. By that time, Charles and Frances were convinced that the baptism in the Holy Spirit was the next step to take in their walk with Christ. They just didn't know how to receive it. When George left, he gave them a cassette tape of one of his teaching sessions. The Hunters lay in bed that night listening to Scriptures from the book of Acts that described the baptism in the Holy Spirit.

In the recording, when George encouraged his listeners to raise their hands to receive, the Hunters raised their hands in the air and invited Jesus to baptize them with the Holy Spirit. They didn't receive their prayer languages that evening, but the very next day, at separate times, they excitedly received a new language to use to praise their Lord.

> **Charles and Frances were convinced that the baptism in the Holy Spirit was the next step to take in their walk with Christ. They just didn't know how to receive it.**

The Flow of God's Power

From the moment they received the baptism in the Holy Spirit, everything changed in the Hunters' ministry. Every time they laid hands on someone to pray or spoke a message from the Bible, they felt the power of God flowing through them unlike anything they had ever experienced before.

But the first thing that happened wasn't exactly positive. They called George Otis in Alaska after they had received the baptism to give him the good news. Even though George was so far away, the news spread like wildfire, and by the very next day, Christians throughout the country were aware of their new experience. A pastor from the Church of God (non-Pentecostal) denomination called to ask Frances if the news concerning the "Holy Spirit baptism" was true. When she admitted that it was, he canceled their upcoming speaking engagement because he was certain that the "wrong spirit" would be present in the meeting. Before the week was up, all of the Hunters' speaking engagements at churches within this denomination were canceled, as well. But in their place, God opened wide a door for the Hunters to minister His power to thousands of people.

In the 1960s, Demos Shakarian of Los Angeles had started the Full Gospel Businessmen's Fellowship International (FGBMFI), which had chapters across the country. It was an organization that encouraged men to share their faith and learn more about God's move in the earth today. There were FGBMFI groups in nearly every city. Frances was the first woman who ever spoke at a Full Gospel Businessmen's meeting. The Hunters' first invitation was to speak at a FGBMFI convention in Seattle, Washington, where Frances gave an altar call for those desiring the baptism in the Holy Spirit. Then, Charles ministered the baptism to those who came forward. Over five hundred people received the baptism that night, and word spread rapidly throughout the entire organization. Invitations from Full Gospel chapters poured into the Hunters' ministry headquarters in Houston from all over the country. Exciting opportunities to share God's message of salvation, power, and healing were multiplying for them.

The Powerful Charismatic Revival

Frances referred to the charismatic flood of the Holy Spirit as a "masculine" revival because, unlike many other revivals and movements in the church, it did not affect primarily women. Instead, men from all walks of life were seeking the power of God represented in the Holy Spirit.[339] Men were discovering that Jesus was the most powerful Man in the world, and they were submitting their lives to Him.

Every denomination was touched by this sweeping movement of God's Spirit. Everyone, from Methodists to Catholics, was hungry for the Holy Spirit of God! At one interdenominational meeting in Wichita, Kansas, Charles asked for every member of the clergy who desired a special anointing of the Holy Spirit to come forward for prayer. Nearly seventy-five pastors and their wives swept forward, weeping and praying in anticipation of a touch by the Spirit of God. "They stood there, Methodist, Presbyterian, Nazarene, Brethren, Mennonite, Assembly of God, Foursquare, Baptist, Congregational, Christian, Friends, Interdenominational pastors, and many others, all wanting everything God had for them. It was a beautiful sight to behold as every single pastor and his wife went under the power of God!"[340]

To the Hunters, the beauty of the charismatic movement was also in the faces and lives of young adults. The 1960s had been a demoralizing decade for the nation, especially for young people. Looking for answers, many were drawn to the baptism in the Holy Spirit and the power of God because they believed it could actually change their lives. They flocked to meetings in droves and were set free from the drug culture and rebellion around them, finding their real hope for change in Jesus Christ alone.

One young man who attended a meeting led by the Hunters was initially cynical about the "emotionalism" around him. But when he saw a close friend healed of a back injury before his very eyes, he cried out for the Lord to save him. This young man accepted Christ, was slain in the Spirit, and was set free from a life of drugs, alcohol, crime, and witchcraft as he lay in God's presence.

Overjoyed at being a part of God's movement, Frances declared,

This is what the Holy Spirit is doing today as He sweeps across the world! He is wooing people into a real love relationship with Jesus! And as hearts are opening up, God is pouring out His Spirit more and more. We are beginning to fulfill the purpose for which we were put on this earth—to have fellowship with God! We're falling in love with Jesus![341]

Marked for Healing

Even before receiving the baptism in the Holy Spirit, Frances Hunter knew that she was marked by God for healing—both to be healed and

Frances Hunter knew that she was marked by God for healing—both to be healed and to bring healing to others in the name of Jesus.

to bring healing to others in the name of Jesus. Even though she initially attended a church that did not believe in divine healing for today, she experienced God's healing power in her own body several times. When she first surrendered to Jesus in the winter of 1966, she was being treated for Addison's disease, a rare disorder of the endocrine glands, which had severely injured her thyroid. Frances was instructed to take a large dosage of steroids every day for the rest of her life. Failure to treat the condition seriously could be fatal.

Then, Frances accepted Jesus Christ as her Savior, and her whole world became a stream of challenging, God-centered opportunities. In her newfound excitement, Frances simply forgot to take her medication. The symptoms of the disease had slipped away without her notice! This may seem strange to some, but not for a woman who moved through life as uproariously as Frances Hunter. Six months later, when she realized that she had neglected her medicine, her first reaction was to panic. Would she die? Quietly, the Lord spoke to her spirit, saying, "I have taken care of the disease. You are healed!" Sure enough, a trip to the doctor confirmed that her thyroid was normal, and her body was completely free of Addison's disease.[342]

Frances's second and third healings came in the next two years. She was having trouble with her right eye, which was her "good" eye. Things had just become blurry. Her eye doctor insisted that without surgery, she would go blind in that eye. If he performed the surgery, though, both eyes would be affected, and she would be without sight for two months during the recovery process. Fear welled up in Frances, and she cried to the Lord to touch her with His healing hand. One day, while Frances was sitting in the beauty parlor, Jesus did just that. She closed her eyes for a moment and woke up with all of the blurriness gone. Frances never had a problem with that eye again.[343]

Frances was healed a third time a year later when she broke her foot while at a Gene Cotton concert in New York City. Gene was a young

Christian friend, and Frances was helping him to manage his new music career. The hospital in New York City determined that her foot was broken in three places. In pain, yet refusing treatment, Frances insisted on returning to Florida to see her own doctor. As she and Gene sped to the airport to catch their late-night flight, she called out to the Lord for a healing. As she walked onto the airplane, Gene realized that Frances was limping on the wrong foot. "The pain is gone," Frances responded. A trip to the local hospital the next morning revealed that her foot was no longer broken.[344] The church that Frances attended at the time may not have believed in divine healing, but she had become a firm believer!

Signs and Wonders Shall Follow

"Faith is not so much believing for miracles as it is knowing you have correctly heard God."[345] The Hunters were certain that God had spoken to them about healing for the multitudes. From that first miracle service they participated in with Pastor Bob Lewis in El Paso, Texas, to their final days on earth, the Hunters believed that God had spoken a healing word to them.

They knew that in the earlier healing ministries, people flocked to special people who had a healing anointing, like Oral Roberts and Kathryn Kuhlman. But once the Hunters received the baptism in the Holy Spirit, Mark 16:17–18 became a central part of their ministry:

And these signs will follow those who believe: in My name they will cast out demons; they will speak with new tongues; they will take up serpents; and if they drink anything deadly, it will by no means hurt them; they will lay hands on the sick, and they will recover. (NKJV)

This was a word for ordinary believers who trusted in the healing power of Jesus Christ. The signs of Jesus' ministry would follow them.

Many healing miracles followed the Hunters through the years and touched many people, including a man named "Stoney" Henry. When he met the Hunters, he had a malignant tumor on his bladder that the doctors had tried to fight with chemotherapy. It had progressed from stage one to stage two and had no signs of remission. Stoney read the testimonies of others who had been miraculously healed of cancer and other diseases. He was invited to attend a Full Gospel Businessmen's meeting to see what God could do, and Charles and Frances Hunter were the speakers at this particular meeting.

After preaching on the power of God to save, baptize, and heal, Charles invited people to come forward for prayer in any of those areas. Stoney came forward, of course—he needed prayer for it all! Unsure if he had been saved, he gave his heart to Christ. As Charles and Frances laid hands on him, he received the baptism in the Holy Spirit with a beautifully flowing new language. They laid hands on him again and rebuked the cancer in the name of Jesus. Stoney walked out of the meeting with great joy, believing that with God, all things are possible. Two trips to MD Anderson Hospital in Houston over the next three months confirmed the Holy Spirit's power that night—Stoney had been completely healed![346]

Miracles upon Miracles

> The woman, who had been crippled with rheumatoid arthritis for twelve years, stood up from her wheelchair and began to walk.

Near the end of a miracle service at a Foursquare church in the Midwest, Frances walked up to a woman in a wheelchair, prayed for her healing, and then laid hands on her and said simply, "Jesus, bless her!" When Frances turned to walk on, she heard the congregation gasp. The woman, who had been crippled with rheumatoid arthritis for twelve years, stood up from her wheelchair and began to walk. Several months later, the Hunters called her to see how she was doing, and she told them, "All I saw was Jesus telling me to get up, and I wasn't about to disobey Him!" She had been completely healed![347]

The Hunters had just finished conducting a marriage ceremony at the Melodyland Christian Center in Anaheim, California, when they noticed a teenage girl walking with a heavy limp. One leg was bent and stiff. When Charles asked her what was wrong,

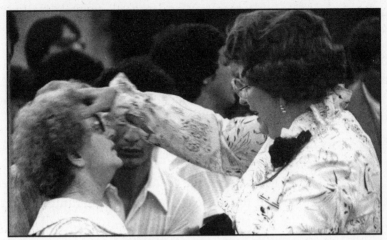

Frances Hunter ministers healing.

she answered, "I was born this way. The tendons in my leg didn't grow correctly." The Hunters had just moments to get to their next seminar, but they laid hands on the girl and said, "Jesus, touch her." Then, they left for their meeting.

A short time later, they were at another meeting in California, and one of the associate pastors from the church in Melodyland, Mike Esses, came up to the microphone and shared the good news of God's healing power in the life of that young girl, saying, "I'm her Sunday school teacher. It was an instant and total healing and her leg is normal."[348]

On their way to minister at a FGBMFI service in Atlanta, Georgia, Charles and Frances were reading Scriptures on healing. Frances read from the ninth chapter of Mark about the healing of a boy who was possessed by a *"deaf and mute spirit"* (Mark 9:25 NIV). They soon realized that God had been preparing their hearts for the meeting, for the third person who came forward for healing that day was a thirty-five-year-old man who was both deaf and mute. He worked in an engineering firm and had been invited to the meeting by his employer.

Laying hands on him, Frances repeated the words of Jesus, saying, "You deaf and dumb spirit, come out of this man now, in the name of Jesus." (See Mark 9:25 NKJV.) The man kept pointing at his ears and looking at Frances. She whispered, "Praise the Lord!" in his ear. Slowly, he spoke his first words ever—"Pwaise" and "Amen"—in a flat-sounding voice but with the biggest smile on his face! Everyone realized this man would have to learn to speak, but he could definitely hear. Tears flowed!

Three weeks later, the Hunters received a letter from the man's employer, reporting that the young man was listening to the radio constantly and "jabbering like a baby" as he was learning to talk. Praise God for His faithfulness!

Frances was deeply touched by the testimony of a woman from Pittsburgh who had been healed at the 1973 Pittsburgh Charismatic Conference. The woman had found a nodule on one of her breasts that her doctor wanted to remove and test for cancer. After the Hunters laid hands on her for healing, she returned to her doctor to find that all signs of the nodule had disappeared! He insisted on taking X-rays to be certain, and they confirmed she was completely healed. The woman joyfully shared, "The thing that perhaps touched me the most is that Jesus had time for me, on that busy night when hundreds were pressing in for healing. It was a needed assurance for me that I am valuable to Him, and I praise and thank Him for this amazing fact."[349]

> **Instead of being limited to personally laying hands on the sick wherever they went, the Hunters had a revolutionary commission to teach the nations how to heal so that believers could lay their hands on the sick and see them recover.**

Covering the Globe with Healing

In early 1980, Frances had a vision of the world with bands of liquid gold running over it. People from every nation were standing on the ribbons of gold throughout the earth. She shared her vision with Charles, and it was clear to them that the Lord was telling them to expand the message of salvation and healing through Christ to the world. But instead of being limited to personally laying hands on the sick wherever they went, they had a revolutionary commission to teach the nations how to heal so that believers could lay their hands on the sick and see them recover. The Lord directed them to multiply themselves by teaching the masses.

How would they reach millions with God's message of healing? Technology became God's answer for their need. The advent of videotapes and the VCR made it possible to teach thousands of people whom the Hunters would never personally meet. Charles and Frances created a fourteen-hour series of videotapes entitled *How to Heal the Sick*, and shared everything that the Lord had revealed to them concerning healing over the last decade.

There were two key teachings that the Hunters wanted to communicate. First, after a close study of the Gospels, they had discovered that Jesus did not pray and ask His Father to heal the sick. Rather, Jesus touched the sick person, spoke a healing word, or commanded the disease to be gone. To deaf ears, Jesus said, *"Be opened"* (Mark 7:34); to the leper, Jesus said *"Be thou clean"* (Mark 1:41) as He touched him; to the man with the withered hand, Jesus said, *"Stretch forth your hand"* (Luke 6:10). It was the touch or the spoken word that brought forth the healing.

The second biblical key to healing the Hunters discovered was to tell people to do something that they were previously unable to do. *"Arise, and take up thy bed, and walk"* (Mark 2:9), Jesus said to the healed paralytic. *"In the name of Jesus Christ of Nazareth, rise up and walk"* (Acts 3:6) was the command of Peter and John to the man at the Beautiful Gate. The sick had to take a step of faith on their own, and the Healer would meet them there! Immediately after the video series was completed and ready for distribution, it was on its way to France, Peru, Bolivia, and several countries in Africa and Asia. And miracle services spread throughout the U.S. and abroad as healing teams were trained in countries around the world.

Healing Explosions

What would you call a meeting where thousands of people came forward for baptism in the Holy Spirit and to receive healing? Charles and Frances would call it a "Healing Explosion."

In 1984, Russ Bixler, president of Channel 40 Christian TV in Pittsburgh, Pennsylvania, invited the Hunters to conduct a healing seminar

✬✬✬✬✬

that would be broadcast on television, followed by a miracle service in the large sports complex then known as the Civic Arena in downtown Pittsburgh. Because the arena could seat over ten thousand people, this was a much bigger venue than any the Hunters had ever experienced. God was opening doors wider for His messages to be shared!

This was the perfect opportunity to put the teachings of *How to Heal the Sick* to work. Charles and Frances did not want the miracle service to focus on them but on Jesus Christ and His Holy Spirit. The Hunters put out a call to Pittsburgh area churches for believers who wanted to be trained to heal the sick. After watching the videos, the participants would receive three days of personal ministry from the Hunters. During the miracle service, the Hunters would be turning the ministry of healing over to ordinary believers, who had the same Holy Spirit power living within them! Frances had initially envisioned a healing team of 120 people, but over one thousand Christians volunteered for the training. There was a tremendous desire to see the power of God move among the sick and heal them.

After praise and worship, Frances opened the service with the gospel message of salvation in Jesus Christ. No one would leave the arena without an opportunity to surrender to a living, loving Christ. Then, Charles ministered the baptism in the Holy Spirit to those who desired to receive this empowering gift from God. Over five thousand people came forward to receive; most spoke in other tongues, and glorified God in their new prayer language.

Finally, the healing teams moved to the front of the arena, where they would meet with anyone who wanted to be prayed for to receive healing. Scores of people gave testimonies of healings that took place—deaf ears were opened, blind eyes could suddenly see, lame people walked. Doctors were on hand, paired with the healing teams, to verify that the healings had taken place.[350] The crowds filtered out of the arena, filled with a sense of wonder. The message of God's love and power they had just heard was not to remain inside the walls of the arena. It would go forth on the lips of people who had sensed the Lord's presence and believed what the Word said about Jesus Christ's having come to give them an abundant life. (See John 10:10 NKJV.)

✷✷✷✷✷

CHARLES & FRANCES HUNTER

A True Explosion

For five years, through more than one hundred fifty Healing Explosions, God moved in His amazing power as the Hunters surrendered to His will. Some of the largest arenas in America were filled with joyful believers seeking the love and power of God in their lives. Thousands responded to become a part of the healing teams—believers ready to be just like Jesus' early disciples, who were sent out in pairs and had the power of God move through their own hands.

Charles at an international Healing Explosion

The Healing Explosions were held in other countries, as well, with crowds of forty to sixty thousand people in countries like Peru, the Philippines, Colombia, and South Africa. In each of these nations, because the need for God was even greater and the belief in His power even stronger than they were in the U.S., even more miracles took place. Frances spoke often of the Healing Explosion in Bogota, Columbia, where they saw more wheelchairs than they had ever seen before. As the healing teams moved out, Frances looked at the pressing needs and thought, *God, if You are not in this, we are sunk!* But God was in it, and that day, more than one hundred people came out of their wheelchairs or dropped their crutches and walked away healed.[351]

Frances at an international Healing Explosion

In the late 1980s, Charles and Frances Hunter ministered the baptism in the Holy Spirit to more people than anyone else had before then—or has since.[352] They never conducted a meeting without giving seeking believers an opportunity to surrender completely to the Spirit of the living God.

World Evangelistic Census

In the early 1990s, Charles and Frances were in their seventies, and the strain of international travel was taking its toll. When they prayed

★★★★★

to the Lord about the next phase of their ministry, Charles received an unusual answer from God: "Take a census of the world."[353] The Hunters were intrigued and uncertain of exactly what the Lord was asking them to do.

A few weeks later, God spoke to Frances in her quiet time and directed her to go back to Honduras and organize an event in which the churches there would share the gospel with every citizen of the nation over a period of two weeks. Because Charles was such a methodical man, he used the basic format of the U.S. Census to divide the nation of Honduras into different sections and then into even smaller segments after that. Teams of two would be assigned thirty-five homes apiece to visit and to share the gospel of the Lord Jesus Christ with. Who knew how many people would profess their faith in Christ after hearing the Word?

At the end of the two weeks, over two million of the five million citizens of Honduras had made a profession of faith in Jesus! Every new Christian was invited to join a church cell group where he could learn more about God and grow in faith. Churches throughout Honduras reported amazing growth in the years that followed, as well.

The success of the Honduras census was not matched in the U.S., however. When the Hunters tried to enact the plan there in 1992, the size of the nation was such that funds were insufficient to cover the costs of large-scale evangelism, and they ended up with unpaid bills and little progress. Although the plan did not work out as they had hoped, they turned their financial troubles over to the Lord, and He brought the increase needed to redeem them. Undaunted, they continued to seek the Lord for new avenues of sharing the gospel.

A New Witnessing Tool

The Hunters were never ready to retire, and God never retired from giving them fresh ideas about new ways to reach the lost. In the late 1990s, someone the Hunters later believed to be an angel shared an amazing witnessing tool with them. This Christian brother would approach someone in his daily routine—a sales clerk in a store, for instance—and say, "May I ask you a question?" If he received an affirmative reply, he would go on and say something like, "Did you know there are two kinds of sales clerks—those who are saved and those who are about to be? Which one are you?" The result was a confession either that the person was already saved or that perhaps he was about to be. If the person admitted to being in the latter group—those who were about to be saved—he would be asked if he wanted to accept Christ as his Lord and Savior. If he gave another affirmative answer, he would be led in the sinner's prayer and then invited to visit a local church or find a place of Christian fellowship to grow in faith.

The Hunters saw this technique as a win-win situation for both parties, and as soon as she heard about this revolutionary witnessing tool, she began to use it. In her caring and forthright manner, she asked the questions of everyone she met, and many people responded that they wanted to know Christ. It happened over and over again! Excited, she and Charles authored a booklet called *There Are Two Kinds Of...*, which was translated into several different languages and distributed worldwide to their international Christian friends and other ministries.

In the Philippines, a network of pastors used the new witnessing tool, as well as the World Census guidelines, to witness to the entire population of the Philippine Islands. Tens of thousands of people accepted the Lord and were welcomed into churches of all denominations throughout the Islands. By the year 2000, believers in one hundred countries were following the Hunters' plan to reach their entire nations for Jesus. As the numbers of those who came to salvation were reported, they grew from tens of thousands to millions and beyond! It was a plan to reach the lost of the world with a personal visit to each household, which they believed to be far more effective than technology alone. The World Evangelistic Census was working! How the Hunters praised God for His supernatural guidance!

By 2009, it was reported that more than one billion people had come to salvation through the World Evangelistic Census.[354] When critics questioned the massive numbers of professions of faith that were being reported, the Hunters' ministry team looked to the Word of God for confirmation. In the parable of the sower and the seed (see Matthew 13:19–23), the seed of

> **The Hunters had been instrumental in the salvation of well over 200 million believers worldwide.**

God's Word was sown on many different types of soil. One-fourth of those who received the Word were "fertile soil" who embraced the Word and grew into vibrant, healthy Christians. With those numbers alone, the Hunters had been instrumental in the salvation of well over 200 million believers worldwide.

From the beginning, soulwinning was at the center of Charles and Frances's Christian walk. As they moved toward the end of their time on earth, "God was able to use them to win millions because *they were faithful to win one.*"[355]

The Final Years

On October 2, 2004, the Houston Astrodome exploded with praise and worship as the 172nd Healing Explosion began. It was the fulfillment of a vision Frances had had years earlier that she and Charles would one day minister in their home stadium. Frances was eighty-eight years old, and Charles was eighty-four. And the vision was fulfilled none too soon, for this was to be the final event in the Astrodome before it was closed for renovation.

Charles and Frances Hunter minister at the Astrodome.

Filled with joy, Frances took the microphone as she had done so many times before and praised God for the opportunity to honor Him once again with other believers in Christ. She assured the people in attendance that it was Jesus' desire to baptize believers with the power of the Holy Spirit. Slowly, Charles joined her on the microphone. He prayed, as he had countless times before, for all those who had come seeking to be filled with the Holy Spirit. He encouraged the members of the congregation to ask Jesus to baptize them in the Spirit, just as they had asked Him to save them from their sins. Thousands prayed to receive the baptism in the Holy Spirit. Then, Frances called on the Lord to move faithfully among them with His healing power, and healing team members from all over the stadium came forward to minister to those in need. Healings were reported that day and for weeks afterward, and the Lord was glorified.

It's Never Quite Over

Two years later, when Frances had passed her ninetieth birthday, the Lord moved in her heart once again. Frances believed that they were to establish a National Day of Healing, when churches of all denominations that wanted to participate could open their doors simultaneously for the sick to come for healing. The date they selected was October 28, 2006. In the months leading up to the event, the Hunters had friends and other ministries spread the word, including Christian television stations and magazines. They distributed material on God's power to heal to every church that requested it.

The mayor of Houston declared that the day would be called "Charles and Frances Hunter Day," and Frances spent twenty minutes on the

Charles and Frances with extended family members at the Healing Explosion

✵✵✵✵✵

phone receiving a commendation from the White House and then-President George W. Bush for planning the day of healing. Ministries in other nations called the Hunters' headquarters and asked if they could join in this time of prayer for healing.

On October 28, telephone lines were open to receive the healing reports, which began to come in from all over the country. A man in Texas was healed in his wheelchair and began to walk. Someone from New Jersey had a tumor on her wrist that disappeared. A helicopter pilot who had been injured in an accident four years earlier was healed, saved, and filled with the Holy Spirit that afternoon.[356]

The Hunters celebrated a victorious day of healing, salvation, and glory to a God who was moving among His people. As the day came to a close, Frances declared that the next Day of Healing would be not quite one year later, on September 22, 2007. But this time, it would be called a "Worldwide Day of Healing" and include brothers and sisters in Christ all over the world. There was no task too large for God, so there was nothing beyond the imagination of this woman who served Him. As others have noted, "Frances was one of the few people over ninety years of age who continued to make plans for the unforeseeable future."[357] Their daughter Joan Hunter continues to lead this effort today.

A Personal Interview

I had the pleasure of interviewing Frances during her ninetieth year of life. She was still a ball of fire who shared with amazing clarity the truths she had learned while working to advance the kingdom of God. During our time together, Frances related many of the stories I have shared with you. She had an uncommonly clear grasp of the purpose of God in their ministry, and she told me her deepest convictions:

God has called me to be an exhorter. I have never forgotten my calling. Whether I am in America or overseas, I remind the people that Jesus is the most exciting Man who ever lived. To this day, at age ninety, I think that is my greatest anointing. Healing, yes, but to get people to know Jesus is alive, and that He lives inside of us. When I learned the truth that Jesus lives inside of me, I spoke out loud to Him, "I shut the door and locked it, Jesus; now

You can never get out!" Since I got saved, I have never wanted anything but Jesus. In one split second, the world lost interest for me![358]

As we spoke, Frances remarked that her view of walking with Christ was much the same as it had been forty years earlier:

The Christian life is the most exciting life in the world. There are only two things you need to do. Number one, do what God tells you to do. Number two, don't do what He tells you not to do. Now, that is the whole secret. It's that simple.

To me, living the Christian life is not a bunch of ups and downs. I think that it takes a total sell-out to Jesus so that nothing else makes a difference. Charles and I do not *talk* about anything else; we do not *do* anything else; and since I was saved, I never *had* anything else.[359]

The Happy Hunters

How did Charles and Frances come to be known as the "Happy Hunters?" Frances once explained it like this: "Charles and I are always ecstatically happy because we've found the secret to life. THE SECRET OF LIVING IS *GIVING*. We've given our entire lives to God, we GIVE to each other, we GIVE to the people we share our faith with, it's a

The Happy Hunters

✵✵✵✵✵

constant time of giving, and because of this, we are ALWAYS happy."[360] An attitude of giving allowed them to share their faith as they did, and it also gave them a happy, fulfilling marriage.

"I think that we have had the most balanced life in the world," Frances shared with me during the interview. "Charles and I have had an incredible marriage. A marriage full of love, love, love. Charles to this day tells me he loves me many times a day."

When Charles asked Frances to marry him back in December 1969, her answer was from the Word of God: *"Wherever you go, I will go; and wherever you lodge, I will lodge; your people shall be my people, and your God, my God."* (Ruth 1:16).

The years sped by, and in 2006, after Charles had back surgery, the doctors put him in a rehabilitation hospital. Frances laughed as she told me, "So, I put myself right in that hospital. He won't go without me, anyway. Where he lodges, I lodge!" When they put Charles in a nursing home, Frances moved right in with him. "I don't care," she exclaimed. "Wherever he lodges, I will lodge." She continued, "I think it's incredible that I'm ninety years old. We are the oldest people in the nursing home, and yet we are the youngest because we are the only ones in here that still work! Nobody else has a purpose in life; we still have a purpose—to spread the gospel of Jesus Christ!"[361]

The Hunters' Legacy

"Precious in the sight of the LORD is the death of His saints" (Psalm 116:15 NKJV).

On Tuesday morning, July 14, 2009, Frances Eileen Hunter went home to heaven. She finally met face-to-face the Jesus whom she loved. Her generous and compassionate heart simply wore out at the age of ninety-three. Up until the final days of her life, she sat at her desk and was even planning the next Worldwide Day of Healing for September 2009.

Over the years, her daughter, Joan Hunter Murrell, had often worked alongside her parents in the ministry. She also established an evangelistic healing ministry of her own and spent a good deal of time ministering overseas. With her mother's death, Joan became the leader of Hunter Ministries in Texas. Frances and Charles were so pleased that Joan had a powerful call of God on her own life, and they had a genuine desire to support Joan and the next generation of ministers. "You have to make room for the younger generation," Frances commented to me. "Fred Price Jr., Joel Osteen, Matthew Hagee, Gordon Robertson, my daughter, Joan. God is moving through the next generation as He has always done, like with Elijah and Elisha. We have to make room for them."

On June 22, 2010, eleven months after Frances went home to be with Jesus, Charles passed away peacefully in his sleep. Never far from Frances's side in their nearly forty years of marriage and ministry together, Charles was ready to join his beloved in heaven.

While family members and the Christian community mourned the passing of these two dynamic saints, they rejoiced that they were together with the Lord. They left a legacy for Jesus that was second to none in its impact over the world. Charles had written a letter to Frances shortly after their marriage in which he proclaimed, "You and I…[are] one in Christ, and one made of two who were brought into one spirit, one body and one soul directly and entirely by God, and so acting as 'one' we will serve God and proclaim Christ Jesus every day for the rest of our lives together."[362] And that is exactly what they did.

"God said it, we believe it, and that settles it!" Over and over in their ministry, this declaration was repeated by Charles and Frances Hunter, two ordinary believers who had unwavering faith in an extraordinary God. In the beginning of their walk with Him, the Hunters had no idea that He would use them to bring His message of salvation, Holy Spirit power, and healing to the 4 corners of the earth. And why would He use them? Because they had been marked by God for His purposes.

Chapter Five

Endnotes

306 Charles and Frances Hunter, *Since Jesus Passed By* (Kingwood, TX: Hunter Books, 1973), 26.
307 Hunter and Hunter, *Since Jesus Passed By*, 41.
308 Ibid.
309 Frances Hunter, *God Is Fabulous* [revised ed.] (Kingwood, TX: Hunter Books, 1998), 101, 102.
310 Frances Hunter, *God Is Fabulous*, 19.
311 Ibid.
312 Ibid., 30.
313 Frances Hunter, interview with the author, Houston, TX, 2006.
314 Frances Hunter, *God Is Fabulous*, 63.
315 Frances Hunter, interview with the author.
316 Frances Hunter, *God Is Fabulous*, 69.
317 Frances Hunter, interview with the author.
318 Richard and Brenda Young, *Messengers of Healing* (New Kensington, PA: Whitaker House, 2009), 79.
319 Young and Young, *Messengers*, 55–61.
320 Ibid., 62.
321 Ibid., 63.
322 Charles Hunter, *Follow Me!* (Kingwood, TX: Hunter Books, 1975), 42.
323 Charles Hunter, *A Tribute to God* (Kingwood, TX: Hunter Books, n.d.), 46.
324 Frances Hunter, *How to Pick a Perfect Husband or Wife* (Kingwood, TX: Hunter Books, 1973), 5.
325 Frances Hunter, *How to Pick*, 21.
326 Ibid., 32.
327 Ibid., 141.
328 Ibid., 142.
329 Ibid., 132.
330 Ibid., 144.
331 Ibid., 115.
332 Frances Hunter, interview with the author.
333 Ibid.
334 Young and Young, *Messengers*, 110.

335 Frances Hunter, interview with the author.
336 Ibid.
337 Ibid.
338 Ibid.
339 Ibid.
340 Hunter and Hunter, *Since Jesus Passed By*, 139–140.
341 Ibid., 139.
342 Young and Young, *Messengers*, 48–49.
343 Ibid., 73.
344 Ibid., 77–78.
345 Charles Hunter, *Follow Me!*, 54.
346 Hunter and Hunter, *Since Jesus Passed By*, 105–106.
347 Ibid., 115.
348 Ibid.
349 Ibid., 136.
350 Young and Young, *Messengers*, 146.
351 Frances Hunter, interview with the author.
352 Ibid.
353 Young and Young, *Messengers*, 163.
354 Ibid., 176.
355 Ibid., 180.
356 Ibid., 195–196.
357 Ibid., 201.
358 Frances Hunter, interview with the author.
359 Ibid.
360 Hunter and Hunter, *Since Jesus Passed By*, 73.
361 Frances Hunter, interview with the author.
362 Frances Hunter, *How to Pick*, 161.

BIBLIOGRAPHY

F. F. Bosworth

Barnes III, Roscoe. *F. F. Bosworth: The Man Behind "Christ the Healer."* Newcastle upon Tyne, England: Cambridge Scholars Publishing, 2009.

Blomgren Jr., Oscar. "Man of God, Fred F. Bosworth," Part IV: Bosworth Begins His Work. *Herald of Faith* (June 1964).

Bosworth, F. F. *Bosworth's Life Story: The Life Story of F. F. Bosworth, as Told by Himself in the Alliance Tabernacle, Toronto.* Toronto: Alliance Book Room, n.d.

—*Christ the Healer.* New Kensington, PA: Whitaker House, 2000.

—*Christ the Healer.* Grand Rapids, MI: Chosen Books, 2000. (Includes a ninth chapter written by Bob Bosworth, F. F.'s son, with details about Bosworth's final ministry year and his death.)

Perkins, Eunice M. *Joybringer Bosworth: His Life's Story.* 1921.

Sumrall, Lester. *Pioneers of Faith.* South Bend, IN: LeSea Publishing, 1995.

George Jeffreys

Boulton, Ernest C. W. *George Jeffreys: A Ministry of the Miraculous*. London: Elim Publishing Company, 1928.

Cartwright, Desmond. *The Great Evangelists: The Remarkable Lives of George and Stephen Jeffreys*. Hants, England: Marshall Pickering, 1986.

Edsor, Albert W. *George Jeffreys Man of God*. London: Ludgate Press Limited, 1964.

Hudson, David Neil. "A Schism and Its Aftermath: An Historical Analysis of Denominational Discerption in the Elim Pentecostal Church, 1939–1940." Ph.D. diss., King's College, 1999.

Hywel-Davies, Jack. *The Kensington Temple Story*. East Sussex, England: Monarch Books, 1998.

Jeffreys, George. *Healing Rays*. London: Elim Publishing Company, 1932.

Lester Sumrall

Sumrall, Lester. *Adventuring with Christ*. South Bend, IN: LeSea Publishing, 1988.

—*Bitten by Devils*. South Bend, IN: LeSea Publishing, 1987.

—*Demons: The Answer Book*. New Kensington, PA: Whitaker House, 1979.

—*Faith Can Change Your World*. South Bend, IN: LeSea Publishing, 1999.

—*Legacy of Faith*. South Bend, IN: LeSea Publishing, 1993.

—*Lester Sumrall's Short Stories*. South Bend, IN: LeSea Publishing, 2005.

—*The Life Story of Lester Sumrall*. Green Forest, AR: New Leaf Press, 1993.

—*Pioneers of Faith*. South Bend, IN: LeSea Publishing, 1995.

Oral Roberts

Harrell Jr., David Edwin. *Oral Roberts: An American Life*. Bloomington, IN: Indiana University Press, 1985.

Roberts, Evelyn. *Evelyn Roberts' Miracle Life Stories*. Tulsa, OK: Roberts Ministries, 1998.

Roberts, Oral. *A Daily Guide to Miracles*. Grand Rapids, MI: Fleming H. Revell Company, 1978.

BIBLIOGRAPHY

—*Expect a Miracle: My Life and Ministry.* Nashville, TN: Thomas Nelson Publishers, 1998.

—*My Story.* Tulsa, OK, and New York, NY: Summit Book Company, 1961.

—*Still Doing the Impossible: When You See the Invisible, You Can Do the Impossible.* Shippensburg, PA: Destiny Image, 2002.

—*When You See the Invisible, You Can Do the Impossible.* Shippensburg, PA: Destiny Image, 2005.

Charles and Frances Hunter

Hunter, Charles. *A Tribute to God.* Kingwood, TX: Hunter Books, n.d.

—*Follow Me!* Kingwood, TX: Hunter Books, 1975.

Hunter, Charles and Frances. *Since Jesus Passed By.* Kingwood, TX: Hunter Books, 1973.

Hunter, Frances. *God Is Fabulous* [revised ed.]. Kingwood, TX: Hunter Books, 1998.

—*How to Pick a Perfect Husband or Wife.* Kingwood, TX: Hunter Books, 1973.

Young, Richard and Brenda. *Messengers of Healing.* New Kensington, PA: Whitaker House, 2009.

ABOUT THE AUTHOR

Roberts Liardon was born in Tulsa, Oklahoma, the first male child born at Oral Roberts University. For this distinction, he was named in honor of the university's founder. To date, he has sold over seven million books worldwide, his works have been translated into more than fifty languages, and he is known internationally, having ministered in over 112 countries. An author of fifty-four books, Roberts continues to have a voice that speaks to this generation of believers, reaching those who are eager to read a relevant message that draws the heart closer to God.

Roberts' career in ministry began in 1979 when he gave his first public address at the age of thirteen. By seventeen, he had published his first book, *I Saw Heaven*, which sold over 1.5 million copies.

God then inspired Roberts to write and produce a book and video series entitled God's Generals, chronicling the lives of some of Christianity's pioneering Pentecostal and charismatic leaders. The books include *God's Generals: Why They Succeeded and Why Some Failed*, *God's Generals: The Roaring Reformers*, and *God's Generals: The Revivalists*. This successful series established Roberts as a leading Protestant church historian, a mantle he wears to this day.

Twice, Roberts was voted Outstanding Young Man in America. He has had the honor of being hosted by presidents, kings, and other political and religious leaders, including former President Ronald Reagan, former Prime Minister Lady Margaret Thatcher, and Dr. Billy Graham. He was also honored by former President George W. Bush and his wife, Laura, for his commitment and contributions to his community.

In 1990, at the age of twenty-five, Roberts Liardon moved to Southern California, where he founded one of the largest Christian churches and Bible colleges in Orange County. Embassy Christian Center would become a base for his apostolic work, which included assistance to the poor and needy in Southern California and throughout the world. From this ministry, he established, financed, and sent forth nearly five hundred men and women to various nations across the globe. Over the years, these humanitarian missionary teams have provided food, clothing, and spiritual teachings to those in need.

Since 2000, Roberts has worked to fulfill a demanding speaking schedule, along with writing new books and mentoring a new generation of world leaders to effect change for the church and society. He continues to manage and expand his international headquarters in Sarasota, Florida, and has an extension office in London, England.

Contact Information

United States office:
Roberts Liardon
P.O. Box 2989
Sarasota, FL 34230
E-mail: Info1@robertsliardon.org
www.robertsliardon.org

United Kingdom/European office:
Roberts Liardon
22 Notting Hill Gate
Suite 125
London, UK W11 3JE